T0192146

Communications
in Computer and Information Science   **1715**

More information about this series at https://link.springer.com/bookseries/7899

Huadong Ma · Xue Wang · Lianglun Cheng ·
Li Cui · Liang Liu · An Zeng (Eds.)

Wireless Sensor Networks

16th China Conference, CWSN 2022
Guangzhou, China, November 10–13, 2022
Proceedings

 Springer

Editors
Huadong Ma
Beijing University of Posts
and Telecommunications
Beijing, China

Lianglun Cheng
Guangdong University of Technology
Guangzhou, China

Liang Liu
Beijing University of Posts
and Telecommunications
Beijing, China

Xue Wang
Tsinghua University
Beijing, China

Li Cui
Institute of Computing Technology
Chinese Academy of Sciences
Beijing, China

An Zeng
Guangdong University of Technology
Guangzhou, China

ISSN 1865-0929   ISSN 1865-0937 (electronic)
Communications in Computer and Information Science
ISBN 978-981-19-8349-8   ISBN 978-981-19-8350-4 (eBook)
https://doi.org/10.1007/978-981-19-8350-4

This Springer imprint is published by the registered company Springer Nature Singapore Pte Ltd.
The registered company address is: 152 Beach Road, #21-01/04 Gateway East, Singapore 189721, Singapore

Preface

The China Conference on Wireless Sensor Networks (CWSN) is the annual conference on the Internet of Things (IoT) which is sponsored by the China Computer Federation (CCF). The 6th CWSN took place in Guangzhou, China, in December 2022. As a leading conference in the field of IoT, CWSN is the premier forum for IoT researchers and practitioners from academia, industry, and government in China to share their ideas, research results, and experiences, which highly promotes research and technical innovation in these fields domestically and internationally.

The conference provided an academic exchange of research and a development forum for IoT researchers, developers, enterprises, and users. Exchanging results and experience of research and applications in IoT, and discussing the key challenges and research hotspots, is the main goal of the forum. As a high-level forum for the design, implementation, and application of IoT, the conference promoted the exchange and application of the theories and technologies of IoT-related topics.

This year, CWSN received 194 submissions, including 82 English papers and 112 Chinese papers. After a careful double-blind review process, with each paper receiving at least 3 reviews, 17 revised and completed papers were selected. The high-quality program would not have been possible without the authors who chose CWSN 2022 as a venue for their publications. We are also very grateful to the members of the Program Committee and Organizing Committee, who put a tremendous amount of effort into soliciting and selecting research papers with a balance of high quality, new ideas, and new applications. We hope that you enjoy reading and benefit from the proceedings of CWSN 2022.

October 2022

Xue Wang
Lianglun Cheng

Organization

Conference Chairs

Huadong Ma   CCF Internet of Things Special Committee, China
Qintai Hu   Guangdong University of Technology, China

Honorary Chair

Hao Dai   Chinese Academy of Engineering, China

Steering Committee Chair

Jianzhong Li   Harbin Institute of Technology, China

Program Committee Chairs

Xue Wang   Tsinghua University, China
Lianglun Cheng   Guangdong University of Technology, China

Program Committee Co-chairs

Liang Liu   Beijing University of Posts and Telecommunications, China
An Zeng   Guangdong University of Technology, China

Outstanding Paper Award Chair

Li Cui   Institute of Computing Technology, Chinese Academy of Sciences, China

Forum Chairs

Aimin Yang   Lingnan Normal University, China
Zheng Yang   Tsinghua University, China
Zhifeng Hao   Shantou University, China
Zhongwen Guo   Ocean University of China, China
Zhibo Wang   Tsinghua University/Zhejiang University, China
Dong Zhao   Beijing University of Posts and Telecommunications, China
Limin Sun   Institute of Information Engineering, Chinese Academy of Sciences, China

Liang Wei	Future Network, China
Huadong Ma	Beijing University of Posts and Telecommunications, China
Lianglun Cheng	Guangdong University of Technology, China

Organization Committee Chairs

Xinbing Wang	Shanghai Jiao Tong University, China
Dongning Liu	Guangdong University of Technology, China
Jing Hu	Guangdong University of Technology, China

Organization Committee Co-chairs

Nong Xiao	Sun Yat-sen University, China
Junlong Chen	South China University of Technology, China
Zhetao Li	Jinan University, China
Hanpin Wang	Guangzhou University, China
Shengyi Jiang	Guangdong University of Foreign Studies, China
Zhun Fan	Shantou University, China
Xiaohong Peng	Guangdong Ocean University, China
Huimin Zhao	Guangdong Normal University of Technology, China
Shuangyin Liu	Zhongkai College of Agricultural Engineering, China
Huaqiang Yuan	Dongguan University of Technology, China
Junjie Yang	Lingnan Normal University, China

Organization Committee

Haiming Jin	Shanghai Jiao Tong University, China
Huanhuan Zhang	Beijing University of Posts and Telecommunications, China
Pinghua Chen	Guangdong University of Technology, China
Guangqiang Xie	Guangdong University of Technology, China
Jian Zhu	Guangdong University of Technology, China
Xiaomin Hu	Guangdong University of Technology, China
Sui Lin	Guangdong University of Technology, China
Si Li	Guangdong University of Technology, China
Lunke Fei	Guangdong University of Technology, China
Shuping Zhao	Guangdong University of Technology, China
Bing Wei	Guangdong University of Technology, China
Jiacheng Diao	Guangdong University of Technology, China

Program Committee

Guangwei Bai	Nanjing University of Technology, China
Ming Bao	Institute of Acoustics, Chinese Academy of Sciences, China
Yuanguo Bi	Northeast University, China
Qingsong Cai	Beijing Business University, China
Shaobin Cai	Overseas Chinese University, China
Bin Cao	Harbin University of Technology, Shenzhen, China
An Zeng	Guangdong University of Technology, China
Deze Cao	China University of Geosciences, Wuhan, China
Fanzai Zeng	Hunan University, China
Shan Chang	Donghua University, China
Guihai Chen	Nanjing University, China
Haiming Chen	Ningbo University, China
Hong Chen	Renmin University of China, China
Honglong Chen	China University of Petroleum (East China), China
Jiaxing Chen	Hebei Normal University, China
Liangyin Chen	Sichuan University, China
Wei Chen	Zhejiang University, China
Xiaojiang Chen	Northwestern University, China
Xi Chen	Tsinghua University, China
Xu Chen	Sun Yat-sen University, China
Yihong Chen	Xihua Normal University, China
Yongle Chen	Taiyuan University of Technology, China
Zhikui Chen	Dalian University of Technology, China
Keyang Cheng	Jiangsu University, China
Xiuzhen Cheng	Shandong University, China
Hongju Cheng	Fuzhou University, China
Lianglun Cheng	Guangdong University of Technology, China
Siyao Cheng	Harbin Institute of Technology, China
Kaikai Chi	Zhejiang University of Technology, China
Li Cui	Institute of Computing Technology, Chinese Academy of Sciences, China
Xunxue Cui	PLA Army Service Academy, China
Haipeng Dai	Nanjing University, China
Xiaochao Dang	Northwest Normal University, China
Qingyong Deng	Xiangtan University, China
Xiaoheng Deng	Central South University, China
Wei Dong	Zhejiang University, China

Hongwei Du	Harbin University of Technology, Shenzhen, China
Juan Fang	Beijing University of Technology, China
Xiaolin Fang	Southeast University, China
Dingyi Fang	Northwestern University, China
Guangsheng Feng	Harbin Engineering University, China
Xiufang Feng	Taiyuan University of Technology, China
Deyun Gao	Beijing Jiaotong University, China
Hong Gao	Harbin University of Technology, China
Ruipeng Gao	Beijing Jiaotong University, China
Jibing Gong	Yanshan University, China
Zhitao Guan	North China Electric Power University, China
Songtao Guo	Chongqing University, China
Zhongwen Guo	Ocean University of China, China
Guangjie Han	Hohai University, China
Jinsong Han	Zhejiang University, China
Yanbo Han	Northern Polytechnic University, China
Zhanjun Hao	Northwest Normal University, China
Daojing He	Harbin University of Technology, Shenzhen, China
Shiming He	Changsha University of Technology, China
Yuan He	Tsinghua University, China
Shibo He	Zhejiang University, China
Chengquan Hu	Jilin University, China
Pengfei Hu	Shandong University, China
Qiangshen Hua	Huazhong University of Science and Technology, China
Zhan Huan	Changzhou University, China
Haiping Huang	Nanjing University of Posts and Telecommunications, China
He Huang	Suzhou University, China
Liusheng Huang	China University of Science and Technology, China
Longbo Huang	Tsinghua University, China
Shuqiang Huang	Jinan University, China
Jie Jia	Northeast University, China
Riheng Jia	Zhejiang Normal University, China
Nan Jiang	East China Jiaotong University, China
Hongbo Jiang	Hunan University, China
Xianlong Jiao	Air Force Engineering University, China
Haiming Jin	Nanjing University of Posts and Telecommunications, China

Qi Jing	Peking University
Bo Jing	Air Force Engineering University, China
Linghe Kong	Shanghai Jiao Tong University, China
Zhufang Kuang	Central South Forestry University, China
Chao Li	Shandong University of Science and Technology, China
Deying Li	Renmin University of China, China
Fan Li	Beijing University of Technology, China
Fangmin Li	Wuhan University of Technology, China
Feng Li	Changsha University of Technology/Donghua University, China
Guanghui Li	Jiangnan University, China
Guorui Li	Northeast University, China
Hongwei Li	University of Electronic Science and Technology, China
Jianqiang Li	Shenzhen University, China
Jianbo Li	Qingdao University, China
Jianzhong Li	Harbin Institute of Technology, China
Jie Li	Northeast University, China
Jinbao Li	Heilongjiang University, China
Minglu Li	Shanghai Jiao Tong University, China
Renfa Li	Hunan University, China
Xiangyang Li	China University of Science and Technology, China
Yanjun Li	Zhejiang University of Technology, China
Zhetao Li	Jinan University, China
Zhiyuan Li	Jiangsu University, China
Chong Li	Zhejiang University of Technology, China
Zhuo Li	Xi'an University of Electronic Science and Technology/Beijing University of Information Technology, China
Hongbin Liang	Southwest Jiaotong University, China
Yongzhen Liang	Changzhou University, China
Wei Liang	Shenyang Institute of Automation, Chinese Academy of Sciences, China
Chi Lin	Dalian University of Technology, China
Feng Lin	Zhejiang University, China
Chao Liu	Shandong University/Chongqing University, China
Chi Liu	Beijing University of Technology, China
Dongning Liu	Guangdong University of Technology, China
Hongbo Liu	University of Electronic Science and Technology, China

Jiajia Liu	Xi'an University of Electronic Science and Technology, China
Kai Liu	Xi'an University of Electronic Science and Technology/Chongqing University/Beijing University of Aeronautics and Astronautics, China
Liang Liu	Beijing University of Posts and Telecommunications, China
Min Liu	Tongji University/Jiangsu University, China
Peng Liu	Guangdong University of Technology, China
Tang Liu	Sichuan Normal University, China
Xingchen Liu	Sun Yat-sen University, China
Yunhao Liu	Tsinghua University, China
Xiang Liu	Peking University, China
Jianfeng Lu	Wuhan University of Science and Technology, China
Chengwen Luo	Shenzhen University, China
Haibo Luo	Neusoft Institute Guangdong/Shenyang Institute of Automation, Chinese Academy of Sciences, China
Juan Luo	Hunan University, China
Junzhou Luo	Southeast University, China
Feng Lv	Central South University, China
Huadong Ma	Beijing University of Posts and Telecommunications, China
Li Ma	Northern Polytechnic University, China
Lianbo Ma	Northeast University, China
Jianwei Niu	Beijing University of Aeronautics and Astronautics, China
Xiaoguang Niu	Wuhan University, China
Hao Peng	Zhejiang Normal University, China
Jian Peng	Sichuan University, China
Li Peng	Jiangnan University, China
Shaoliang Peng	Hunan University, China
Yuanyuan Pu	Yunnan University, China
Wangdong Qi	Army Engineering University of PLA, China
Kaiguo Qian	Kunming University, China
Jiefan Qiu	Zhejiang University of Technology, China
Tie Qiu	Tianjin University, China
Fengyuan Ren	Tsinghua University, China
Ju Ren	Central South University, China
Yanzhi Ren	University of Electronic Science and Technology, China

Shikai Shen	Kunming University, China
Yiran Shen	Harbin Engineering University, China
Yulong Shen	Xi'an University of Electronic Science and Technology, China
Jian Shu	Nanchang Hangkong University, China
Xiaoxia Song	Shanxi Datong University, China
Geng Sun	Dalian Ocean University/Jilin University, China
Lijuan Sun	Nanjing University of Posts and Telecommunications, China
Limin Sun	Institute of Information Engineering, Chinese Academy of Sciences, China
Weifeng Sun	Dalian University of Technology, China
Fengxiao Tang	Central South University, China
Dan Tao	Beijing Jiaotong University, China
Xiaohua Tian	Shanghai Jiao Tong University, China
Shaohua Wan	Zhongnan University of Economics and Law, China
Yang Wang	China University of Science and Technology, China
En Wang	Jilin University, China
Jiliang Wang	Tsinghua University, China
Kun Wang	Nanjing University of Posts and Telecommunications, China
Lei Wang	China University of Science and Technology, China
Liangmin Wang	Southeast University, China
Pengfei Wang	Dalian University of Technology, China
Ping Wang	Xihua University, China
Qi Wang	Institute of Computing Technology, Chinese Academy of Sciences, China
Qingshan Wang	Hefei Polytechnic University, China
Ruchuan Wan	Nanjing University of Posts and Telecommunications, China
Rui Wang	Changchun University of Technology/Beijing University of Science and Technology, China
Shuai Wang	Southeast University, China
Tian Wang	Beijing Normal University, China
Xiaoming Wang	Shaanxi Normal University, China
Xiaodong Wang	Kunming University of Technology/Fuzhou University, China
Xiaoliang Wang	Hunan University of Science and Technology, China
Xinbing Wang	Shanghai Jiao Tong University, China

Xue Wang	Chongqing University, China
Yiding Wang	Northern Polytechnic University, China
Guoren Wang	Beijing University of Technology, China
Zhibo Wang	Zhejiang University, China
Zhi Wang	Tsinghua University, China
Zhu Wang	Harbin Institute of Technology, China
Wei Wei	Xi'an University of Technology, China
Zhenchun Wei	Hefei Polytechnic University, China
Hui Wen	Guilin University of Electronic Science and Technology, China
Zhongming Weng	Tianjin University, China
Hejun Wu	Sun Yat-sen University, China
Honghai Wu	Henan University of Science and Technology, China
Xiaojun Wu	Northwestern Polytechnical University, China
Xingjun Wu	Tsinghua University, China
Kaishun Wu	Shenzhen University, China
Chaoshen Xiang	Chongqing University, China
Deqin Xiao	South China Agricultural University, China
Fu Xiao	Nanjing University of Posts and Telecommunications, China
Liang Xiao	Hubei University of Technology, China
Ling Xiao	Hunan University, China
Kun Xie	Hunan University, China
Lei Xie	Northwestern Polytechnical University, China
Mande Xie	Zhejiang Gongshang University, China
Xiaolan Xie	Guilin University of Technology, China
Yongping Xiong	Beijing University of Posts and Telecommunications, China
Jia Xu	Nanjing University of Posts and Telecommunications, China
Wenzheng Xu	Sichuan University, China
Chenren Xu	Peking University, China
Guangtao Xue	Shanghai Jiao Tong University, China
Geng Yang	Nanjing University of Posts and Telecommunications, China
Guisong Yang	Shanghai University of Technology, China
Hao Yang	Chongqing University, China
Panlong Yang	China University of Science and Technology, China
Weidong Yang	Henan University of Technology, China
Zheng Yang	Tsinghua University, China
Weidong Yi	Chinese Academy of Sciences, China

Zuwei Yin	Information Engineering University, China
Ruiyun Yu	Northeast University, China
Jiguo Yu	Qilu University of Technology, China
Peiyan Yuan	Henan Normal University, China
Deyu Zhang	Central South University, China
Jiao Zhang	Beijing University of Posts and Telecommunications, China
Lan Zhang	China University of Science and Technology, China
Lei Zhang	Sichuan University, China
Lichen Zhang	Guangdong University of Technology, China
Lianming Zhang	Hunan Normal University, China
Shigeng Zhang	Central South University, China
Shuqin Zhang	Zhongyuan University of Technology, China
Yanyong Zhang	China University of Science and Technology, China
Yin Zhang	Northeast University/Zhejiang University/University of Electronic Science and Technology, China
Yongmin Zhang	Central South University, China
Yunzhou Zhang	Northeast University, China
Dong Zhao	Beijing University of Posts and Telecommunications, China
Jumin Zhao	Taiyuan University of Technology, China
Junhui Zhao	East China Jiaotong University, China
Liang Zhao	Xi'an University of Electronic Science and Technology/Sichuan University/Lanzhou Institute of Chemical Physics, Chinese Academy of Sciences, China
Zenghua Zhao	Tianjin University, China
Zhiwei Zhao	University of Electronic Science and Technology, China
Jiping Zheng	Nanjing University of Aeronautics and Astronautics, China
Meng Zheng	Shenyang Institute of Automation, Chinese Academy of Sciences, China
Xiaolong Zheng	Beijing University of Posts and Telecommunications, China
Ping Zhong	Central South University, China
Anfu Zhou	Beijing University of Posts and Telecommunications, China

Jian Zhou	Nanjing University of Posts and Telecommunications/Southwest University, China
Ruiting Zhou	Wuhan University, China
Changbing Zhou	Beijing University of Science and Technology/China University of Geosciences, China
Hongzi Zhu	Shanghai Jiao Tong University, China
Hongsong Zhu	Institute of Information Engineering, Chinese Academy of Sciences, China
Peidong Zhu	National University of Defense Science and Technology, China
Weiping Zhu	Wuhan University/Nanjing University of Posts and Telecommunications, China
Yihua Zhu	Zhejiang University of Technology, China
Liehuang Zhu	Beijing University of Technology, China
Shihong Zou	Beijing University of Posts and Telecommunications, China

Contents

MmLiquid: Liquid Identification Using mmWave

Dingyue Cao[1], Yuxiang Lin[1], Geng Ren[2], Yi Gao[1,3], and Wei Dong[1,3(✉)]

[1] College of Computer Science, Zhejiang University, Hangzhou, China
{caody,linyx,gaoy,dongw}@emnets.org
[2] Alibaba Group, Hangzhou, China
rengeng.rengeng@alibaba-inc.com
[3] Alibaba-Zhejiang University Joint Institute of Frontier Technologies,
Hangzhou, China

Abstract. Liquid identification is an essential technology for water safety monitoring. This paper shows the feasibility of identifying liquid using millimeter wave (mmWave) signals. The inherent principle comes from that the fine-grained mmWave signals can capture signal attenuation, phase shift, and propagation delay when penetrating the liquid. We have conducted a preliminary experiment to prove the effectiveness of using mmWave for liquid identification. However, after moving the container, the identification accuracy will drop significantly. To address this challenge, we propose a robust mmWave-based liquid identification approach MmLiquid, which uses a container position information filtering (CPIF) scheme to eliminate the influence of different container positions. MmLiquid will extract container position-independent information from the original mmWave signals and train a deep complex model (DCN) for accurate liquid identification. To further improve the identification performance, we set up an identification environment with two reflective surfaces to capture effective mmWave signals that contain more liquids information. We implement MmLiquid using commercial mmWave devices. Experimental results on 16 kinds of liquids at 24 different container positions show that MmLiquid can achieve an average liquid identification accuracy of 97.6%.

Keywords: Liquid identification · mmWave · Signal processing

1 Introduction

Liquid identification is an essential technology to enable various important applications, ranging from water quality monitoring to liquid safety testing. Traditional liquid identification methods usually rely on laboratory testing with

This work is supported by NSFC under grant no. 62072396, Zhejiang Provincial Natural Science Foundation for Distinguished Young Scholars under grant no. LR19F020001, the Fundamental Research Funds for the Central Universities (no. 226-2022-00087), and Alibaba-Zhejiang University Joint Institute of Frontier Technologies.

expensive and huge equipment [3,17,22,25]. Recently, an extensive amount of mobile computing researches have been proposed to identify liquids based on wireless signals [9–11,20,38]. These approaches can distinguish a variety of liquids at a low cost outside the lab environment, in a non-invasive manner. However, these methods entail numerous hard-to-satisfy requirements, including (1) need to know a certain prior property of the liquid (e.g., density) [38], (2) need a specialized setup (a container at a specific location) [7,11], or (3) use wireless signals that are usually unavailable to the general population (e.g., UWB, RFID readers) [7,9,10].

In this paper, we aim to achieve accurate liquid identification *using commercially available wireless signals, without any prior knowledge*. This paper intends to take a step towards this vision by answering the following questions.

What Wireless Signal Can the Public Use to Effectively Identify Liquids? Among existing wireless signals, millimeter wave (mmWave) has been widely used for sensing the physical world due to its wide frequency band and high sensing resolution [5,12,13,15,19,34]. Moreover, mmWave has entered the lives of the public since because it is an essential part of 5G NR, and has been widely adopted and embedded in commercial phones [39]. In this paper, we propose MmLiquid, a liquid identification approach based on mmWave.

Without Prior Knowledge, How to Accurately Identify Different Liquids? The mmWave mixer combines the transmitted and received mmWave signal to generate the intermediate frequency (IF) signal. Based on a deep complex network (DCN), MmLiquid designs a deep learning model as the classifier, which takes the complex IF signals as its input and learns the signal variation caused by different liquids.

Will Different Container Positions Affect the Identification Accuracy? If So, How to Eliminate its Interference? To investigate the impact of different container positions, we conduct a preliminary study. We collect mmWave signals that penetrate the liquid in a known setup. Results show that when identifying 16 kinds of liquids, our learning model can achieve an accuracy of 100.0%, which proves the feasibility of using mmWave for liquid identification. However, after changing the position of the container, the identification accuracy will drop.

To address this issue, MmLiquid uses a container position information filtering (CPIF) scheme to filter out the changed signal parts that correspond to position changes of the container. To amplify the signal that penetrates the liquid, we design an identification environment with two steel plates as reflective surfaces. MmLiquid will use the multiple reflection enhanced mmWave signals to improve its identification accuracy.

We have implemented MmLiquid using commercial mmWave devices. We evaluate the identification performance of MmLiquid in normal indoor scenarios using 16 kinds of liquids. For each kind of liquid, we place the container at 24 different positions and collect 2 samples in each position. In total, 768 samples are collected for performance evaluation, where the size of each sample is around 0.2M. Results show that MmLiquid achieves an average identification accuracy of 97.6%.

In summary, we make the following key contributions in this paper:

- We propose MmLiquid, a liquid identification approach using mmWave signals. We have conducted a preliminary study to prove the effectiveness of mmWave in liquid identification and show the performance will drop when the position of containers varies.
- We propose a CPIF scheme to filter out the changed part corresponding to the position changes of containers. We also design a simple but effective identification environment to help enhance the liquid information contained in the received signal.
- We implement MmLiquid using commercial-off-the-shelf devices. Evaluation on 16 kinds of liquids shows that MmLiquid can achieve a high identification accuracy with changing container positions.

The rest of the paper is organized as follows. Section 2 reviews the related work of MmLiquid. Section 3 introduces the background of mmWave and the motivation of using it for liquid identification. Section 4 describes the system overview. Section 5 shows the essential system design in detail. In Sect. 6, we present implementation details and evaluation results of MmLiquid. Finally, Sect. 7 concludes this paper.

2   Related Work

2.1   Wireless Sensing

Wireless sensing refers to the technology that perceives the physical world using wireless signals [1,16,28,37,40], which are ubiquitous in our daily life. These wireless signals can realize the physical world perception without contact. Existing literature uses various wireless signals to enable plenty of novel applications, including WiFi [2,8,21,27,29,30], bluetooth [24], and RFID [26,33,35].

Compared to the above wireless signals, mmWave has a finer-grained sensing resolution due to its higher frequency and millimeter-level wavelengths. As mmWave has been widely deployed worldwide [18], exploiting mmWave for sensing the physical world has attracted increasing research interests. There exists works that use mmWave for positioning [15], tire wear detection [19], temperature measurement [5], electronic equipment detection [13], and voice recognition [12,34]. In particular, many studies [31,36] have explored the feasibility of non-destructive material classification using mmWave signals. However, it is inconvenient to need to place the materials in a fixed position. In this paper, we focus on achieving low-cost and fast liquid identification using mmWave signals.

2.2   Liquid Identification

The ability to identify an unknown liquid is of great importance for many security areas, including liquid safety inspection, water pollution detection, food safety identification, and urine test. Traditional liquid identification methods rely on high-precision instruments. However, these devices are expensive and in specialized laboratories [3,17]. Besides, it takes time and human efforts to manually sample liquid for electrochemical tests.

To achieve low-cost and fast liquid identification, extensive passive liquid identification approaches have been proposed. They can be divided into two categories. One is to identify an unknown liquid based on a specific physical property of the liquid. Dhekne et al. [7] use UWB to measure and calculate the dielectric constant of liquids. Huang et al. [11] use the vibration of a smartphone to measure the viscosity of the liquid, but this solution requires fixing the smartphone to a special container. All these approaches require customized containers. Yue et al. [38] use the smartphone camera to measure the surface tension of the liquid. However, this approach cannot work with opaque liquids and need the prior knowledge of the density of different liquids.

Another category is to using machine learning/deep learning models to classify different liquids. For example, Nutrilyzer [20] uses the optical properties of liquids and an artificial neural network to classify liquids. However, it requires sampling the liquid to an electrode of piezoelectric sensor, which is not usually used in our daily life. Ha et al. [9,10] use RFID to measure liquid data and a 3-layer DNN to classify liquids in different environments. However, this approach only considers a two-class liquid classification problem.

On the other hand, all the above approaches cannot work well after moving the container due to the changes in wireless signals. FG-LiquID [14] uses mmWave and RC-Net for liquid classification, but the containers of FG-LiquID are also placed in relatively fixed locations. In this paper, we manage to achieve container position-independent liquid identification using a novel CPIF scheme.

3   Background and Motivation

3.1   mmWave Background

mmWave refers to electromagnetic waves with a millimeter-level wavelength and a frequency between 30 GHz and 300 GHz. mmWave signals usually adopt beamforming technology to enable directional propagation and are commercialized as mmWave radar. Unlike traditional pulse radar systems that periodically emit short pulses, mmWave radar uses frequency modulated continuous waves (FMCWs). FMCW can differentiate the reflective objects due to its continuously changing frequency. The FMCWs reflected at different positions can be distinguished in the frequency domain, while they are mixed in the time domain. Therefore, FMCW can perceive the position of a liquid container placed in the environment. The mmWave radar mixer mixes the transmit signal (TX) and the received signal (RX) together to generate an intermediate frequency (IF) signal. Specifically, the TX $T(t)$ at time t is:

$$T(t) = exp[j(2\pi f_0 t + \int_0^t 2\pi \rho t \, dt], \tag{1}$$

where $0 < t < T_r$, T_r is one chirp cycle, f_0 is the carrier frequency, and ρ is the chirp rate. With a round trip delay t_d lagged behind the transmitted chirp signal, the RX $R(t)$ can be represented as:

$$R(t) = \Gamma exp[j(2\pi f_0(t - t_d) + \int_0^{t-t_d} 2\pi \rho t \, dt], \tag{2}$$

where $t_d < t < T_r + t_d$, Γ denotes the amplitude normalized to the transmitted chirp signal. Assuming that the distance between the object and the mmWave radar is X, we can get t_d as:

$$t_d = \frac{2X}{c}. \tag{3}$$

For each chirp, when $t_d < t < T_r$, the IF signal of a chirp after mixing is:

$$H(t) = T(t) \times R^*(t) = \Gamma exp[j(2\pi \rho t_d t + 2\pi f_0 t_d)], \tag{4}$$

where $*$ represents a conjugate transpose operation, $\times$ is the mixer. For a reflective object, its frequency of IF signal:

$$F = \rho t_d = \rho \frac{2X}{c}, \tag{5}$$

is the frequency difference between the transmit signal and the reflected signal. As there may be multiple objects on the propagation path, the frequency spectrum of an IF signal can be a superposition of multiple signals reflected by multiple objects, and thus will have multiple peaks. Each frequency peak F is proportional to the distance between the object and the radar. Therefore, We can easily identify the positions of objects along the propagation path (i.e., containers and reflective surfaces in our experiments) in the frequency spectrum of IF signals.

3.2 Liquid Properties and mmWave

The properties of liquid through which the mmWave passes will affect its propagation. As shown in Fig. 3, starting from the mmWave radar, a part of mmWave signals will be reflected by the container. The rest will penetrate the liquid and be reflected by the reflective surface placed in the identification environment. The reflection, absorption, and refraction of the mmWave by different liquids can be different since they have different properties, such as dielectric constant, refractive index, etc. Figure 1 shows the effects of two different liquids on mmWave signals. In our settings, the first peak appears near the position of the container. We can see that for these two liquids, the amplitude of the first peak is significantly different. This is because the signal absorption capabilities of different liquids are different, leading to diverse Γ in Eq. 4.

Taking a closer look at Fig. 1, the frequency of the second peak, which appears near the position of the reflective surface, has been changed. Assuming that the width of the container is d, the refractive index of the liquid is n, the time delay

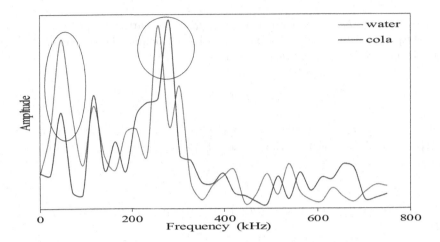

Fig. 1. The mmWave signals of water and cola, and the two liquids is placed in the same position.

t'_d of the mmWave signal returning from the reflective surface after penetrating the liquid is:

$$t'_d = \frac{2(X - d)}{c} + \frac{2d}{v} = t_d + \frac{2d(n - 1)}{c}. \tag{6}$$

The frequency shift ΔF of the first received signal from the reflective surface caused by different liquids can be represented as:

$$\Delta F = \rho(t'_d - t_d) = \frac{2\rho d(n - 1)}{c}. \tag{7}$$

As different liquids have different refractive indices, when the liquid in the container changes, the position of the second peak corresponding to the reflective surface will change accordingly. Therefore, different liquids will also cause changes in the peak position, as shown in Fig. 1. Based on the above properties, we can use mmWave signals to identify different liquids in MmLiquid.

3.3   Preliminary Study and Motivation

We have conducted a preliminary study and found that changing the container position leads to a decrease in the accuracy of mmWave for liquid identification. In our work, we leverage a Texas Instruments AWR1642 mmWave radar (TX Power = 12.5 dBm, RX Gain = 30 dB) [23] to emit the signal and capture the received data. The mmWave radar has 1 transmitting antenna and 4 receivers. The key parameters of mmWave radar are shown in Table 1. We use 16 types of liquids (e.g., water, milk) in our preliminary study. The weight of each liquid is 200.0 g. We put these liquids in a plastic beaker container.

As shown in Fig. 3, we place the container in front of the mmWave radar. The distance between the container and the mmWave radar is 20 cm. We also place a reflective surface behind the container for reflecting all mmWave signals back. The reflective surface is around 1.0 m away from the mmWave radar.

Table 1. mmWave waveform design.

Start freq	77.00 GHz	Frequency slope	40.024 MHz/μs
ADC start time	6.00 μs	Bandwidth	2401.44 MHz
ADC samples	256	Sample rate	6000 ksps
Frames	4	Chirps/frame	64

In this way, we can get more liquid information with multiple reflections. Some mmWave signals will be reflected by the container and some can penetrate the liquid and be reflected by the reflective surface.

The received IF signals are complex values. We design a Deep complex networks (DCN) model to identify these 16 liquids (see model details in Sect. 5.3). Experimental results show that our DCN model can achieve a classification accuracy of 100.0% for these 16 liquids, as shown in Fig. 2(a). As a result, mmWave has the ability of high-precision liquid identification.

However, there is no guarantee that the containers are placed in the same position during liquid identification in practice. Therefore, we change the position of the container and repeat the experiment. For each kind of liquid, we place the container at 24 different positions in an area of 10 cm × 16 cm. As shown in Fig. 2(b), the classification accuracy will drop to 93.6% with such small movements. Results show that mmWave signals are sensitive to environmental changes. When the position of test liquids changes (even in millimeters), the

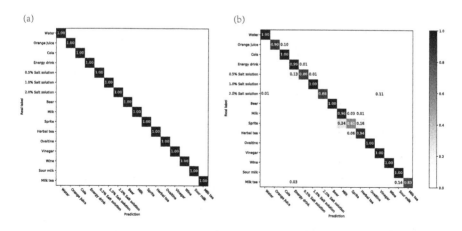

Fig. 2. (a) Classification results of 16 common liquids, when these liquids are in the same position. (b) Classification results of 16 common liquids, when testing liquids are in different positions.

mmWave signal will change significantly, leading to poor identification accuracy. The impact of different liquids on mmWave signal can easily be submerged in the impact of different container positions. The classification module uses a deep learning model to extract liquid-related information and classify candidate liquids.

In this paper, we aim to propose an accurate liquid identification approach that will not be affected by the position of the container.

4   Overview

In this paper, we propose MmLiquid, a mmWave-based liquid identification system. Figure 3 shows the overview of MmLiquid, which consists of three modules: a data collection module, a data reconstruction module, and a classification model.

The mmWave radar sends FMCW signals to the container and receives the response signals reflected from the liquid and reflective surfaces. The collected signals are then input into the data reconstruction module, which is responsible for obtaining effective liquid information. This module will filter out frequency bands that hurt the classification accuracy using FFT and a CPIF scheme and feed the processed data into the classification module.

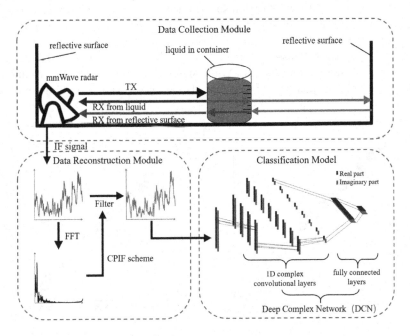

Fig. 3. The overview of MmLiquid. MmLiquid mainly consists of a data collection module to sense the liquid information, a data reconstruction module to filter out the complex frequency band, and a classification module to identify different liquids.

5   MmLiquid Design

5.1   Data Collection Module

In MmLiquid, the data collection module consists of a mmWave radar and two vertically placed steel plates with a size of 30 cm × 30 cm, as shown in Fig. 3. The distance between the two steel plates is around 1 m. The mmWave radar has 4 signal receivers, and the distance between every 2 receivers is about 3 mm. Based on our preliminary study, such distance can make a completely different mmWave link. Therefore, we take the data collected by each receiver in a chirp as a raw data sample.

5.2   Data Reconstruction Module

In this module, we use a container position information filtering (CPIF) scheme to filter out the changed signal parts that correspond to position changes of the container.

Since the IF signal is related to the distance X between the object and the mmWave radar, we can determine the position of the container and the reflective surface through the frequency spectrum of the mmWave signal. We perform Fourier transform on Eq. 4 and get the IF signal in the frequency domain $H(X)$:

$$H(X) = \frac{1}{T_r} \int_{T_0}^{T_0+T_r} H(t)exp[-j2\pi\rho\frac{2X}{c}t] \, dt = \Gamma exp(j\frac{4\pi f_0 X}{c}). \qquad (8)$$

Equation 8 shows that the peaks of frequency spectrum of mmWave signals corresponds to the positions of object/reflective surfaces. By scanning the peak positions, we can find the positions of the liquid container and reflective surfaces. As shown in Fig. 1, the first peak attributes to the container, while the second peak attributes to the reflective surface behind the container. The mmWave signals reflected from the reflective surfaces will repeatedly penetrate the liquid. That is, when the liquid in the container changes, the amplitude and phase differences will be amplified in our experimental settings. Therefore, both the two peaks and the subsequent multiple reflection peaks carry valuable liquid information.

In theory, when the signal penetrates the liquid multiple times, the frequency shift of the signal peak will be more obvious:

$$\Delta F = k\frac{2\rho d(n-1)}{c}, \qquad (9)$$

where k indicates the times the signal penetrating the liquid. The amplitude and frequency of all these peaks can reflect the attenuation and change caused by the liquid. Based on the above principles, we propose a CPIF scheme to filter out the signals whose frequency band corresponds to the changing position of the container.

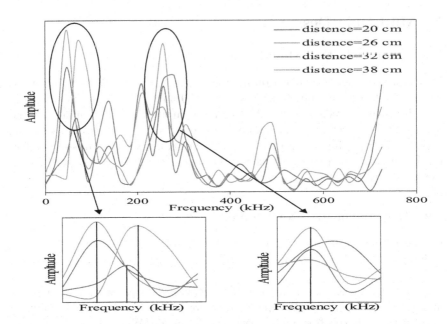

Fig. 4. mmWave signals of water placed in different positions, the distances from the container to the mmWave radar are 20 cm, 26 cm, 32 cm and 38 cm respectively.

We first aim to extract the mmWave signals that are reflected by the container and by the reflective surfaces after the mmWave signal penetrates the liquid. These signal segments can contain liquid-related information, which can be used to distinguish different liquids. Then, as shown in the Fig. 4, for the same liquid, the mmWave signal reflected by the container will vary with the distance. Comparing the liquid information collected at different positions, the information reflected by the reflective surface is relatively similar. The information reflected by the container is messier, with different frequencies and amplitudes. Therefore, the information returned by the reflective surface is more conducive to the extraction of the liquid feature. This is because the distance between the container and the mmWave radar is changed and the reflective surface is fixed.

Based on the above facts, we can conclude that the information reflected by the container hurts the result of liquid classification.

Therefore, our CPIF scheme will first calculate the distance between the container and the mmWave radar as:

$$X = \frac{1}{2}c \times t_d = \frac{c \times F}{2\rho}. \tag{10}$$

Then the scheme will calculate the frequency band corresponding to the position where the container is placed. Finally, our CPIF scheme will eliminate the harmful frequency band and retain the more similar frequency bands (the signals reflected by the reflective surface) to improve the classification accuracy of MmLiquid.

5.3 Classification Model

The collected IF signals are complex values that have richer characterization capabilities. Deep complex networks (DCN) [6] provide the key atomic components for complex-valued deep neural networks. Therefore, in MmLiquid, we directly extract the liquid-related features from IF signals using DCN. The DCN model in our classification module includes 3 1D complex convolutional layers and 2 fully connected layers. In DCN [6], the real part A and imaginary part B of a complex number are represented as logically different real-valued entities. DCN uses real-valued algorithms to simulate complex number operations. We use a filter in the form of Eq. 11:

$$W * h = (A * x - B * y) + j(B * x + A * y), \qquad (11)$$

where W represents the weight, h represents the filter. For mmWave signals, the use of complex numbers in neural networks makes neural networks more expressive [4,32], and retains the liquid information as much as possible.

6 Performance Evaluation

In this section, we first introduce the implementation of MmLiquid. Then we will present the detailed liquid identification results and the impact of different practical conditions.

6.1 Implementation

Our experimental setup for evaluating MmLiquid is shown in Fig. 5. In our experiments, we leverage a Texas Instruments AWR1642 mmWave radar to emit the signal and capture the data. The cost of the hardware is $299.

We place the mmWave radar vertically to ensure that the mmWave signals can penetrate the candidate liquid. We use two vertical steel plates as reflective surfaces to set up the liquid identification environment. These vertical plates can increase signal reflections, thereby increasing the amount of liquid information carried in the received signal.

The container we use in our experiments has a height of 8.5 cm and a diameter of 7.0 cm. The diameter is much larger than the signal wavelength of mmWave to avoid signal diffraction. The container is placed in a 10 cm × 16 cm area in front of the mmWave radar. In each experiment, we use a high-precision balance to ensure that the liquid quality is the same and sufficient. We use 16 types of liquids collected at 24 different positions in our experiments. At each position, each liquid is tested 2 times to eliminate the impact of measurement noise. In total, we have collected 768 data traces.

Fig. 5. Implementation.

All experiments are run in a lab setting with standard multipath effects. All liquids are at room temperature between 20 °C and 25 °C. NaCl solutions of different concentrations are prepared by mixing non-iodized salt in drinking water. The mmWave signals of different liquids are collected, processed, and classified on a DELL desktop with Intel Core i7-7700 CPU and 12G RAM. We use the end-to-end identification accuracy as the evaluation metric.

6.2 Liquid Identification Performance

Figure 6 shows the confusion matrix for identifying the 16 liquids using MmLiquid. Results show that MmLiquid can achieve a liquid identification accuracy of 97.6% for all liquids. Compared to the original identification accuracy of 93.6% shown in Sect. 3, our CPIF scheme manages to improve the accuracy by 4.0%. These results indicate that MmLiquid can effectively identify the liquid even when the container is in different positions. Because MmLiquid use CPIF scheme to filter out the frequency bands that hurt the classification to improve its classification accuracy.

Impact of Selected Frequency Band. To verify which frequency band (i.e., physical position) contributes more to the liquid identification accuracy, we choose the sliding filter windows with window sizes of $8 \times Fs/N$ in the frequency spectrum.

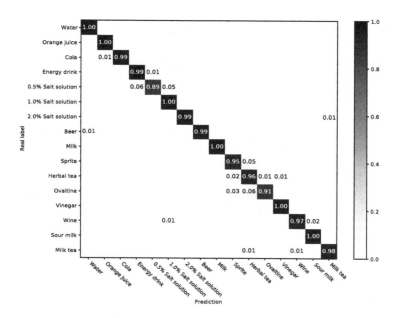

Fig. 6. MmLiquid's classification result of 16 common liquids in different positions.

Figure 7(a) shows the performance of different frequency bands. We observe that the accuracy changes periodically with the movement of the filter window and the accuracy and the peak accuracy gradually decreases. Results show that the frequency bands between 164 kHz and 352 kHz and between 539 kHz and 727 kHz provide the best identification accuracy since these frequencies can successfully capture the mmWave signals that are affected by the liquids. The positions of these two peaks correspond to the distance from the mmWave device to the reflector and three times the distance, respectively.

We can also observe that some bad frequency bands (e.g., when we select the frequency band between 23 kHz and 234 kHz, the accuracy is just 18.06%) have negative impacts on identification accuracy, and even worse than the classification results of some high-frequency bands whose signals reflected multiple times between two reflecting surfaces. This indicates that these frequency bands will lead to poor accuracy. This frequency band corresponds to the container position. The signal changes introduced by liquids' property can be easily overwhelmed by container position changes. Therefore, we should not use these frequency bands for liquid property extraction. When we filter out the signal segments corresponding to the container position, the liquid identification accuracy can be greatly improved. As for the signal reflected by reflective surface, its change is mainly caused by the different liquid properties since the relative surface position between the mmWave and the reflector will remain the same. Therefore, these frequency bands of information can be used for liquid identification.

As shown in Fig. 7(a), there are peaks whose frequencies are multiple times than that of the reflective surface. When the sliding window moves toward high frequencies, the accuracy of peaks shows a downward trend. Therefore, we believe that high-frequency signals (signals that are reflected multiple times by two reflective surfaces) also have little effect on classification accuracy. Therefore, these high-frequency bands are also eliminated in our CPIF scheme.

Impact of Reflective Surface. In our implementation, we have designed a liquid identification environment with strong reflectors (i.e., the steel plates). These reflectors can increase the strength of the received mmWave signal and increase the number of liquid penetrations. To validate the effectiveness of the reflector, we compare the liquid identification performance with and without reflective surface in Fig. 7(b). As seen, without a reflective surface, the identification

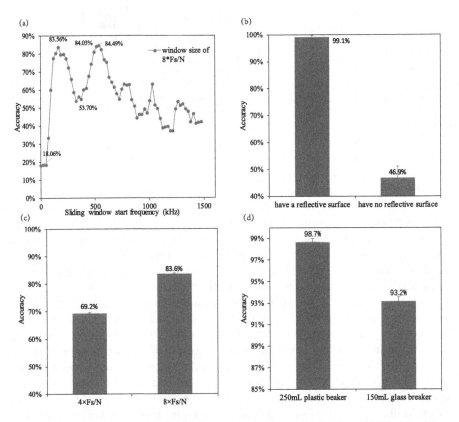

Fig. 7. (a) Contribution of sliding window to 12 liquids classification. (b) The classification accuracy of 6 liquids with and without the reflective surface. (c) The classification accuracy of 8 liquids when the slope of FMCW is 29.982 MHz/μs and 40.024 MHz/μs. (d) The classification accuracy of 8 liquids when these liquids in a plastic beaker and a glass beaker.

accuracy will drop to 46.9%, a decrease of 52.2% compared to that with reflector. This is because the reflector can effectively increase the liquid information carried in the signal. On the other hand, since the identification environment usually remains unchanged after deployment, our identification system will not introduce much extra deployment overhead.

Impact of the Slope of FMCW. A larger slope of FMCW can carry more signal information. Note that this also proportionally increases the bandwidth. Thus intuitively: The greater the Bandwidth carry more information. We set the slope of the FMCW to 29.982 MHz/μs and 40.024 MHz/μs. Figure 7(c) shows that a slope of 40.024 MHz/μs can achieve an identification accuracy of 99.1%, 11.5% higher than that when setting the slope to 29.982 MHz/μs. This experiment validates that a slope of 40.024 MHz/μs can lead to better liquid identification accuracy than the slope of 29.982 MHz/μs. Therefore, MmLiquid chooses a slope of 40.024 MHz/μs to collect data.

Impact of Container. The different containers can introduce different multipath effects to the received signals. To investigate the identification performance with different containers, we use the data collected using different containers, including a 250 mL plastic beaker and a 150 mL glass beaker, in this experiment. We use these two kinds of beakers to carry out experiments, realize the classification of 8 liquids. The experimental results are shown in Fig. 7(d). The average classification accuracy of 8 liquids in plastic breaker is 98.7%, but when the container is a glass breaker, the average classification accuracy drops to 93.2%. This may be due to the fact that glass is more reflective than plastic. In addition, the diameter of the glass beaker is only 6 cm, which is smaller than the diameter of the plastic beaker. Therefore, when the liquid is placed in a plastic beaker, it has a greater impact on the mmWave signal. Different containers have a small influence on the classification accuracy of MmLiquid.

7   Conclusion

mmWave signals will suffer from different signal changes when passing through different liquids. Based on this property, we conduct a preliminary experiment to prove the effectiveness of mmWave signals in liquid identification. However, the identification accuracy will decrease after moving the container. To address this issue, we propose an accurate and robust mmWave-based liquid identification approach MmLiquid. MmLiquid can identify the frequency bands that correspond to position changes of the container and will hurt liquid identification. MmLiquid will automatically filter out these frequency parts and use the filtered data for training a deep learning-based classifier built on DCN. MmLiquid can be implemented using commercial mmWave devices. For 16 kinds of liquids, MmLiquid can achieve a 97.6% identification accuracy when placing the container at 24 different locations.

References

1. Adib, F., Kabelac, Z., Katabi, D., Miller, R.C.. 3D tracking via body radio reflections. In: 11th USENIX Symposium on Networked Systems Design and Implementation (NSDI 2014), pp. 317–329 (2014)
2. Adib, F., Katabi, D.: See through walls with Wifi! In: Proceedings of the ACM SIGCOMM 2013 Conference on SIGCOMM, pp. 75–86 (2013)
3. Alocilja, E.C., Radke, S.M.: Market analysis of biosensors for food safety. Biosens. Bioelectron. **18**(5–6), 841–846 (2003)
4. Arjovsky, M., Shah, A., Bengio, Y.: Unitary evolution recurrent neural networks. In: International Conference on Machine Learning, pp. 1120–1128. PMLR (2016)
5. Chen, B., Li, H., Li, Z., Chen, X., Xu, C., Xu, W.: ThermoWave: a new paradigm of wireless passive temperature monitoring via mmWave sensing. In: Proceedings of the 26th Annual International Conference on Mobile Computing and Networking, pp. 1–14 (2020)
6. Chiheb, T., Bilaniuk, O., Serdyuk, D., et al.: Deep complex networks. In: International Conference on Learning Representations (2017). https://openreview.net/forum
7. Dhekne, A., Gowda, M., Zhao, Y., Hassanieh, H., Choudhury, R.R.: Liquid: a wireless liquid identifier. In: Proceedings of the 16th Annual International Conference on Mobile Systems, Applications, and Services, pp. 442–454 (2018)
8. Feng, C., et al.: WiMi: target material identification with commodity Wi-Fi devices. In: 2019 IEEE 39th International Conference on Distributed Computing Systems (ICDCS), pp. 700–710. IEEE (2019)
9. Ha, U., Leng, J., Khaddaj, A., Adib, F.: Food and liquid sensing in practical environments using RFIDs. In: 17th USENIX Symposium on Networked Systems Design and Implementation (NSDI 2020), pp. 1083–1100 (2020)
10. Ha, U., Ma, Y., Zhong, Z., Hsu, T.M., Adib, F.: Learning food quality and safety from wireless stickers. In: Proceedings of the 17th ACM Workshop on Hot Topics in Networks, pp. 106–112 (2018)
11. Huang, Y., Chen, K., Huang, Y., Wang, L., Wu, K.: Vi-liquid: unknown liquid identification with your smartphone vibration. In: Proceedings of the 27th Annual International Conference on Mobile Computing and Networking, pp. 174–187 (2021)
12. Li, H., et al.: Vocalprint: exploring a resilient and secure voice authentication via mmWave biometric interrogation. In: Proceedings of the 18th Conference on Embedded Networked Sensor Systems, pp. 312–325 (2020)
13. Li, Z., Yang, Z., Song, C., Li, C., Peng, Z., Xu, W.: E-eye: hidden electronics recognition through mmWave nonlinear effects. In: Proceedings of the 16th ACM Conference on Embedded Networked Sensor Systems, pp. 68–81 (2018)
14. Liang, Y., Zhou, A., Zhang, H., Wen, X., Ma, H.: FG-LiquID: a contact-less fine-grained liquid identifier by pushing the limits of millimeter-wave sensing. Proc. ACM Interact. Mob. Wearable Ubiquitous Technol. **5**(3), 1–27 (2021)
15. Lu, C.X., et al.: milliEgo: single-chip mmWave radar aided egomotion estimation via deep sensor fusion. In: Proceedings of the 18th Conference on Embedded Networked Sensor Systems, pp. 109–122 (2020)
16. Marin, G., Dominio, F., Zanuttigh, P.: Hand gesture recognition with leap motion and kinect devices. In: 2014 IEEE International Conference on Image Processing (ICIP), pp. 1565–1569. IEEE (2014)

17. McLachlan, M., Hamann, R., Sayers, V., Kelly, C., Drimie, S.: Fostering innovation for sustainable food security: the Southern Africa food lab. In: Bitzer, V., Hamann, R., Hall, M., Griffin-EL, E.W. (eds.) The Business of Social and Environmental Innovation, pp. 163–181. Springer, Cham (2015). https://doi.org/10.1007/978-3-319-04051-6_9

18. Polese, M., Mezzavilla, M., Rangan, S., Kessler, C., Zorzi, M.: mmWave for future public safety communications. In: Proceedings of the First CoNEXT Workshop on ICT Tools for Emergency Networks and DisastEr Relief, pp. 44–49 (2017)

19. Prabhakara, A., Singh, V., Kumar, S., Rowe, A.: Osprey: a mmWave approach to tire wear sensing. In: Proceedings of the 18th International Conference on Mobile Systems, Applications, and Services, pp. 28–41 (2020)

20. Rahman, T., Adams, A.T., Schein, P., Jain, A., Erickson, D., Choudhury, T.: Nutri-lyzer: a mobile system for characterizing liquid food with photoacoustic effect. In: Proceedings of the 14th ACM Conference on Embedded Network Sensor Systems CD-ROM, pp. 123–136 (2016)

21. Ren, Y., Tan, S., Zhang, L., Wang, Z., Wang, Z., Yang, J.: Liquid level sensing using commodity Wifi in a smart home environment. Proc. ACM Interact. Mob. Wearable Ubiquitous Technol. 4(1), 1–30 (2020)

22. Shi, C., Zhu, J., Xu, M., Wu, X., Peng, Y.: An approach of spectra standard-ization and qualitative identification for biomedical materials based on terahertz spectroscopy. Sci. Program. 2020, 1–8 (2020)

23. Singh, J., Ginsburg, B., Rao, S., Ramasubramanian, K., et al.: AWR1642 mmWave sensor: 76–81-Ghz radar-on-chip for short-range radar applications. Texas Instruments, pp. 1–7 (2017)

24. Stange, H., Liebig, T., Hecker, D., Andrienko, G., Andrienko, N.: Analytical work-flow of monitoring human mobility in big event settings using bluetooth. In: Proceedings of the 3rd ACM SIGSPATIAL International Workshop on Indoor Spatial Awareness, pp. 51–58 (2011)

25. Tsiminis, G., Chu, F., Warren-Smith, S.C., Spooner, N.A., Monro, T.M.: Identi-fication and quantification of explosives in nanolitre solution volumes by Raman spectroscopy in suspended core optical fibers. Sensors 13(10), 13163–13177 (2013)

26. Wang, J., Xiong, J., Chen, X., Jiang, H., Balan, R.K., Fang, D.: Tagscan: Simulta-neous target imaging and material identification with commodity rfid devices. In: Proceedings of the 23rd Annual International Conference on Mobile Computing and Networking. pp. 288–300 (2017)

27. Wang, W., Liu, A.X., Shahzad, M., Ling, K., Lu, S.: Understanding and modeling of Wifi signal based human activity recognition. In: Proceedings of the 21st Annual International Conference on Mobile Computing and Networking, pp. 65–76 (2015)

28. Wang, W., Liu, A.X., Sun, K.: Device-free gesture tracking using acoustic signals. In: Proceedings of the 22nd Annual International Conference on Mobile Computing and Networking, pp. 82–94 (2016)

29. Wang, Y., Liu, J., Chen, Y., Gruteser, M., Yang, J., Liu, H.: E-eyes: device-free location-oriented activity identification using fine-grained Wifi signatures. In: Proceedings of the 20th Annual International Conference on Mobile Computing and Networking, pp. 617–628 (2014)

30. Wang, Y., Wu, K., Ni, L.M.: WiFall: device-free fall detection by wireless networks. IEEE Trans. Mob. Comput. 16(2), 581–594 (2016)

31. Weiß, J., Santra, A.: One-shot learning for robust material classification using millimeter-wave radar system. IEEE Sens. Lett. 2(4), 1–4 (2018)

32. Wisdom, S., Powers, T., Hershey, J., Le Roux, J., Atlas, L.: Full-capacity unitary recurrent neural networks. In: Advances in Neural Information Processing Systems 29 (2016)
33. Xie, B., et al.: Tagtag: material sensing with commodity RFID. In: Proceedings of the 17th Conference on Embedded Networked Sensor Systems, pp. 338–350 (2019)
34. Xu, C., et al.: WaveEar: exploring a mmWave-based noise-resistant speech sensing for voice-user interface. In: Proceedings of the 17th Annual International Conference on Mobile Systems, Applications, and Services, pp. 14–26 (2019)
35. Yang, L., Lin, Q., Li, X., Liu, T., Liu, Y.: See through walls with COTS RFID system! In: Proceedings of the 21st Annual International Conference on Mobile Computing and Networking, pp. 487–499 (2015)
36. Yeo, H.S., Flamich, G., Schrempf, P., Harris-Birtill, D., Quigley, A.: RadarCat: radar categorization for input & interaction. In: Proceedings of the 29th Annual Symposium on User Interface Software and Technology, pp. 833–841 (2016)
37. Youssef, M., Mah, M., Agrawala, A.: Challenges: device-free passive localization for wireless environments. In: Proceedings of the 13th Annual ACM International Conference on Mobile Computing and Networking, pp. 222–229 (2007)
38. Yue, S., Katabi, D.: Liquid testing with your smartphone. In: Proceedings of the 17th Annual International Conference on Mobile Systems, Applications, and Services, pp. 275–286 (2019)
39. Zhang, X., Zhu, X., Guo, Y.E., Qian, F., Mao, Z.M.: Poster: characterizing performance and power for mmWave 5G on commodity smartphones. In: 11th ACM Workshop on Wireless of the Students, by the Students, and for the Students, S3 2019, co-located with MobiCom 2019, p. 14. Association for Computing Machinery (2019)
40. Zhang, Z.: Microsoft kinect sensor and its effect. IEEE Multimedia 19(2), 4–10 (2012)

PASD: A Prioritized Action Sampling-Based Dueling DQN for Cloud-Edge Collaborative Computation Offloading in Industrial IoT

Wei Qin[1], Haiming Chen[1,2(✉)] (iD), and Lei Wang[1]

[1] Faculty of Electrical Engineering and Computer Science, Ningbo University, Ningbo 315211, Zhejiang, China
chenhaiming@nbu.edu.cn
[2] Zhejiang Provincial Key Laboratory of Mobile Network Application Technology, Ningbo 315211, Zhejiang, China

Abstract. Due to restricted resources such as computing power and battery capacity of Industrial Internet of Things (IIoT) equipments, computation-intensive tasks need to be migrated to edge or cloud servers for execution. To improve the processing efficiency of tasks with limited computation and network resources, we study the problem of joint allocation of network and computational resources in the cloud-edge collaborative IIoT, with the goal of minimizing the average task delay and total system energy consumption. To address this issue, we propose a prioritized action sampling-based Dueling DQN (PASD) algorithm to determine task offloading and resource allocation strategies. Finally, we evaluate PASD through large-scale simulation experiments and NBUFlow, which is an IoT experimental platform equipped with object recognition and pose detection applications. Compared with baselines, PASD has significant advantages in reducing the total energy consumption of the system, and has a good performance in reducing task delay and task throw rate.

Keywords: IIoT · Cloud-Edge collaboration · Computation offloading · Deep reinforcement learning

1 Introduction

With the rapid development of the Industrial Internet of Things (IIoT), IIoT task processing will also bring in a large amount of energy consumption. Therefore, a low-latency and low-energy production environment is an urgent problem to be solved. The traditional approach is that IIoT equipments (IIoTEs) can offload their tasks to the mobile cloud computing (MCC) server [1]. However, the inherent limitation of MCC is high transmission delay and energy caused by the long transmission distance [2]. The rise of the mobile edge computing (MEC) has compensated for the shortcomings of MCC. Some delay-sensitive tasks can

H. Ma et al. (Eds.): CWSN 2022, CCIS 1715, pp. 19–30, 2022.
https://doi.org/10.1007/978-981-19-8350-4_2

be migrated to the edge of the network, which dramatically decreases the high transmission delay and the energy consumption of IIoTEs [3].

However, the limited network and computational resources of IIoTEs becomes a significant factor affecting offloading performance [4]. Therefore, in order to enhance the offloading performance and cut down the task delay and system overhead, it is a prerequisite to optimize the offloading decision and allocate the limited resources reasonably. Therefore, Seid [5] proposed a method based on Multi-Agent Deep Reinforcement Learning (MADRL) to obtain the optimal resource allocation and computation offloading strategy. Hence, we propose a deep reinforcement learning (DRL)-based task offloading and coordinated network and computational resource allocation scheme, and put forward the remaining bandwidth allocation strategy. The main contributions of this paper are as follows.

1) In this paper, we study the network and computational resource management problems of cloud-edge collaboration in the IIoT. The optimization goal is to minimize the average task completion time and total energy consumption of the system and improve bandwidth utilization.
2) This paper proposes an improved Dueling DQN, named PASD, which utilizes the prioritized action sampling strategy in the prioritized Experience Replay (PER) mechanism to improve the learning efficiency of the agent.
3) We conduct extensive simulation experiments and use the IoT experimental platform in real IIoT environment, named NBUFlow [6], to evaluate the performance of the PASD. Results show that PASD has good performance advantages compared with existing baselines.

The rest of this paper is organized as follows: In Sect. 2, we review related work. Section 3 presents the proposed system model. In Sect. 4, we introduce the design of the PASD algorithm. In Sect. 5, we describe our algorithm evaluation. Finally, we conclude our work in Sect. 6.

2   Related Work

The agent of computation offloading determines where to offload tasks based on currently available network resources and available computational resources on the server. Alfakih [7] proposed a State-Action-Reward-State-Action (RL-SARSA) based on reinforcement learning to solve the bandwidth and computational resource management problem of edge servers. In contrast, Chen [8] investigated the dynamic resource management problem of joint power control and computational resource allocation for MEC in IIoT.

In recent years, many scholars have conducted a series of researches on the offloading decision method. Traditional methods such as game theory [9] etc., which are not suitable for solving the computation offloading problem of large-scale cloud-edge collaboration. Therefore, Yadav [10] proposed a computation offloading scheme based on reinforcement learning (CORL). In addition, for problems with large-scale state or action space, RL-based offloading schemes are also somewhat stretched. Deep reinforcement learning, which combines RL with deep neural network (DNN), can significantly improve the generalization ability of computation offloading policies [11].

3 System Model

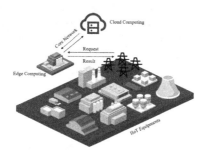

Fig. 1. Cloud-Edge collaborative computation offloading in IIoT.

Figure 1 depicts the cloud-edge collaborative computation offloading model in this paper. We suppose that there are a total of N IIoTEs n ($n \in \{1, 2, 3, ..., N\}$) and M edge servers m ($m \in \{1, 2, 3, ..., M\}$), which are connected through wireless links, and the edge servers pass through the core network connect to cloud server C. Furthermore, we divide time into equally spaced discrete time slot t ($t \in \{1, 2, 3, ..., T\}$) with a fixed time interval τ in each time slot t.

3.1 Task Model

At the beginning of time slot t, the IIoTE generates a task, which is expressed as $R_n^i(t) = \{B_n^i(t), D_n^i(t), \tau_n^i(t)\}$, ($i \in \{1, 2, 3, ..., R\}$). $B_n^i(t)$ represents the size of the task, and $D_n^i(t)$ represents the required computational resources. $\tau_n^i(t)$ is expressed as the maximum tolerable delay, where $\tau_n^i(t) \leq \tau$. When the task arrives, the task can be executed directly on the local device, or offloaded to the server. The offloading decision can be expressed as $\alpha_n^i(t) = [\alpha_{n\_n}^i(t), \alpha_{n\_m}^i(t), \alpha_{n\_c}^i(t)]$, $\alpha_{n\_n}^i(t), \alpha_{n\_m}^i(t), \alpha_{n\_c}^i(t) \in (0, 1)$, and $\alpha_{n\_n}^i(t) + \alpha_{n\_m}^i(t) + \alpha_{n\_c}^i(t) = 1$.

3.2 Transmission Model

At each time slot, we record the remaining bandwidth $b_i(t)$ ($i \in I$) of the link. For time slot t, bandwidth with all links remaining non-zero will be allocated for each task $R_n^i(t)$, then the allocated bandwidth is $W_n^i(t) = min b_i(t)$ ($i \in I$). Here, $W_n^i(t)$ should not exceed the maximum communication bandwidth W_{max} of the link. After bandwidth allocation, $b_i(t)$ can be updated as: $b_i(t) = b_i(t) - W_n^i(t)$. So we obtain the maximum upload rate from the IIoTE to the edge server according to Shannon's equation $r_{n\_m}^i(t) = W_n^i(t) \log \left(1 + \frac{P_n(t) h_{n\_m}(t)}{N_0} \right)$, where

$P_n(t)$ represents the transmission power allocated for IIoTE n in time slot t, $h_{n\_m}(t)$ represents the wireless channel gain from IIoTE n to the server, and N_0 is the channel white Gaussian noise.

3.3 Computing Model

Local Computing Model. Due to the heterogeneity of devices, there are differences in the computational capabilities F_n of different IIoTEs. It is assumed that $f_{n\_n}^i(t)$ is the computational resource allocated by IIoTE n to the task $R_n^i(t)$. Since local limited computational resources, the number of tasks is limited by the current device: $\sum f_{n\_n}^i(t) \le F_n$. Furthermore, since the IIoTE is battery powered, the energy consumption needs to satisfy $\sum E_{n\_n}^i(t) \le E_n$. The delay of the task $R_n^i(t)$ consists of the waiting calculation delay $w_{n\_pn}^i(t)$ and the calculation delay, then the total local delay of the task is $T_{n\_n}^i(t) = w_{n\_pn}^i(t) + \frac{D_n^i(t)}{f_{n\_n}^i(t)}$. The energy consumption of task $R_n^i(t)$ running in the local can be calculated as $E_{n\_n}^i(t) = \varphi\left(f_{n\_n}^i(t)\right)^2 D_n^i(t)$, where $\varphi = 10^{-26}$ [12].

Edge Computation Model. When the agent decides to offload the task to the edge server, $\alpha_{n\_m}^i(t) = 1$. Each edge server m has F_m computational resource. The processing time of each task is $T_{n\_m}^i(t)$ which includes transmission waiting delay $w_{n\_tm}^i(t)$, transmission delay $T_{n\_tm}^i(t) = \frac{B_n^i(t)}{r_{n\_m}^i(t)}$, computational waiting delay $w_{n\_pm}^i(t)$, and computational delay $\frac{D_n^i(t)}{f_{n\_m}^i(t)}$, where $f_{n\_m}^i(t)$ is allocated by edge server m for the task $R_n^i(t)$, which satisfies $\sum f_{n\_m}^i(t) \le F_m$. Therefore, the total processing delay is $T_{n\_m}^i(t) = w_{n\_tm}^i(t) + \frac{B_n^i(t)}{r_{n\_m}^i(t)} + w_{n\_pm}^i(t) + \frac{D_n^i(t)}{f_{n\_m}^i(t)}$.

Similarly, the total energy consumption $E_{n\_m}^i(t)$ is composed of the transmission energy consumption $E_{n\_tm}^i(t) = P_n(t)\frac{B_n^i(t)}{r_{n\_m}^i(t)}$ and the computational energy consumption $E_{n\_pm}^i(t) = \varphi\left(f_{n\_m}^i(t)\right)^2 D_n^i(t)$. So $E_{n\_m}^i(t)$ is expressed as $E_{n\_m}^i(t) = E_{n\_tm}^i(t) + E_{n\_pm}^i(t)$.

Cloud Computing Model. In addition to edge servers and local processing, tasks can also be offloaded to the cloud when $\alpha_{n\_c}^i(t) = 1$. In the network model, the cloud server has enough computational resources F_c. When task are offloaded to cloud, the processing time of a task consists of transmission waiting delay $w_{n\_tc}^i(t)$, transmission delay $T_{n\_tc}^i(t) = \frac{B_n^i(t)}{r_{n\_c}^i(t)}$, where $r_{n\_c}^i(t)$ is the transmission rate between the IIoTE and the cloud server, and computation delay. The processing time for offloading the task $R_n^i(t)$ to the cloud is $T_{n\_c}^i(t) = w_{n\_tc}^i(t) + \frac{B_n^i(t)}{r_{n\_c}^i(t)} + \frac{D_n^i(t)}{f_{n\_c}^i(t)}$, where $f_{n\_c}^i(t)$ is the computational resource allocated by the cloud server. The energy consumption of offloading the task $R_n^i(t)$ to the cloud server is defined as $E_{n\_c}^i(t) = P_n(t)\frac{B_n^i(t)}{r_{n\_c}^i(t)} + \varphi\left(f_{n\_c}^i(t)\right)^2 D_n^i(t)$.

Therefore, the total delay $T_n^i(t)$ of the task $R_n^i(t)$ can be expressed as $T_n^i(t) = \left[T_{n\_n}^i(t), T_{n\_m}^i(t), T_{n\_c}^i(t)\right] \cdot \left[\alpha_{n\_n}^i(t), \alpha_{n\_m}^i(t), \alpha_{n\_c}^i(t)\right]^T$. Meanwhile, the total energy consumption of task can be represented by $E_n^i(t)$, which is specifically expressed as $E_n^i(t) = \left[E_{n\_n}^i(t), E_{n\_m}^i(t), E_{n\_c}^i(t)\right] \cdot \left[\alpha_{n\_n}^i(t), \alpha_{n\_m}^i(t), \alpha_{n\_c}^i(t)\right]^T$.

3.4 Problem Formulation

The purpose of this paper is to optimize the task offloading and resource allocation in the IIoT cloud-edge collaborative computation environment based on the resource constraints of nodes.

In the range of time slot t, we define the practical optimization problem as:

$$\mathbb{P}: min\frac{1}{T}\sum_{t=1}^{T}\frac{1}{N}\sum_{n=1}^{N}\frac{1}{R}\sum_{i=1}^{R}T_n^i(t) \ and \ \sum_{t=1}^{T}\sum_{n=1}^{N}\sum_{i=1}^{R}E_n^i(t),$$

$$s.t. \ C1: T_n^i(t) \leq \tau_n^i(t),$$

$$C2: W_{min} \leq W_n^i(t) \leq W_{max}, \tag{1}$$

$$C3: \sum_{t=1}^{T}\sum_{n=1}^{N}\sum_{i=1}^{R}f_{n\_n}^i(t) \leq F_n,$$

$$C4: \sum_{t=1}^{T}\sum_{n=1}^{N}\sum_{i=1}^{R}E_{n\_n}^i(t) \leq E_n.$$

Here, $C1$ constrains the completion time of the delay-sensitive task, and $C2$ constrains the communication bandwidth. W_{min} and W_{max} denote the minimum and the maximum transmission bandwidth of the link, respectively. $C3$ indicates that the computational resources of the IIoTE allocated by the local computing task in the time slot t. $C4$ indicates the total battery capacity of IIoTE n.

4 Computation Offloading and Resources Allocation with PASD

In this section, we transform problem $\mathbb{P}$ into Markov Decision Process (MDP) and design a DRL-based for computation offloading and resource allocation.

4.1 MDP

We regard the cloud-edge collaborative environment as a MDP with internal state transition probability ρ. The MDP consists of a quintuple $\mathbf{M} = \{S, A, \rho, R, \gamma\}$, where S represents the state space. A represents the action space, ρ represents the state transition probability, R denotes the reward, and γ represents the discount factor. The details of our designed MDP are as follows:

1) *State Space.* The system state space $s_n^i(t)$ is a four tuple, including the computational resources of the IIoTE, the edge server and the cloud, and the remaining bandwidth resources of the wireless channel.

$$s_n^i(t) = \{F_n(t), F_m(t), F_c(t), b_i(t)\}. \tag{2}$$

2) *Action Space.* The action space $a_n^i(t)$ consists of the nodes or servers selected for computation offloading and resources allocation.

$$a_n^i(t) = \left\{ \alpha_n^i(t), f_{n\_n}^i(t), f_{n\_m}^i(t), f_{n\_c}^i(t), W_n^i(t) \right\}. \tag{3}$$

3) *Reward.* The reward $r_n^i(t)$ indicates that the reward is obtained according to the action $a_n^i(t)$ executed in the state $s_n^i(t)$. When action $a_n^i(t)$ is done, the agent will feedback a reward $r_n^i(t)^+ = -\left(\delta * T_n^i(t) + \mu * E_n^i(t) \right)$. Here, δ and μ are the proportional coefficients of the average task completion time and the total energy consumption, respectively. In addition, when task fails, we set the punishment $r_n^i(t)^- = -\left(\delta * maxT_n^i(t) + \mu * maxE_n^i(t) \right)$. Therefore, the cumulative reward of deep reinforcement learning is $r_n^i(t) = \sum_{t=1}^{T} \left(r_n^i(t)^+ + r_n^i(t)^- \right)$.

4.2 PASD Model

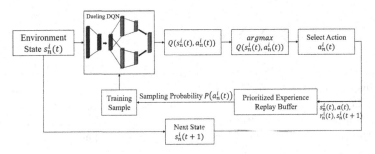

Fig. 2. The training process of PASD.

PASD based on Dueling DQN is shown in Fig. 2, where the Q function is represented by the action value function $A^\pi \left(s_n^i(t), a_n^i(t) \right)$ and state value function $V^\pi \left(s_n^i(t) \right)$ outputs, where π indicates the strategy adopted. Because V and A cannot accurately and uniquely estimate the Q value. Therefore, it is necessary to force the output sum of the action function to 0, then the Q function can be expressed as:

$$Q \left(s_n^i(t), a_n^i(t) \right) = V \left(s_n^i(t) \right) + A \left(s_n^i(t), a_n^i(t) \right) - \sum_{a_n^i(t+1)} A \left(s_n^i(t), a_n^i(t+1) \right) / |A|. \tag{4}$$

To obtain special actions, the traditional approach is based on the $\epsilon - greedy$ strategy to select an action. This kind of action selection algorithm means that the initial high error value actions will be repeatedly sampled frequently, lack of action diversity [13]. Therefore, we propose a prioritized action sampling strategy (PASD) based on Prioritized Experience Replay (PER) [14] to overcome this problem. Under this strategy, we guarantee that the action sampling probability $P\left(a_n^i(t)\right)$ and the state-action value are monotonic.

$$P\left(a_n^i(t)\right) = \frac{p_i^\partial}{\sum_{j=1}^{A} p_j^\partial} \ \ and \ \ p_i = Q\left(s_n^i(t), a_n^i(t)\right). \tag{5}$$

Here, $p_i > 0$ is the priority of the action a_i, and ∂ decides how many priorities to use. Since we use PER, it changes the probability distribution of actions, which can bias the agent towards actions with high priority values. To reduce this bias, we use Importance Sampling (IS) weights, which adjust updates by reducing the weights $\omega_{a_n^i(t)} = \left(\frac{1}{N} \cdot \frac{1}{P(a_n^i(t))}\right)^\sigma$ of frequently used samples, where N represents the size of PER buffer, σ controls the degree of IS influence on learning. The details of the PASD-based are presented in Algorithm 1.

Algorithm 1: Computation Offloading and Resources Allocation with PASD Algorithm

---

1: At the beginning of slot 0: Initialize state S, action A, and PER memory N
2: **for** each episodes **do**
3:     Load tasks from datasets
4:     Reset the IIoT system environment
5:     **while** True **do**
6:         Get $a_n^i(t)$ from A
7:         Execute $a_n^i(t)$, observe $s_n^i(t+1)$, and obtain $r_n^i(t)$
8:         Store $\left(s_n^i(t), a_n^i(t), r_n^i(t), s_n^i(t+1)\right)$ into the prioritized experience replay buffer
9:         Obtain a batch of samples from the buffer N based on equation (5)
10:         Calculate $Q\left(s_n^i(t), a_n^i(t)\right)$ with equation (4)
11:         **if** task $R_n^i(t)$ is finished
12:             break
13:         **end if**
14:     **end while**
15: **end for**

---

5 Evaluation

We first conduct the simulation experiments, and then adopt NBUFlow, an IoT task orchestration and offloading platform, to evaluate PASD.

- *Simulation experiments based on dataset.* Comparison of training speed, average delay, energy consumption, task throw rate and network resource utilization, which indicators were evaluated by simulation experiments with baselines.
- *Platform experiments based on NBUFlow.* Through platform experiments, we compared average delay, energy consumption and task throw rate of PASD with other baselines.

5.1 Experimental Environment

This paper uses 10–50 IIoTEs, 2–6 edge servers and a cloud server to build NBUFlow. The camera collects data, and we use four Raspberry Pies running Ubuntu 18.04 as IIoTEs to generate tasks. Two hosts are simultaneously used as edge servers. In addition, this paper uses a server equipped with NVIDIA Quadro K2200 as a cloud server. The experimental equipments and system monitoring status are shown in Fig. 3.

Fig. 3. Experimental equipments.

Table 1. Experimental parameter settings.

Parameters	Values
Number of IIoTEs	[10, 50]
Number of edge servers	[2, 6]
Number of cloud servers	1
Task arrive rate	[0, 1]
Learning rate	0.001
Batch size	32
Discount factor	0.99

5.2 Parameter Settings

The influence of different DRL network parameter settings (such as learning rate, discount factor and batch size) on the proposed algorithm is analyzed. The parameter settings of this experiment are shown in Table 1.

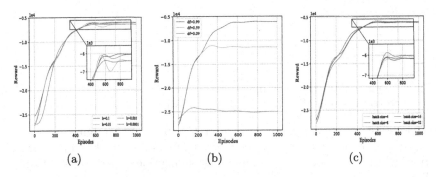

(a)   (b)   (c)

Fig. 4. Parameter evaluation. (a) The effect of different learning rate. (b) The effect of different discount factor. (c) The effect of different batch size.

1) *Effect of learning rate on convergence.* It can be seen from the Fig. 4(a) that the larger the learning rate, the faster the convergence. Because the smaller the loss function at each step, the slower the convergence and the more time required for optimization. Therefore, the learning rate is chosen to be 0.001.

2) *Effect of discount factor on convergence.* As shown in Fig. 4(b), the larger the discount factor, the higher the reward and the better the system performance optimization. This experiment selects a discount factor of 0.99.

3) *Effect of batch size on convergence.* In the Fig. 4(c), the convergence speed is improved dramatically, when increasing from 16 to 32. Therefore, the experiment set batch size = 32 to reduce the training time.

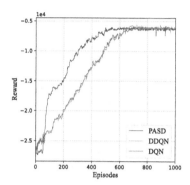

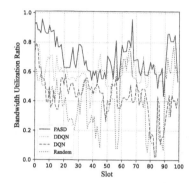

Fig. 5. Comparison of training speed of PASD, DDQN and DQN.

Fig. 6. Comparison of bandwidth utilization ratio.

5.3   Experimental Results

We compare PASD with other baselines, including DQN [15], DDQN [16] based on Dueling DQN, no offload decision (No) and random offload decision (Random). At the same time, the performance of PASD is evaluated from the following four aspects using the first 1600 tasks of the Alibaba Cluster [17] dataset.

Simulation Results. 1) *Training speed.* In Fig. 5, PASD converges at 500 episodes, while the DQN and DDQN start to converge at 700 episodes and 800 episodes, respectively, which means that PASD outperforms others by at least 40%.

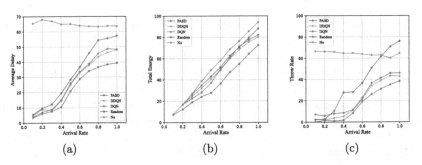

Fig. 7. Comparison of (a) average delay, (b) system total energy, (c) throw rate for different task arrival rates.

2) *Performance comparison with different task arrival density.* As shown in Fig. 7(a), PASD reduces the average task completion delay by 39.08% and 21.15% compared to DDQN and DQN, respectively. From Fig. 7(b), we can see that the total energy consumption of the PASD is reduced by 28.73% compared to the baseline when the task arrival rate increases to 0.3. From Fig. 7(c), we can see that when the task arrival rate is more than 0.7, the throw rate of PASD can be reduced by 28.57% compared with DQN.

3) *Performance comparison with different numbers of IIoTEs.* Figure 8 compares the adaptability of different algorithms to the system with various numbers of IIoTEs. From Fig. 8(a), we can see that the average task completion delay of PASD is always around 8.09. From Fig. 8(b), we can see that the total system energy consumption is reduced by 55.21% compared with the baseline, when the number of IIoT devices increases to 30. As shown in Fig. 8(c), the task throw rate of PASD remains around 0.55%.

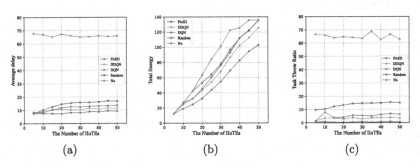

Fig. 8. Comparison of (a) average delay, (b) system total energy, (c) task arrive rate, with different number of IIoTEs.

4) *Performance comparison in Bandwidth utilization.* As shown in Fig. 6, compared with other baselines, the average bandwidth utilization of PASD is maintained at 70%, so the average bandwidth utilization of the time slot is improved by 22.8%.

Platform Experimental Results. In the platform experiment, we generate 100 tasks. The deployed process of experiments in the NBUFlow platform is shown in Fig. 9.

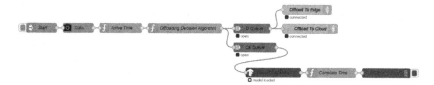

Fig. 9. Offloading process in the platform.

As shown in Fig. 10, PASD reduces the average task completion delay by at least 8.3%, while reducing the total energy consumption of the system and maintaining a relatively low task throw ratio. It is because DDQN and DQN offload more tasks to the cloud, reducing the computational delay of tasks, but generating a large amount of transmission energy consumption.

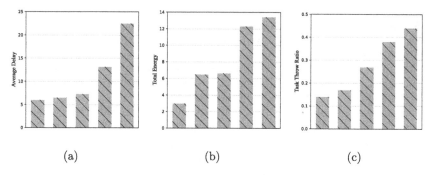

(a)   (b)   (c)

Fig. 10. Comparison of different algorithms in the experimental platform. (a) The average delay. (b) The system total energy. (c) The task throw ratio.

6   Conclusion

In this work, we propose a DRL-based computation offloading and resource allocation algorithm, named PASD, which optimizes the average task completion time and total energy consumption of the system while reducing the task throw rate, to realize efficient cloud-edge collaborative computing in IIoT. Its performance is evaluated by a large number of simulation experiments, and by using the NBUFlow IoT experimental platform in real scenarios. Compared to the baselines, PASD can significantly reduce the total energy consumption of the system. It also reduces the completion delay and throw rate of tasks, and has good performance in improving bandwidth utilization.

Acknowledgements. This work was supported by the Natural Science Foundation of Ningbo City (2021J090) and Ningbo Manicipal Commonweal S&T Project (2022S005).

References

1. Ko, H., Pack, S., Leung, V.C.: Performance optimization of serverless computing for latency-guaranteed and energy-efficient task offloading in energy harvesting industrial IoT. IEEE Internet Things J. (2021)
2. Huang, W., Huang, Y., He, S.: Cloud and edge multicast beamforming for cache-enabled ultra-dense networks. IEEE Trans. Veh. Technol. **69**(3), 3481–3485 (2020)
3. Sun, Z., Yang, H., Li, C.: Cloud-edge collaboration in industrial internet of things: a joint offloading scheme based on resource prediction. IEEE Internet Things J. **9**(18), 17014–17025 (2021)
4. Seid, A.M., Boateng, G.O.: Collaborative computation offloading and resource allocation in multi-UAV-assisted IoT networks: a deep reinforcement learning approach. IEEE Internet Things J. **8**(15), 12203–12218 (2021)
5. Seid, A.M., Boateng, G.O., Mareri, B.: Multi-agent DRL for task offloading and resource allocation in multi-UAV enabled IoT edge network. IEEE Trans. Netw. Serv. Manage. **18**(4), 4531–4547 (2021)
6. Wang, L., Chen, H., Qin, W.: NBUFlow: a dataflow based universal task orchestration and offloading platform for low-cost development of IoT systems with cloud-edge-device collaborative computing. In: Lai, Y., Wang, T., Jiang, M., Xu, G., Liang, W., Castiglione, A. (eds.) ICA3PP 2021. LNCS, vol. 13156, pp. 665–681. Springer, Cham (2021)
7. Alfakih, T., Hassan, M.M., Gumaei, A.: Task offloading and resource allocation for mobile edge computing by deep reinforcement learning based on SARSA. IEEE Access **8**, 54074–54084 (2020)
8. Chen, Y., Liu, Z., Zhang, Y.: Deep reinforcement learning-based dynamic resource management for mobile edge computing in industrial internet of things. IEEE Trans. Industr. Inf. **17**(7), 4925–4934 (2020)
9. Shakarami, A., Shahidinejad, A., Ghobaei-Arani, M.: A review on the computation offloading approaches in mobile edge computing: a game-theoretic perspective. Softw. Pract. Exp. **50**(9), 1719–1759 (2020)
10. Yadav, R., Zhang, W., Elgendy, I.A.: Smart healthcare: RL-based task offloading scheme for edge-enable sensor networks. IEEE Sens. J. **21**(22), 24910–24918 (2021)
11. Feng, C., Han, P., Zhang, X.: Computation offloading in mobile edge computing networks: a survey. J. Netw. Comput. Appl. **202**, 103366–103381 (2022)
12. Ale, L., Zhang, N., Fang, X., Chen, X., Wu, S., Li, L.: Delay-aware and energy-efficient computation offloading in mobile-edge computing using deep reinforcement learning. IEEE Trans. Cogn. Commun. Netw. **7**(3), 881–892 (2021)
13. Zheng, B., Ming, L., Hu, Q.: Supply-demand-aware deep reinforcement learning for dynamic fleet management. ACM Trans. Intell. Syst. Technol. (TIST) **13**(3), 1–19 (2022)
14. Schaul, T., Quan, J., Antonoglou, I.: Prioritized experience replay. arXiv preprint arXiv:1511.05952 (2015)
15. Huang, L., Feng, X., Zhang, C.: Deep reinforcement learning-based joint task offloading and bandwidth allocation for multi-user mobile edge computing. Digit. Commun. Netw. **5**(1), 10–17 (2019)
16. Jiang, F., Ma, R., Gao, Y.: A reinforcement learning-based computing offloading and resource allocation scheme in F-RAN. EURASIP J. Adv. Signal Process. **2021**(1), 1–25 (2021)
17. Alibaba trace. https://github.com/alibaba/clusterdata. Accessed 18 Aug 2022

Automatic Construction of Large-Scale IoT Datasets with Multi-strategy Fusion

Weifeng Wang[1,2], Peipei Liu[3,4], Zhiyu Wang[1,2], Yimo Ren[3,4], Hong Li[3,4], and Fang Zuo[2,5(✉)]

[1] Henan International Joint Laboratory of Intelligent Network Theory and Key Technology, Henan University, Kaifeng 475000, China
[2] School of Software, Henan University, Kaifeng 475000, China
[3] School of Cyber Security, University of Chinese Academy of Sciences, Beijing 100193, China
[4] Institute of Information Engineering, Chinese Academy of Sciences, Beijing 100193, China
[5] Subject Innovation and Intelligence Introduction Base of Henan Higher Educational Institution-Software Engineering Intelligent Information Processing Innovation and Intelligence Introduction Base of Henan University, Kaifeng 475000, China
zuofang@henu.edu.cn

Abstract. With the advent of the "Internet+" era, the IoT has developed rapidly and is gradually penetrating into all fields of life. While the scale of IoT devices is showing an explosive growth trend, the importance of IoT security is also becoming more and more prominent in the rapid development of the IoT. In order to assist the identification of Internet-connected devices and further identify the vulnerability information of devices to achieve security protection for IoT devices, we construct a large-scale, diverse, and high-coverage dataset of IoT devices by automated and semi-automated means. In this dataset, each piece of data contains the information of the category, brand, and product model of the device. The large-scale, diverse, and high-coverage properties of the dataset are fully validated through our statistical analysis and experimental applications.

Keywords: Large-scale dataset · Web crawler · Bi-LSTM+CRF · TF-IDF · Regular expression

1 Introduction

Large-scale datasets are the premise for machines to learn knowledge and the basis for many downstream tasks. The construction of datasets usually includes the crawling of source data and the regularization of data. The technical problem we mainly solve in this paper is to design a data set construction system for downstream tasks such as device identification and IoT device knowledge graph

---

W. Wang and P. Liu—These authors contributed equally to this work.

construction, and to automatically collect the type, brand, product model and other information of IoT devices on a large scale [1]. The construction process of the system includes 6 parts, which are crawling of raw data, screening of IoT device categories, automatic identification of brand and model information, inspection and completion of brand and model information, Chinese-English alignment of categories and brands, and data deduplication. Among them, the automatic identification of brand and model information is implemented using two different methods (NER and Regular Expressions) (Fig. 1). We also use two methods to verify and complete the brand and model information, the utilization of the URL page information of the product details page and the search engine + TF-IDF to obtain key information and a total of 384,875 pieces of data including 12 categories, 115 sub-categories, and 5,950 brands were obtained [2]. This article uses the python development language to start with a series of starting web pages using breadth-first, and automatically collects information in web pages in a tree structure. For some data irregularities, we use the regularization method pattern = '[A-Za-z0-9 \s\-\ + \.\(\)/]+') and named entity recognition based on Bi-LSTM+CRF method to process and extract the brand and model of each piece of data. [3] Finally, we check and correct the data based on the structural information that may appear in the actual situation of each piece of data to complete the missing information.

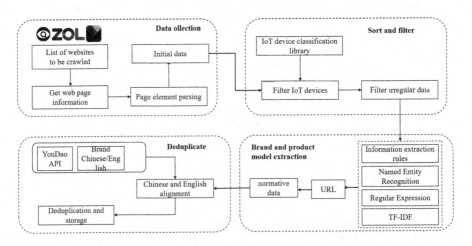

Fig. 1. Overall architecture of dataset construction

2 Dataset Construction Methods

In this part, we will focus on the construction of original data, data classification and filtering, refinement of the data, and data standardization. For different problems in the data, we will use different methods to process and achieve the standardization and regularization of the dataset.

2.1   Construction of Original Data

The original data construction mainly starts from the regularized static websites such as industrial control network, security network, and product shopping guide network (Table 1), and adopts the crawler strategy of breadth-first search to capture the IoT device information (brand, model, product details page url, etc.) on these websites.

Table 1. Introduction to the categories of IoT devices

Website name	URL	Abbreviation	Data volume
Zhongguancun Online Network	http://detail.zol.com.cn/subcategory.html	zol	508521
Pacific Internet	https://product.pconline.com.cn/category.html	pconline	197025
IT168	http://product.it168.com/category.html	it168	671938
Mobile Home Network	http://product.imobile.com.cn/phone.html	mobile	11496
Celestial net	http://product.yesky.com/category.shtml	yesky	261158
International Industrial Control Network	http://www.iianews.com/ca/sitemap.html	iianews	22808
Pacific Security Network	http://www.tpy888.cn	tpy888	338563
Huaqiang Wisdom Network	http://b2b.hqps.com/	hqps	41921
Security Knowledge Network	http://product.asmag.com.cn/	asmag	45930
China PLC Network	http://www.chinaplc.net/plcsupply/	plc	144875
China Security Industry Network	http://b2b.21csp.com.cn/	21csp	327144
Huaqiang Core City Network	http://www.hqchip.com/	hqchip	49316
Smart Home	http://www.znjj.tv/product/	znjj	40907
Hikvision official website	https://www.hikvision.com/cn/prnav_2.html	hikvision	2085
RFID World Network	http://www.rfidworld.com.cn/	rfidworld	3157

For the above website, we use the breadth-first [4] crawler to start from a series of starting web pages, extract all the sub-directory URLs in the web page, and put them into the queue for crawling in sequence.

In the specific implementation process, we first set up an empty crawler queue, sent the URL1 to be crawled into the crawler queue, and then read the URL1 in the queue in turn and collected all device types and corresponding URL2 in each URL1 page, and add the data to the queue in the format of <type,

URL2>. Then we delete all URL1 in the queue, and read the <type, URL2> in the queue in turn, and get all the trademarks and brands in each URL2 page and the corresponding URL3, also add data to the queue in the format <type, brand, URL3>. In this process, if the brand information is "other", then add data to the queue in the format of <type, "other", URL3> and delete all <type, URL2> in the queue.

Finally, read the <type, brand, URL3> in the queue one by one, if there is model data in the current URL3 page, directly store the device model and the corresponding URL4, namely <type, brand, model, URL4>;If the model does not exist in the current URL3 page, then obtain the model through URL4 to the details page of the device, and store it in the data format of <type, brand, model, URL4>; If the model information cannot be obtained from the details page of the device, store it in the data format of <type, brand, "NULL", URL4> and delete all <type, brand, URL3> in the queue, so that the construction of the original data set has been completed [5].

2.2 Data Classification and Filtering

For the captured raw data, the device types (as shown in Tables 2 and 3) and the data in the IoT range were screened out to obtain 115 types (such as network cameras), which were semi-automatically processed in Chinese and English. The filtered data types are merged to obtain 12 relatively broad categories of IoT (such as video systems, each category contains several types), and semi-automatic processing in Chinese and English is carried out. The original data we collected may have a series of problems, such as the model field including product model information, brand information and other redundant content, and the lack of brand field or model field in some data. Therefore, it is necessary to check the integrity and standardization of each data.

Storage of Complete Data. For complete and pure data, first use these data to build a brand library, and then store it in json format after data standardization. Our dataset includes various IoT device information, and in Table 4 we show a part of the dataset for H_PersDev class.

Processing of Data Redundancy. In our original data, if the brand field is redundant (more than 6 characters), the brand field is used as the input content. If the brand field is missing, input the content of the model field into the trained BiLSTM+CRF named entity recognition model to extract the brand information in the field. The model is obtained by training 16,000 pieces of data manually annotated (as shown in Table 5).

The model we used has 5 layers (as shown in Fig. 2), which are input layer, embedding layer, Bi-LSTM [6,12] layer, CRF layer, and output layer from bottom to top.

The input layer is the first layer. In this layer, the brand field X that needs to be recognized by the name body is input into the model in the form of a single character.

Table 2. Introduction to the categories of IoT devices

English abbreviation	English full name	Details
H_PersDev	Personal Device	Mobile phones, computers and other equipment used by major individual users
H_ServDev	Server Device	Main server and other equipment
M_RSS	Routing Switching System	There are mainly switches/gateways/routers and other equipment
M_CSS	Cyber Security System	Mainly refers to intrusion detection/firewall and other equipment
M_VSS	Video Surveillance System	Video surveillance equipment, etc.
M_ICS	Industrial Control System	Mainly refers to industrial control DCS/PLC and other equipment
M_OAS	Office Automation System	Mainly refers to equipment such as printers/scanners
M_VCS	Video Conference System	Mainly refers to video conference system equipment
M_HAS	Home Automation System	Mainly refers to smart TV/smart water heater and other equipment
M_SAD	Security Alarm Device	Alarm, alarm host, alarm system, etc.
M_BAS	Building Automation System	Control/elevator/access control equipment/air conditionin ventilation monitoring system, etc.
M_OthCateDev	Other Category Device	Product category not listed

The embedding layer is the second layer, which performs word embedding for each input sentence (that is, converts each input character into a vector), and its purpose is to convert logical characters into mathematical variables that the computer can recognize and calculate. In this model, we use randomly initialized word embeddings.

Table 3. Introduction of several types of M_VSS

English abbreviation	Category	English full name
IPCam	M_VSS	IP Camera
OCD	M_VSS	Other Camera Device
NVR	M_VSS	Network Hard Disk Video Recorder
DVR	M_VSS	Digital Video Recorder
VSD	M_VSS	Video Server Device
VOT	M_VSS	Video Optical Transceiver
NSD	M_VSS	Network Storage Device
VAR	M_VSS	Video Analyse Recoder
VMS	M_VSS	Video Management System
OMD	M_VSS	Other Monitor Device

Table 4. Partial data of H_PersDev class

Category	Type	Vendor	Product model
H_PersDev	Computer	Think pad	tablet 236793gc
H_PersDev	Computer	Sony	Svt11227scw
H_PersDev	Computer	Dell	Latitude 2120
H_PersDev	Computer	Lenovo	ideapad s100-nfo
H_PersDev	Computer	Asus	fl5700u
H_PersDev	Computer	Samsung	nc110-p03

Table 5. Data annotation format

Labels	Full name	Representative entity
BV	Begin-Vendor	Start character of brand field
IV	Inside-Vendor	Brand field non-starting character
BP	Begin-Product	Start character of model field
IP	Inside-Product	Model field non-starting character
O	Other	Other characters

The Bi-LSTM layer is the third layer and its main purpose is to model text data [7]. At a certain point in the sequence, the forward-LSTM network is used to obtain the above information, and the backward-LSTM network is used to obtain the following information. By concatenating the output vectors of forward-LSTM and backward-LSTM, and the hidden layer output at the current moment is obtained through softmax calculation. Between the embedding layer and the Bi-LSTM layer, a Dropout parameter is also used. Dropout ran-

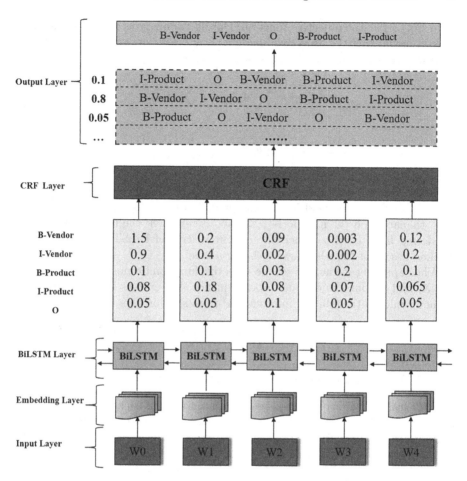

Fig. 2. Brand and product model extraction models.

domly invalidates some units in the forward calculation process to reduce the co-adaptation relationship between hidden units, which solves the overfitting problem and makes the neural network more robust to noisy data.

The CRF layer is the fourth layer, which takes the hidden layer output of Bi-LSTM as input and outputs all possible predicted label sequences Y. In the output layer, a (K+2) * (K+2) state transition matrix A is initialized during model training, and each element in the matrix represents the score (i.e. likelihood [8]) of the transition between labels. Here K represents the number of tags and 2 is the special tag for start and end. Equation (1) is used to calculate the likelihood of the predicted label sequence output by the CRF, and the probability of the true label sequence among all predicted label sequences is maximized (as in Eq. (2)) as the objective function. During training, according to the principle of maximizing the objective function, A and the corresponding weights of the BiLSTM+CRF model are obtained by training.

$$s(X,y) = \sum_{i=0}^{n} A_{y_i,y_{i+1}} + \sum_{i=1}^{n} P_{i,y_i} \tag{1}$$

$$obj : max\left\{p(y|X) = \frac{e^{s()}}{\sum_{\tilde{y} \in Y_X} e^{X,\tilde{y}}}\right\} \tag{2}$$

In the above formula, it represents all predicted label sequences output by CRF for a given input field X. For the predicted label sequence output by the CRF, the labels on the ith and i+1 characters represent the likelihood of being transferred from label to label; the output matrix of BiLSTM represents the likelihood score of the ith character being a label.

When applying the model, set the objective function formula (3) for the input field X, and output the optimal label sequence. We extract the corresponding character information (brand information) from specific tags (BV, IV) [9]

$$y^* = \underset{y \in Y_X}{argmax} \ s(X, \tilde{y}) \tag{3}$$

2.3   Refinement of the Data

Network search (Baidu) to obtain model information for each piece of data, and use the TF-IDF [10,11] algorithm to process the first 15 search results (Based on Baidu Baike corpus to find the most important 10 words in each result). We take the top 10 words with the highest frequency. If a word appears in the established brand library, the word will be used as the brand information, otherwise the word with the highest frequency will be used as the brand information. After doing a general statistics and analysis of the crawled data, it is found that the model field has the following characteristics: the model information of the device is a combination of letters, numbers and symbols, which is relatively regular and regular compared to other fields. So we use a regular expression (pattern =‘[A-Za-z0-9 \s\-\+\.\(\)/]+’) [12,13] to extract the model information in the model field. But if there are multiple model data in a sentence, take the longest one in the returned model list as the data model. At this point, the model information in the field is supplemented.

2.4   Data Standardization

We check and correct brand and model information based on possible structured information based on the URL and detail page content of each piece of data. If the corresponding information cannot be extracted from the details page, the content of the obtained data will not be changed. In addition, the brand names of equipment captured by the website are confusing, for example: "Hikvision",

"Hikvision", "HIKVISION", "Hikvision" all refer to the same brand - Hikvision, therefore, it is necessary to convert all brands to a unified standard. With the help of Youdao dictionary API, we have realized the perfect mapping between Chinese and English in the brand library (if there are multiple translation results, we choose the one with the highest frequency), and replaced all device brands in the IoT device database with the corresponding lowercase English. For complete and purely data containing <type, brand, model, URL>, we store the dataset in the MongoDB database in json format.

3   Data Analysis and Application

After statistics, it is found that the dataset we constructed has a total of 15 categories of IoT device information and 164 subcategories (Table 6). In terms of scale, it has reached the million level. In terms of diversity, from the number of brands in the table, we can see that each subcategory includes almost all brands in this category. In terms of coverage, as shown in the line chart in Fig. 3, whether it is subcategory, brand or product model, the number of each type in our dataset is much higher than the number of types in the Cydar system(we will introduce in the application of our dataset). In addition, we did more than 1000 random lookup validations and found that only 3 random lookups resulted in results not included in our dataset. Finally, we apply our dataset to the Cydar system(as show in Fig. 4), which is constructed through extensive screening of our dataset and some other datasets to quickly find relevant information about IoT devices. At the same time, we took the category of personal devices as an example to search and verify, we found that we have two more sub-categories than Cydar, and the number of brands is more than 1,000. In addition, we have more than 60,000 product models(as show in Table 6) than the Cydar system (as shown in Fig. 3 (a), (b), (c)). From the line chart in Fig. 3, we can find that our data set is largely superior to the data in the Cydar system, and we can also find that our data set has many brands and product models that the Cydar system does not have.

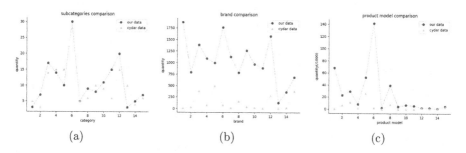

(a)   (b)   (c)

Fig. 3. (a) subcategories comparsion (b) brand comparsion (c) product model comparsion

Fig. 4. Home page of the Cydar system.

Table 6. Detailed number of main categories and subcategories

Main categories	Subcate-gories	Number of brands	Product model
Personal device	3	1869	68402
Server device	7	792	23077
Routing switching system	17	1386	29378
Cyber security system	14	1092	8265
Video surveillance system	10	997	52684
Industrial control system	30	1766	141366
Building automation system	5	1128	2451
Office automation system	9	786	39260
Video conference system	8	1262	4614
Home automation system	11	968	6742
Electirc system	15	887	5662
Intelligent healthcare system	20	1576	2316
Internet of vehicles	3	126	2152
Security alarm device	5	362	974
Other category device	7	688	4802
Total number	164	15685	392145

In addition, the categories and sub-categories in the practical Cydar system are shown in Fig. 5. After analysis we can find that there are fewer main categories and subcategories in Cydar system than ours, which verifies the diversity of our dataset. This is because the classification methods used by the two are different. The classification method of our dataset is more detailed, while the classification method of the Cydar system is more general.

We queried the two brands Thor and Hisense (as show in Fig. 6) in the Cydar system and found no results, which verifies the high coverage of our dataset. Then we queried the hikvision brand (Part of the results are shown in Fig. 7), we found a total of 1918 product models, which is close to the product model of hikvision in our dataset. Since one IP corresponds to multiple product models, we collect all product models, while the Cydar system only collects one product model in each IP, which leads to a gap in quantity.

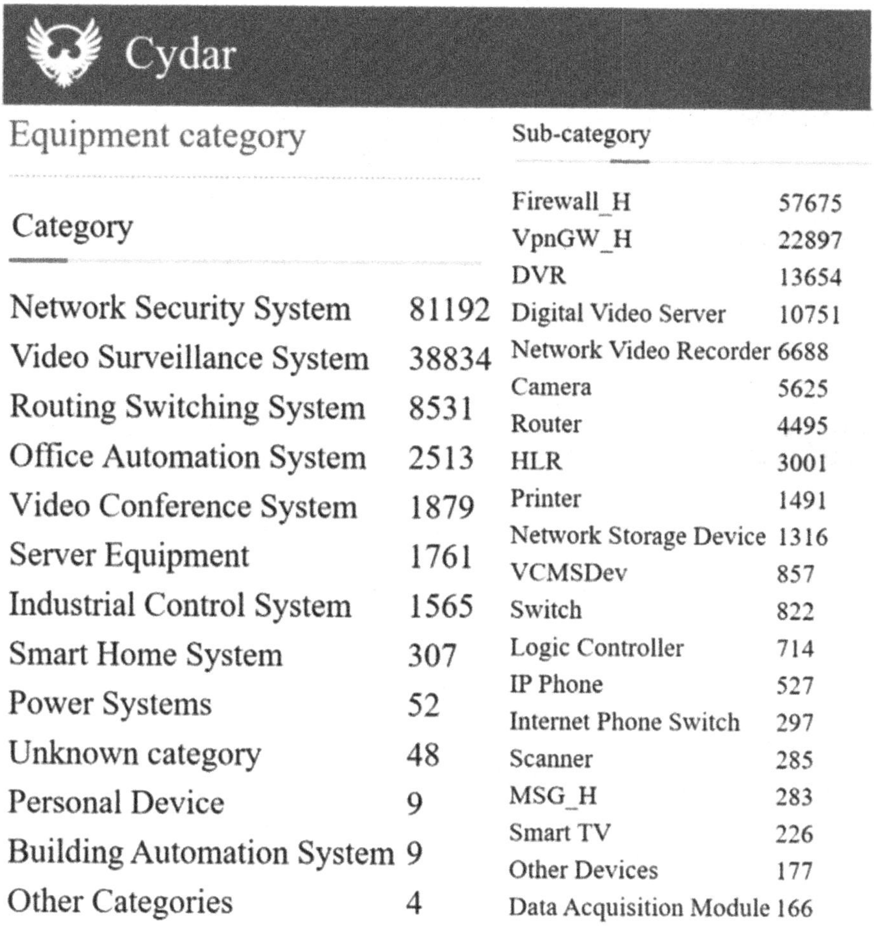

Cydar

Equipment category		Sub-category	
Category		Firewall_H	57675
		VpnGW_H	22897
		DVR	13654
Network Security System	81192	Digital Video Server	10751
Video Surveillance System	38834	Network Video Recorder	6688
Routing Switching System	8531	Camera	5625
		Router	4495
Office Automation System	2513	HLR	3001
Video Conference System	1879	Printer	1491
Server Equipment	1761	Network Storage Device	1316
		VCMSDev	857
Industrial Control System	1565	Switch	822
Smart Home System	307	Logic Controller	714
Power Systems	52	IP Phone	527
		Internet Phone Switch	297
Unknown category	48	Scanner	285
Personal Device	9	MSG_H	283
Building Automation System	9	Smart TV	226
		Other Devices	177
Other Categories	4	Data Acquisition Module	166

Fig. 5. Categories and sub-categories in the Cydar system.

After the log4j vulnerability appeared not long ago, we combined the vulnerability warning system with this dataset to quickly and accurately give the relevant IoT device information with this vulnerability, which greatly reduced the loss caused by the vulnerability.[5]

---

[5] Fig. 4 to Fig. 7 are obtained by translating the Chinese Cydar system into English. (System Link: https://cydar.cn/).

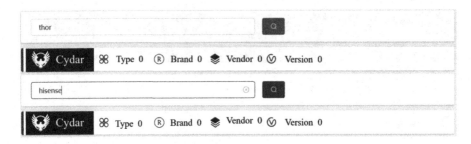

Fig. 6. Search results for thor and hisense brands.

Fig. 7. Search results for the hikvision brand.

4 Conclusion

In order to assist in the identification of Internet-connected devices and further identify the vulnerability information of devices to achieve the security protection requirements for IoT devices, We design a dataset construction system and build a large-scale, diverse and high-coverage dataset based on this system, and through statistical analysis and application of the dataset, we demonstrate these three characteristics of the dataset. We hope that this dataset will play a driving role in future research on IoT device identification and IoT device security protection.

Acknowledgement. This work is supported by Graduate Education innovation and quality improvement Action Plan project of Henan University (No. SYLJD2022008 and No. SYLKC2022028), 2022 Discipline Innovation Introduction Base cultivation project of Henan University and Key Technology Research and Development Project of Henan Province under Grant 222102210055.

References

1. Ananadharaj, G., Balaji, K.: A study internet of things is a revolutionary approach for future technology enhancement. Int. J. Eng. Adv. Technol. **10**(4), 114–119 (2021)

2. Kandasamy, K., Srinivas, S., Achuthan, K., Rangan, V.P.: IoT cyber risk: a holistic analysis of cyber risk assessment frameworks, risk vectors, and risk ranking process. EURASIP J. Inf. Secur. **1**, 2020 (2020)
3. Alfonso, I., Garcs, K., Castro, H., Cabot, J.: Self-adaptive architectures in IoT systems: a systematic literature review. J. IoT. **12**, 1–8 (2021)
4. Liu, H., Wang, K., Liu, Z.: Application and research of heuristic search algorithm in crawler field. In: 2020 2nd International Conference on Information Technology and Computer Application (ITCA) (2020)
5. Stambuk, E., Gros, S., Vukovic, M.: Analyzing web security features using crawlers: study of Croatian web. In: 2021 16th International Conference on Telecommunications (ConTEL) (2021)
6. Hou, T.J., Zhou, L.: Ship fault named entity recognition based on bilayer BI-LSTM-CRF. In: 2020 13th International Congress on Image and Signal Processing, BioMedical Engineering and Informatics (CISP-BMEI) (2020)
7. Zhenqiang, Z. et al.: Chinese named entity recognition in power domain based on Bi-LSTM-CRF (2019)
8. Wang, Z., Hamza, W., Florian, R.: Bilateral multi-perspective matching for natural language sentences. In: Twenty-Sixth International Joint Conference on Artificial Intelligence (2017)
9. Thattinaphanich, S., Prom-On, S.: Thai named entity recognition using Bi-LSTM-CRF with word and character representation. In: The 4th International Conference on Information Technology (InCIT 2019) (2019)
10. Rahmah, A., Santoso, H.B., Hasibuan, Z.A.: Exploring technology-enhanced learning key terms using TF-IDF weighting. In: 2019 Fourth International Conference on Informatics and Computing (ICIC) (2019)
11. Yang, Y.: Research and realization of internet public opinion analysis based on improved TF-IDF algorithm. In: 2017 16th International Symposium on Distributed Computing and Applications to Business, Engineering and Science (DCABES) (2017)
12. Jin, H., Rui, Y, Wang, X., Huang, L.: Validation of query expression based on regular expression IEEE (2011)
13. Zhu, Z., Ping, L., Chen, L., Zhang, K.: Memory-efficient regular expression matching for Chinese network content audit. IEEE

Research on Argo Data Anomaly Detection Based on Improved DBSCAN Algorithm

YongGuo Jiang[✉], Ce Kang, Yan Shen, TingTing Huang, and GuangDa Zhai

Ocean University of China, Qingdao, Shandong, China
{jiangyg,kc,shenyan,htt9211}@stu.ouc.edu.cn

Abstract. The problem of anomaly detection in marine Argo data is studied. Based on the common and widely used DBSCAN (Density-Based Spatial Clustering of Applications with Noise) algorithm for anomaly detection in Argo data, as in other fields, there is a major problem in the application of DBSCAN algorithm, which is how to choose the appropriate parameter pairs. To solve this problem, this paper proposes an improved version of DBSCAN, namely CCMD-DBSCAN (DBSCAN based on the classification characteristics of marine data), which solves the above problem by studying the characteristics and laws of Argo data and is successfully applied to anomaly detection of marine data. The experimental results show that the new algorithm can not only determine the appropriate parameter pairs but also has a good anomaly detection effect.

Keywords: Argo · DBSCAN · Anomaly detection

1 Introduction

With the rapid development of the Big Data era, the volume of data is increasing exponentially, and people must find ways to eliminate abnormal data from the huge amount of data to obtain real and reliable data for scientific research or commercial use.

The international Argo program, proposed in 1998 and implemented in early 2000, is a global real-time ocean observation program consisting of about 3000 buoys. Argo has become a major source of data for physical oceanographic studies from basin to global scale, and Argo data have been widely used for operational ocean and atmospheric forecasting and prediction [1], and as one of the regular global real-time ocean observation data sources, how to effectively detect data anomalies has been an important research element [2].

An anomaly is data that is significantly different from the rest of the data in the sample set. An anomaly is defined in the literature [3,4] as an anomaly that is an observation that appears to deviate significantly from the other sample members in the sample set in which it is located, and it can also be said that an anomaly is an observation that is inconsistent with the rest of the current data set. Data anomalies in Argo buoys may be because their observation profiles are prone to inaccuracies or even errors due to abnormal environmental changes, data transmission, and aging and corrosion of Argo buoys during their operation. Given the above problems, with the rapid development of marine science, the subject of Argo buoys abnormal data detection has received high research interest in recent year [5].

An anomaly detection algorithm based on distance as a criterion to improve k-mean clustering for ocean anomaly data determination is proposed in literature [6]. A new method for identifying anomalous ocean temperature and salinity from Argo profiling buoys is proposed in literature [7], which classifies anomalous data by using convex packets, constructing an n-sided polygon with the minimum area containing all climate points using the Jarvis March algorithm, and subsequently using the PIP principle in the polygon implemented by the light projection algorithm for classifying temperature and salinity data as being in the acceptable or unacceptable range.

DBSCAN is a typical representative algorithm of the density-based clustering algorithm, which has good performance for spatial database clustering, is fast in processing spatial data, effective in handling noise points, and finds arbitrary shape clusters [8]. It also has many problems, such as the difficulty of parameter pair selection. Many methods have been proposed for the selection of parameter pairs in recent years, such as the dual-grid method proposed in the literature [9], yet numerous variants of the grid method are almost useless in high-dimensional space [10]. The selection of parameter pairs highly affects the clustering results and thus directly affects the accuracy and high quality of anomaly detection. To make the algorithm better applicable to Argo data, this paper proposes an improved anomaly detection algorithm for marine data based on the study of data characteristics of Argo data and the improved DBSCAN algorithm.

In the experimental part, we first processed the original data of Argo, then we reduced the dimensionality of the data while highly preserving the correlation between each dimension, after that, we defined a threshold value according to the data characteristics of Argo and found the appropriate threshold size according to the performance index and accuracy of the algorithm, and finally, we compared the improved algorithm with the original algorithm and K-means algorithm for anomaly detection experiments, and the results showed that our algorithm has better performance.

The relevant contributions of this paper are as follows:

1) Comparison of our sampled data with the Argo dataset resulted in a more accurate and identifiable set of ocean data.
2) Reducing the dimensionality of the data while retaining a high degree of correlation between the various dimensions of Argo data makes the data more suitable for anomaly detection algorithms.
3) According to the data and the characteristics of the anomaly detection algorithm, a threshold value is defined, and the anomaly detection algorithm parameter pair selection is performed according to the threshold value, which

makes the parameter pair selection no longer rely on manual experience and improves the efficiency and accuracy of the parameter pair selection.

The rest of the paper is organized as follows. In Sect. 2, the improvement work related to the DBSCAN clustering algorithm is described. Section 3 introduces the proposed clustering algorithm, namely CCMD -DBSCAN, which describes the Argo dataset and data processing, algorithm parameters selection, basic algorithm flow, and clustering process description, respectively. In Sect. 4, experiments are conducted to compare the performance of the CCMD-DBSCAN algorithm with the commonly used clustering algorithms K-means and the original DBSCAN. Conclusions are drawn in Sect. 5.

2 Related Work

Recent research on the DBSCAN clustering algorithm has focused on improving the way the algorithm determines parameter pairs and reducing the process of calculating the neighborhood for each data point. Most of the improvements are made by applying different methods to determine one of the two parameters after manually determining the other one. However, few methods address the application of the DBSCAN algorithm to high-dimensional data with specific optimization for the data, so these are somewhat limited.

A new efficient TI-DBSCAN algorithm and its variant TI-DBSCAN-REF are proposed in literature [11] for speeding up the most time-consuming process of computing the neighborhood of each data point in DBSCAN. The improved algorithm uses the triangle inequality property instead of spatial indexing to rapidly reduce the neighborhood search space. This results in a speedup of three orders of magnitude compared to the original algorithm and allows efficient clustering of low and high-dimensional data. A performance-improved distributed parallel clustering algorithm KDSG-DBSCAN is proposed in the literature [12], which uses K-D Tree neighborhood queries to reduce the number of interpoint distance calculations, uses graph concatenation algorithms to optimize the local class cluster merging process and achieves parallelization of the computational process based on the Apache Spark MapReduce platform, which has good scalability and acceleration ratio. The literature [13] presents a sliding window DBSCAN clustering algorithm that uses Gridding and local parameters to deal with uneven data by dividing the dataset into several grids, each of which is sized and shaped depending on the specimen density specification. Then for each grid, the parameters are adjusted for the local clustering and the final combined data region. Similar to literature [13], a dual-grid based DBSCAN clustering algorithm (DG-DBSCAN) is proposed in literature [14], which uses two types of grids (i.e., inner and outer grids) to solve the difficulty and time-consuming problem of choosing suitable external parameters for the original DBSCAN algorithm.

In this paper, based on the research of the above algorithm and other related algorithms, and combined with the analysis of the characteristics of Argo data, we propose an improved DBSCAN-based anomaly detection algorithm for ocean data.

3   Improved Algorithm

In this section, we will introduce the application of the improved DBSCAN algorithm on the Argo buoy dataset. First, we will introduce the dimensionality of Agro data, then we will describe how to process the Argo dataset and find out its data characteristics, and finally, we will improve the parameter pair selection mechanism of DBSCAN according to the data characteristics.

3.1   Argo Buoy Dataset

Since its inception 2000, the International Argo Program, through the joint efforts of more than 30 countries and international organizations, the international Argo program has deployed more than 15,000 automated profiling buoys in the global ocean. The total number of temperature and salinity profiles and some biogeochemical elements has exceeded 2.3 million. Currently, there are nearly 4,000 buoys in operation at sea, providing about 150,000 profiles per year. As time progresses, the global ocean Argo data set will become more accessible. The Argo data has become a major data source for basic research and operational forecasting in the field of ocean and atmospheric sciences.

However, in the transfer and storage of Agro buoy data, the core Argo (temperature, salinity, and pressure) data file and a biogeochemical element data file hold separate data and the data do not correspond, e.g., only some of the dimensions may be transferred smoothly at the same time, while others fail or have large amounts missing due to problems such as encoding and satellite transmission. This makes it necessary to first filter the complete dataset, i.e., containing the core data and the important biogeochemical data. We ended up with a complete Argo dataset containing nine dimensions (pressure, temperature, salinity, dissolved oxygen, chlorophyll, particulate matter backscatter coefficient, yellow matter, irradiance, and pH). After obtaining the complete Argo dataset, we compared it with the dataset we derived from data sampling on multiple trips to the sea and found that the error rate of the Argo dataset is generally around 2%.

3.2   Dataset Processing

After obtaining the complete dataset, we use the PCA algorithm to reduce its dimensionality. Principal component analysis (PCA) is a technique for reducing the dimensionality of such large datasets, increasing interpretability but at the same time minimizing information loss. It does so by creating new uncorrelated variables that successively maximize variance. Finding such new variables, the principal components, reduces to solving an eigenvalue/eigenvector problem, and the new variables are defined by the dataset at hand, not a priori, hence making PCA an adaptive data analysis technique [15]. Thanks to the advantages and applicability of the PCA algorithm, we obtained a dataset that is more suitable for our algorithm based on a high degree of preservation of the connections between the dimensions of the dataset.

3.3   Parameter Pair Selection Mechanism

We want to derive the automatic determination of two parameters in the DBSCAN algorithm: Eps and MinPts, based on the study of Argo data.

$$\varepsilon = \frac{n}{C} \times D \tag{1}$$

In this equation, n represents the number of anomalous data points detected, C represents the number of clusters, and D represents the DBI (Davies-Bouldin Index).

We first perform the PCA algorithm to reduce the dimensionality of the read Argo data, followed by nested iterative loops of the two parameters to derive the corresponding n, C, D, and finally calculate ε.

If $\varepsilon \geq 0.75$, then the corresponding parameter pair is appropriate. Our algorithm is described as shown in Fig. 1.

Input: Argo dataset
Output: the detection result
 1: PCA
 2: Mark all objects as unvisited
 3: Randomly select an unvisited object p
 4: Mark p as visited
 5: **for** eps in np.arange(0.5, 10, 0.5)
 6:       **for** MINPTS in range(2, 21)
 7:             **If** The eps neighborhood of p has at least minpts of objects
 8:                   Create a new cluster C and add p to C
 9:                   Let N be the set of objects in the neighborhood of p
10:                 **for** p in N
11:                         **If** p is unvisited
12:                               Mark p as visited
13:                               **If** The eps neighborhood of p has at least minpts of objects,add this to N
14:                               **If** p is not yet a member of any cluster, add p to c
15:                   **end for**
16:                 **else** mark p as Anomalies
17:                   **Until** No objects marked as unvisited
18:       **end for**
19: **end for**
20: calculate ε
21: **If** $\varepsilon \geq 0.75$
22: **result** p eps MINPTS

Fig. 1. Algorithm 1 CCMD-DBSCAN

3.4   Algorithm Clustering Process

Density clustering, also known as density-based clustering, is a type of algorithm that assumes that the clustering structure can be determined by the closeness of the sample distribution. Usually, density clustering algorithms examine the connectivity between samples from the perspective of sample density and continuously expand the clusters based on the connectable samples to obtain the final clustering results.

As a well-known density clustering algorithm, DBSCAN is based on a set of neighborhood parameters (ϵ, MinPts) to portray the closeness of the sample distribution. In the data set $D = \{x_1, x_2, \ldots, x_m\}$, the following concepts are defined:

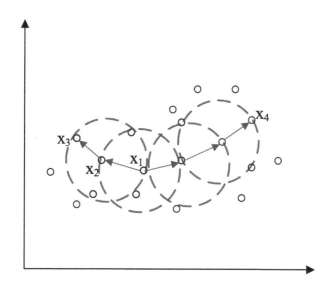

Fig. 2. Conceptual schematic.

- ϵ-neighborhood: for $x_j \in D$, the neighborhood contains the samples in the sample set D whose distance from x_j is not greater than ϵ, $N_\epsilon(x_j) = \{x_i \in D \mid dist(x_i, x_j) \leq \epsilon\}$;
- core object: if x_i neighborhood contains at least MinPts samples, $|N_\epsilon(x_j)| \geq$ MinPts, then x_j is a core object;
- directly density-reachable: If x_j lies in a ϵ-neighborhood of x_i and x_i is a core object, then x_j is said to be directly reached by the density of x_i;
- density-reachable: for x_i and x_j, if there exists a sequence of samples $p_1, p_2, \ldots, p_n$, and $p_1 = x_i, p_n = x_j$, p_{i+1} is directly reachable by p_i density, then x_j is said to be reachable by x_i density;
- density-connected: for x_i and x_j, if there exists x_k is of x_i and x_j both reachable by x_k density, then x_i is said to be connected to x_j density.

Figure 2 gives a visual display of the above concept, where MinPts = 3, the dashed line shows the ϵ-neighborhood, x_1 is the core object, x_2 is directly reachable by x_1 density, x_3 is reachable by x_1 density, and x_3 is connected to x_4 density.

After the clustering is completed, each data point is classified into the cluster with the highest similarity, where the cluster is defined as the largest set of densely connected samples derived from the density reachability relation.

Figure 3 shows an example graph of the results of the anomaly detection algorithm, where the normal data are clustered into 4 clusters, and the anomalous data are samples that are not included in any of the clusters, as shown by the fork marks in the figure.

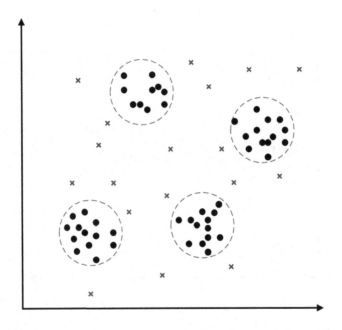

Fig. 3. Example diagram of anomaly detection algorithm results.

4   Experimental Results and Discussion

In this section, the algorithm performance is compared and tested on real and artificial datasets. The compared algorithms are K-means based anomaly detection algorithm, DBSCAN based anomaly detection algorithm, and the improved anomaly detection algorithm in this paper. The experimental environment is Intel(R) Core(TM) i7 with 16 GB of RAM, DDR4, and 1T hard disk. The experimental IDE is Pycharm-Prefessional 2021.2.3. Python3 is the programming language.

The dataset used in this experiment is from the Argo Real-Time Data Center in China (http://www.argo.org.cn/). The Argo profiling buoy data are constantly changing in different seasons or years, and there are significant differences in the measured data between the four seasons of the year. Therefore, the data selected for this experiment are the same time (2019/11/28 10:30:00AM), same location (125.094, 17.704), controlling for a single variable, with different depths (0–10 m) for the experiment. The data format is CSV. The basic information in the data file is mainly the instrument model, data model, date of placement, and number, as well as information on measurement time, depth, temperature, salinity, pressure, dissolved oxygen, chlorophyll, particle backscatter coefficient, yellow matter, irradiance, pH, and other measurement data.

4.1 Dataset Processing

The initial data of the Argo profiling buoy contains many dimensions that are not related to anomaly detection, so the data file needs to be filtered to eliminate the dimensions before importing them, and these possibly irrelevant dimensions These may be irrelevant dimensions, mainly including the basic information of the device, measurement time, latitude and longitude. After eliminating the irrelevant dimensions, the data is abnormal The data to be detected include pressure, temperature, salinity, dissolved oxygen, chlorophyll, particle backscatter coefficient, yellow matter, irradiance, pH, and other measurement data information. 9 dimensions, a total of 1068 pieces of data.

4.2 Threshold Selection

First, we use the clustering algorithm performance index DBI and TPR (the probability that abnormal data are discriminated as abnormal data normally) to determine the size of the threshold we defined. As shown in Fig. 4, when the threshold reaches 0.75, the DBI is the smallest, and the highest anomaly detection accuracy indicates that the threshold is appropriate at this time.

4.3 Analysis of Experimental Results

The results of the three algorithms are shown in Table 1. TPR indicates the probability that abnormal data are discriminated as abnormal data normally, FPR indicates the probability that normal data are incorrectly discriminated as abnormal data, and the internal metric of clustering performance measure DBI. The TPR of the improved DBSCAN is 0.98, which can discriminate most of the abnormal data, while the TPR of the original DBSCAN using elbow method to determine parameter pairs is only 0.83, and the TPR of K-means is 0.65. The TPR of DBSCAN is only 0.83 and the TPR of K-means is 0.65, both of which have a lot of data that should be anomalous but are not correctly discriminated. The FPR of the improved DBSCAN is 0.03, and a few normal data are misjudged as abnormal data, but the FPR of the original DBSCAN

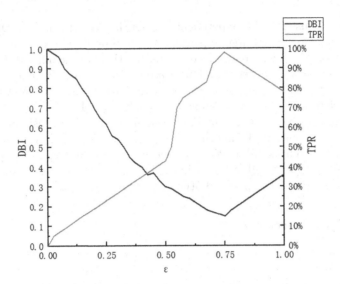

Fig. 4. Example of a figure caption.

Table 1. Experimental results for the Argo dataset

Algorithm	Performance indicators		
	TPR	FPR	DBI
DBSCAN	0.83	0.18	0.68
K-means	0.65	0.23	0.73
CCMD-DBSCAN	0.98	0.03	0.15

with the elbow method to determine the parameter pairs is 0.18, and the FPR of K-means is 0.23 indicating that more normal data are misjudged as abnormal data, and the DBI of the improved DBSCAN is 0.15, saying that the clustering effect is very well, while the DBI of the original DBSCAN algorithm is 0.68 and the DBI of K-means is 0.73, which indicates that the clustering effect of these two algorithms is poor. From the detection results of the three algorithms, the improved DBSCAN algorithm, i.e., CCMD-DBSCAN, has higher accuracy in detecting abnormal data and lower false detection rate. It shows good anomalous data detection on the Argo dataset.

5   Conclusion

Based on the research of marine Argo buoy data, anomaly detection and DBSCAN algorithm, an improved algorithm is proposed in this paper. The algorithm firstly reduces the dimensionality of Argo data with high latitude and strong correlation, and secondly defines the threshold value of marine data based on the research of anomaly detection algorithm and DBSCAN related improvement direction, and determines the selection of algorithm parameters automatically based on the threshold value, which reduces the labor cost and improves the efficiency of the algorithm and the accuracy of anomaly detection. At the same time, the improved algorithm in this paper retains the advantages of the original algorithm and has high scalability. According to the results of multiple experiments, based on the improved DBSCAN algorithm, our proposed CCMD-DBSCAN algorithm has better Argo data applicability and is more scientific compared with other comparative algorithms, which presents a new idea and a resolute solution for anomaly detection of marine data.

References

1. Liu, Z., et al.: China Argo project: progress in China Argo ocean observations and data applications. Acta Oceanol. Sin. **36**(06), 1–11 (2017). https://doi.org/10.1007/s13131-017-1035-x
2. Rettig, L., Khayati, M., Cudré-Mauroux, P., Piórkowski, M.: Online anomaly detection over big data streams. In: 2015 IEEE International Conference on Big Data (Big Data), Santa Clara, CA, USA, pp. 1113–1122 (2015). https://doi.org/10.1109/BigData.2015.7363865
3. Grubbs, F.E.: Procedures for detecting outlying observations in samples. Technometrics **11**(1), 1–21 (1969)
4. Lewis T.: Outliers in Statistical Data, 3rd edn. (1994)
5. Ding, J., Wang, L., Shen, D., et al.: An anomaly detection system on big data. Nat. Sci. J. Hainan Univ. (2015)
6. Jiang, H., Yao, W.U., Lyu, K., et al.: Ocean data anomaly detection algorithm based on improved k-medoids. In: 2019 Eleventh International Conference on Advanced Computational Intelligence (ICACI) (2019)
7. Bhaskar, T., Shesu, R.V., Boyer, T.P., et al.: Quality control of oceanographic in situ data from Argo floats using climatological convex hulls. MethodsX **4**(2), 469–479 (2017)
8. He, Z.-S., Liu, Z.T., Zhuang, Y.B.: Data-partitioning-based parellel DBSCAN algorithm. J. Chin. Comput. Syst. (2006)
9. Zhu, Q., Tang, X., Liu, Z., et al.: Revised DBSCAN clustering algorithm based on dual grid. In: 2020 Chinese Control and Decision Conference (CCDC) (2020)
10. Chen, Y., Zhou, L., Bouguila, N., et al.: BLOCK-DBSCAN: fast clustering for large scale data. Pattern Recogn. **109**, 107624 (2020)
11. Kryszkiewicz, M., Lasek, P.: TI-DBSCAN: clustering with DBSCAN by means of the triangle inequality. In: Szczuka, M., Kryszkiewicz, M., Ramanna, S., Jensen, R., Hu, Q. (eds.) RSCTC 2010. LNCS (LNAI), vol. 6086, pp. 60–69. Springer, Heidelberg (2010). https://doi.org/10.1007/978-3-642-13529-3_8
12. Gao, X., Gui, Z.P., Long, X., et al.: KDSG-DBSCAN: a high performance DBSCAN algorithm based on K-D tree and spark GraphX. Geogr. Geo-Inf. Sci. **33**(6), 1–7 (2017)
13. Ohadi, N., Kamandi, A., Shabankhah, M., Fatemi, S.M., Hosseini, S.M., Mahmoudi, A.: SW-DBSCAN: a grid-based DBSCAN algorithm for large datasets. In: 2020 6th International Conference on Web Research (ICWR), Tehran, Iran, pp. 139–145 (2020)

14. Zhu, Q., Tang, X., Liu, Z.: Revised DBSCAN clustering algorithm based on dual grid. In: Chinese Control And Decision Conference (CCDC), Hefei, China, pp. 3461–3466 (2020)
15. Jolliffe, I.T., Cadima, J.: Principal component analysis: a review and recent developments. Philos. Trans. A Math. Phys. Eng. **374**(2065), 20150202 (2016)

Fog Federation Pricing and Resource Purchase Based on the Stackelberg Model in Fog Computing

Chenxiang Zhang, Yujie Sun[(✉)], Wenqing Liu, and Chenbin Huang

Zhejiang Normal University, Jinhua 321004, China
202025201030@zjnu.edu.cn, zjnuminnasun@163.com

Abstract. Fog computing, which provides low-latency computing services at the network edge, is an enabler for the emerging Internet of Things (IoT) systems. However, due to the limited capacity of the fog devices, a large number of tasks will still be offloaded to the cloud for processing. This can overload the backbone network and cause excessive delays. In addition, the distribution of IoT devices is uneven. This paper groups fog nodes into a fog federation to increase the number of tasks that fog nodes can handle. The boom in fog computing has made fog pricing an important issue. But so far, no one has set a price for the federation. This article uses the Stackelberg model to simulate the interaction process between fog federation and IoT devices. First, fog devices bundle certain computing power, memory, and some other resources into a computing resource block (CRB). Then, fog devices act as a leader to release the price of CRB, and IoT devices act as a follower to determine the amount of CRB purchased. This article introduces how IoT can buy the right amount of CRB to minimize its cost and how CRB is priced to maximize the revenue of the fog federation.

Keywords: Fog computing · Cloud computing · Stackelberg · Internet of Things

1 Introduction

International Data Corporation (IDC) predicts that the number of sensors connected to the network will increase to 30 billion, and the number of connected devices will increase from 50 billion to 1 trillion by 2021. All these devices are connected to the network and construct the Internet of Things (IoT) systems [1]. As the increasing number of computation-intensive applications (e.g., augmented reality and face recognition) appears, higher requirements of computing power are placed on IoT devices. The IoT devices with limited memory and computing power cannot handle computation-intensive applications effectively. How to deal with the data generated by a large number of devices has become a problem. It is inefficient to offload tasks to the cloud data center. This will cause network bandwidth overhead, as much of the data can be filtered due to high redundancy. Besides, the long distance between the IoT devices and the cloud data center leads to unacceptable task processing delay, huge transmission energy consumption, poor support for mobility, and problems of security [2–5]. Therefore, the CISCO proposed

H. Ma et al. (Eds.): CWSN 2022, CCIS 1715, pp. 55–65, 2022.
https://doi.org/10.1007/978-981-19-8350-4_5

fog computing, sending tasks on the IoT devices to fog device which is closer to IoT devices for processing. Fog computing can handle low-latency tasks effectively and reduce network congestion. However, due to the limited capacity of the fog devices, a large number of tasks will still be offloaded to the cloud for processing. In addition, the distribution of IoT devices is uneven, and fog devices cannot be effectively used. Therefore, this article uses fog-to-fog offloading in this article. Combine fog devices from different areas into a fog federation to increase the number of tasks that fog devices can handle. The fog in the fog federation can offload tasks to other members of the fog federation. Therefore, it greatly improves the utilization of fog equipment. As the fog market is very large, how to price fog devices is a very important issue. If fog resources are priced too high, it will result in a small number of users. If the price is too low, it will result in less profit for the fog provider. This article combines the Stackelberg model and fog federation to maximize the profits of the fog provider while ensuring that the cost for IoT users will not be too high. Subsequent paragraphs, however, are indented.

The contributions of this article are as follows:

1) This article considers the cooperation between fog devices, and bundles certain computing power, memory, and some other resources into a computing resource block (CRB).
2) This article uses the Stackelberg model to simulate the pricing and purchase process between fog federation and IoT devices. First, fog federation is priced, and then IoT devices determine the number of CRB purchased according to the fog federation pricing. And this article deduces how IoT can buy the right amount of CRB to minimize its cost and how CRB is priced.

2   Related Works

[6] once proposed the concept of fog federation. The fog-to-fog offloading method is prosed in [7–9]. Fog-to-fog offloading means that fog with insufficient computing power can offload tasks to other fog with sufficient resources for processing. Each fog device can be offloaded from the other in the fog federation. Regrettably, none of these articles considers the pricing of fog federation. Even though fog federation pricing is concerned in [10], it does not propose how to set a price for fog federation, but directly gives a definite value.

Fog resource pricing has already had much research in this area. In [11], the article utilizes the Alternating Direction Method of Multipliers (ADMM) as a large-scale optimization tool to obtain the Optimal price of fog devices. ADMM obtains prices through multiple iterations, which will cause a waste of time. A multi-attribute-based double auction mechanism in Vehicular fog computing was proposed, which considers both the price and nonprice attributes for constructing reasonable matching in [12]. Literature [13] introduces the design of an optimal auction based on deep learning for resource allocation in fog computing. Both articles are priced using a bilateral auction, the auction process will take some extra time and they do not consider fog federation. Stackelberg model is used to price for data service operator (DSO) in [14]. [15] proposes multi-objective factors that should be considered in computational offloading. We also consider those factors when IoT devices buy CRB. This article proposes to use the Stackelberg model to pricing for fog federation and introduces how IoT can buy the right amount of CRB to minimize its cost and how CRB is priced. This article meets the needs of IoT devices while ensuring that the fog.

3 System Model

The traditional three-tier model of Fog computing is shown in Fig. 1 IoT devices can offload tasks to fog devices for processing, or they can offload tasks to the cloud for processing through fog devices. Due to fog devices' limited computing power and storage capacity, the number of tasks that fog devices can handle is limited. In addition, due to the uneven distribution of IoT devices, the distribution of tasks among fog nodes is unbalanced, and fog nodes are not effectively used. On the one hand, to reduce the traffic from fog devices to the cloud, on the other hand, to make full use of fog devices, we use the system model shown in Fig. 2 in this article.

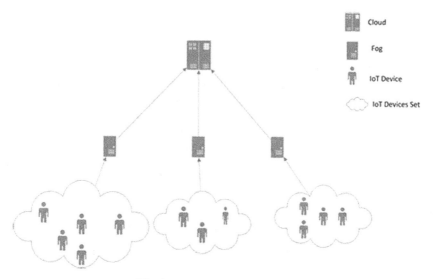

Fig. 1. Traditional system model.

As shown in Fig. 2, fog nodes form a fog federation. IoT devices can offload the task to the connected fog node. Each fog device can be offloaded from the other in the fog federation. Fog devices with insufficient resources can offload tasks to other idle or resource-sufficient fog devices for calculation. This not only improves the utilization of fog devices but also effectively reduces the traffic between fog devices and the cloud. Furthermore, the task is offloaded to other fog devices for processing, instead of being transmitted to a remote cloud for processing, effectively reducing the task completion time and improving the task success rate. For time-sensitive tasks, the time cost of transferring to the cloud is too high, and the model in Fig. 2 is a suitable method.

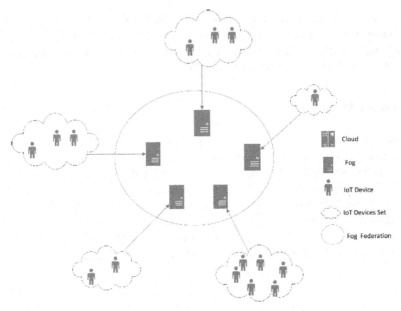

Fig. 2. System model.

We assume that the considered system consists of N fog devices. In this paper, we consider the traffic model at the fog devices as an M/M/1 queue. There are M_j IoT devices in the area of fog device j. These IoT devices in M_j can only offload tasks to the main fog device j. For each IoT device, it can offload its tasks to the main fog device through the wireless channel or process tasks locally. We assume that the tasks generated from IoT i ($i \in M_j$) follow a Poisson process with an average arrival rate of λ_i. The average length of the task is θ bit. The IoT device i choose to offload the service request with a probability $\pi_i, 0 \le \pi_i \le 1$. Accordingly, the tasks which are offloaded to the fog follow a Poisson process with an average rate of $\pi_i\lambda_i$. The tasks that are processed locally also follow a Poisson process with an average rate of $(1 - \pi_i)\lambda_i$. The response time T_i^{total} for locally processing tasks is expressed as follows:

$$T_i^{local} = \frac{(1 - \pi_i)\lambda_i\theta}{u_i} \tag{1}$$

The u_i denotes the computing capability of IoT device i. When IoT device i transmits the data to the fog node, with the consideration of the interference caused by other IoT devices, we can get the transmission rate [16] as follows:

$$R_i = W\log_2\left(1 + \frac{P_i h_i}{w_0 + \sum_{j \in M_j, j \ne i} P_j h_j}\right) \tag{2}$$

This is derived from the Shannon formula. Where W is the channel bandwidth and P_i is the transmission power of the IoT device i. h_i is the channel gain between IoT device i and fog node j. w_0 denotes the noise power. We do not study the impact of power here, so we assume that the power of each IoT device is the same. The transmission time of IoT i for offloading the data to fog devices is as follows:

$$T^t = \frac{\theta \pi_i \lambda_i}{R_i} \tag{3}$$

IoT devices are heterogeneous. Therefore, the processing power and memory requirements of different IoT devices are inconsistent. We bind the processing power u_0 and the memory m_0 into a computing resource block (CRB). The IoT device i is in the area of fog device j, so IoT device i offload its task to fog device j. Suppose IoT device i needs q_i CRBs, the total processing time of offloaded tasks in fog device j is expressed as follows:

$$T_j^F = \frac{\pi_i \lambda_i}{u_0 q_i} \tag{4}$$

From [15], we can get the average waiting time of the individual task is expressed as follows:

$$t = \frac{1}{u_0 q_i - \pi_i \lambda_i} \tag{5}$$

To ensure that the tasks on the fog devices can be successfully processed, the t should be less than the maximum tolerable delay t^{max}.

$$\frac{1}{u_0 q_i - \pi_i \lambda_i} \leq t^{max} \tag{6}$$

From (6) we can get the minimum number of CRBs that need to be purchased.

$$q_i \geq \frac{1}{t^{max} u_0} + \frac{\pi_i \lambda_i}{u_0} \tag{7}$$

High-speed wireless transmission is used between fog devices, and the transmission time can be ignored. If the CRBs of fog device j is not enough, fog device j will use the resource block provided by the fog federation.

We assume the energy required to process one bit in IoT device i is k_i. Therefore, we can get the energy needed for local processing as follows:

$$E_i^{local} = (1 - \pi_i)\lambda_i \theta k_i \tag{8}$$

The energy required to offload the task to the fog device is expressed as follows:

$$E_i^T = P_i T^t \tag{9}$$

Therefore, the total processing time and total energy are expressed as follows:

$$T_i^{total} = T_i^{local} + T^t + T_j^F \tag{10}$$

$$E_i^{total} = E_i^{local} + E_i^T \tag{11}$$

4 Problem Statement

We consider the time and energy of IoT devices and the cost of purchasing fog devices. In general, there are two kinds of algorithms to solve multi-objective optimization problems, which are traditional optimization algorithms and intelligent optimization algorithms. The traditional optimization method is the weighted method. Therefore, we express the objective function of IoT device i as follows:

$$\underset{q_i}{Min} a^T T_i{}^{total} + a^E E_i{}^{total} + a^C q_i P_j^f \tag{12}$$

$$St: u_0 q_i - \pi_i \lambda_i > 0 \tag{13}$$

a^E, a^T and a^C are the weights of time and energy respectively, where $0 \le a^T, a^E, a^C \le 1$ and $a^E + a^T + a^C = 1$. If we pay more attention to time, should be the biggest weight. Constraint (13) represents the tasks processed locally cannot exceed the amount that the IoT device can handle. The P_j^f is the cost of one CRB in fog device j. If the difference between the data is too large, we can also normalize and then plus together.

We express the objective function of fog federation as follows:

$$\underset{P_j^f}{Max} \sum_{j=1}^{N} \sum_{i=1}^{M_j} P_j^f q_i - \max(0, q^{\max} - \sum_{j=1}^{N} \sum_{i=1}^{M_j} q_i) P^c - c \sum_{j=1}^{N} \sum_{i=1}^{M_j} q_i \tag{14}$$

$$c \le P_j^f \le P^c \tag{15}$$

P^c represents the penalty for task failure. c represents the maintenance and operation cost of a CRB.

We set the pricing process of the fog devices as the Stackelberg Game model. Stackelberg Game is a two-stage dynamic game with complete information, and the time of the game is sequential. The main idea is that both parties choose their strategies according to the other's possible strategies to ensure that they maximize their interests under the other's strategies. In this game model, the party that makes the decision first is called the leader. After the leader, the remaining players make decisions based on the leader's decisions, which are called followers, and then the leader adjusts their own decisions according to the decisions of the followers. Repeat until it reaches the Nash equilibrium. In this article, we will use fog devices as the leader and IoT devices as the followers. First, the fog devices set the price, and then the IoT device determines the amount of offloading according to the price set by the fog federation. Ensure that both fog federation and IoT devices can achieve their objective functions.

Stage A: Fog Federation(leader):

$$\underset{P_j^f}{Max} \sum_{j=1}^{N} \sum_{i=1}^{M_j} P_j^f q_i - \max(0, \sum_{j=1}^{N} \sum_{i=1}^{M_j} q_i - q^{\max}) P^c - c \sum_{j=1}^{N} \sum_{i=1}^{M_j} q_i$$

Stage B: IoT devices in the area of fog device j (followers)

$$\underset{q_i}{Min} \, a^T T_i{}^{total} + a^E E_i^{total} + a^C q_i P_j^f$$

We first present the analysis of stage B. In this stage, IoT devices try to minimize their object function by purchasing suitable CRBs at a given P_j^f. We first define the objective function of IoT device i as $o_1(q_i)$. $o_1(q_i)$ is expressed as follows:

$$
\begin{aligned}
o_1(q_i) &= a^T T_i^{total} + a^E E_i^{total} + a^C q_i P_j^f \\
&= a^T \left(\frac{(1 - \pi_i)\lambda_i\theta}{u_i} + \frac{\pi_i\lambda_i}{u_0 q_i} + \frac{\theta\pi_i\lambda_i}{R_i} \right) + a^E \left((1 - \pi_i)\lambda_i\theta k_i + P_i\frac{\theta\pi_i\lambda_i}{R_i} \right) + a^C q_i P_j^f
\end{aligned}
$$

So we can get the second derivative of the objective function as follows:

$$
\frac{\partial o_1}{\partial^2 q_i} = \frac{2a^T\pi_i\lambda_i}{u_0 q_i^3} > 0 \tag{16}
$$

From (16), the second derivative of the objective function is more than zero. o_1 is a convex function. Therefore, the minimum value is obtained when the first derivative of the objective function is equal to zero.

$$
\frac{\partial o_1}{\partial q_i} = -\frac{a^T\pi_i\lambda_i}{u_0 q_i^2} + a^C P_j^f = 0 \tag{17}
$$

From (18), when $q_i = \sqrt{\frac{a^T\pi_i\lambda_i}{a^C u_0 P_j^f}}$, $o_1(q_i)$ can get the minimum value. Since q_i can only be an integer, we define $q_i = \lceil \sqrt{\frac{a^T\pi_i\lambda_i}{a^C u_0 P_j^f}} \rceil$. [d] represents the rounded up of d. Then, we present the analysis of stage A. In this stage, the fog federation tries to maximize its income. Only (18) is true, and the objection of the fog federation can be achieved.

$$
q^{max} - \sum_{j=1}^{N}\sum_{i=1}^{M_j} q_i \geq 0 \tag{18}
$$

We can get the minimum price $P_j^{min}.\max(c, P^{min}) \leq P_j^f < P^c$, P_j^{min} is the approximate solution of (19). The minimum price set by the Fog federation is all CRB just sold out.

$$
\sum_{j=1}^{N}\sum_{i=1}^{M_j} \sqrt{\frac{a^T\pi_i\lambda_i}{a^C u_0 P_j^f}} = q^{max} \tag{19}
$$

$$
P_j^{min} = \left(\frac{\sum_{j=1}^{N}\sum_{i=1}^{M_j} \sqrt{\frac{a^T\pi_i\lambda_i}{a^C u_0}}}{q^{max}} \right)^2 \tag{20}
$$

From (7), we can get (21).

$$q_i \geq \frac{1}{t^{\max} u_0} + \frac{\pi_i \lambda_i}{u_0} \Rightarrow \sqrt{\frac{a^T \pi_i \lambda_i}{a^C u_0 P_j^f}} \geq \frac{1}{t^{\max} u_0} + \frac{\pi_i \lambda_i}{u_0} \tag{21}$$

To ensure the successful offloading of half of the IoT devices, from (22) P_j^{max} is expressed as follows:

$$P_j^{\max} = \frac{1}{M_j} \sum_{i=1}^{M_j} \frac{a^T \pi_i \lambda_i}{a^C u_0 (\frac{1}{t^{\max} u_0} + \frac{\pi_i \lambda_i}{u_0})^2} \tag{22}$$

In the case of satisfying condition (18), the objective function of fog federation is $o_2(P_j^f)$.

$$o_2(P_j^f) = \sum_{j=1}^{N} \sum_{i=1}^{M_j} P_j^f q_i - c \sum_{j=1}^{N} \sum_{i=1}^{M_j} q_i$$

$$\Rightarrow \sum_{j=1}^{N} \sum_{i=1}^{M_j} P_j^f [\max(\sqrt{\frac{a^T \pi_i \lambda_i}{a^C u_0 P_j^f}}, \frac{\pi_i \lambda_i}{u_0})] - c \sum_{j=1}^{N} \sum_{i=1}^{M_j} \sqrt{\frac{a^T \pi_i \lambda_i}{a^C u_0 P_j^f}}$$

$o_2(P_j^f)$ is an increasing function of price. To get the maximum profit. We can take $\max(P_j^{max}, P_i^{min})$.

5 Simulation

In this section, we consider the fog federation composed of three fog devices. M_1, M_2, M_3 are 10, 50, 100 respectively. Moreover, the processing capability of three fog devices is uniformly distributed over $[6 \times 10^7, 7 \times 10^7]$ bit/s [5, 6]. In addition, the processing capability of IoT devices is uniformly distributed over $[1 \times 10^5, 2 \times 10^5]$. The processing capability u_0 of a CRB is 100 tasks/s. θ is 1000 bit. We further assume that a^T, a^E, a^C are 0.6, 0.1, 0.4 respectively. The average arrival rate λ of IoT devices in the area of fog 1 are uniformly distributed over [1000,5000], λ in fog 2 is uniformly distributed over [2000,3000], and λ in fog 3 is uniformly distributed over [1000,2000].

Table 1. The states of all fog devices.

Fog device	Price	Total CRB	Remain CRB	Revenue (no federation)	Revenue (federation)
Fog 1	0.0677	670	448	15.0294	15.0294
Fog 2	0.0837	695	−96	58.1715	66.2067
Fog 3	0.1359	679	−324	88.27	130.39

From Table 1, we can see the RCB usage status and pricing of each fog node. We can know that our proposed fog federation strategy is effective according to the total revenue.

We can see from Fig. 3 when q reaches a point, it begins to rent fog devices, so the total cost begins to drop. As q continues to increase, the total cost reaches a minimum. However, when q continues to increase, the total cost will not decrease but will increase. This is due to the fact that when the demand for RCB becomes larger, the price of fog will increase. So the cost will be higher. Since we pay more attention to time, IoT devices can achieve better benefits when the value of π is larger.

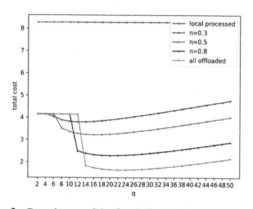

Fig. 3. Cost change of the first IoT device in the fog 1 area

Through the comparison of the two curves in Fig. 4, we can see that the fog federation can make the total revenue of fog devices higher. Looking at each curve separately, we can see that as the number of total IoT devices increases, the total revenue increases. When all the CRBs in the fog federation are rented, the total revenue begins to decline.

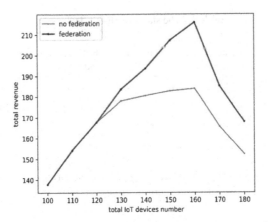

Fig. 4. Total revenue of fog federation

6   Conclusion

This paper proposes the Stackelberg model to simulate the interaction between fog devices and IoT devices. The article introduces how fog devices should be priced for RCB, and also introduces the optimal number of RCBs for IoT devices. We combined the Stackelberg model with Fog federation to give the fog federation pricing and proved the effectiveness of fog federation through experiments. Experiments also show that the number of RCBs we selected is the best.

More things can be further studied and discussed in fog Federation pricing and resource purchase. In the future, we will continue to allocate funds for members of fog federation, and rationally optimize the current model, so that it can describe the mathematical and physical meaning of fog federation pricing and resource purchase more concretely and vividly.

References

1. Gubbi, J., Buyya, R., Marusic, S., Palaniswami, M.: Internet of Things (IoT): a vision, architectural elements, and future directions. Futur. Gener. Comput. Syst. **29**(7), 1645–1660 (2013)
2. Chiang, M., Ha, S., ChihLin, I., Risso, F., Zhang, T.: Clarifying fog computing and networking: 10 questions and answers. IEEE Commun. Mag. **55**(4), 18–20 (2017)
3. Ahmedet, E.: Process state synchronization for mobility support in mobile cloud computing. In: IEEE International Conference on Communication (ICC), pp. 1–6 (2019)
4. Gai, K., Qiu, M., Zhao, H., Tao, L., Zong, Z.: Dynamic energy-aware cloudlet-based mobile cloud computing model for green computing. J. Netw. Comput. App. **59**, 46–54 (2016)
5. Chen, X., Jiao, L., Li, W., Fu, X.: Effificient multi-user computation offloading for mobile-edge cloud computing. IEEE/ACM Trans. **24**(5), 2795–2808 (2016)
6. Mukherjee, M., Kumar, V., Lloret, J., Zhang, Q.: Revenue maximization in delay-aware computation offloading among service providers with fog federation. IEEE Commun. Lett. **24**, 1799–1803 (2020)

7. Lyu, X., Ren, C., Ni, W., Tian, H., Liu, R.P.: Distributed optimization of collaborative regions in large-scale inhomogeneous fog computing. IEEE J. Sel. Areas Commun. **36**, 574–586 (2018)

8. Lyu, X., et al.: Distributed online optimization of fog computing for selfish devices with out-of-date information. IEEE Trans. Wirel. Commun. **17**, 7704–7717 (2018)

9. Xiao, Y., Krunz, M.: Distributed optimization for energy-efficient fog computing in the tactile internet. IEEE J. Sel. Areas Commun. **36**, 2390–2400 (2018)

10. Kim, D., Lee, H., Song, H., Choi, N., Yi, Y.: Economics of fog computing: interplay among infrastructure and service providers, users, and edge resource owners. IEEE Trans. Mob. Comput. **19**, 2609–2622 (2020)

11. Raveendran, N., Zhang, H., Song, L, Wang, L.-C., Hong, C.S., Han, Z.: Pricing and resource allocation optimization for IoT fog computing and NFV: an EPEC and matching based perspective. In: IEEE Transactions on Mobile Computing, September 2020

12. Peng, X., Ota, K., Dong, M.: Multiattribute-based double auction toward resource allocation in vehicular fog computing. IEEE Internet Things J. **7**, 3094–3103 (2020)

13. Luong, N.C., Jiao, Y., Wang, P., Niyato, D., Kim, D.I., Han, Z.: A machine-learning-based auction for resource trading in fog computing. IEEE Commun. Mag. **58**, 82–88 (2020)

14. Zhang, H., Xiao, Y., Bu, S., Niyato, D., Yu, F.R., Han, Z.: Computing resource allocation in three-tier IoT fog networks: a joint optimization approach combining Stackelberg game and matching. IEEE Internet Things J. **4**(5), 1204–1215 (2017)

15. Liu, L., Chang, Z., Guo, X., Mao, S., Ristaniemi, T.: Multiobjective optimization for computation offloading in fog computing. IEEE Internet Things J. **5**, 283–294 (2018)

16. Adhikari, M., Mukherjee, M., Srirama, S.N.: DPTO: a deadline and priority-aware task offloading in fog computing framework leveraging multilevel feedback queueing. IEEE Internet Things J. **7**, 5773–5782 (2020)

Bandwidth Scheduling Scheme with AoI Guarantee for Heterogeneous Mobile Edge Caching

Yiying Sun, Hui Wang[✉], Hongba Bao, Fangbin Chen, and Minghui Sheng

School of Mathematics and Computer Science, Zhejiang Normal University, Jinhua 321004, China
hwang@zjnu.cn

Abstract. In recent years, the wide spread adoption of mobile applications exerts a great burden on backhaul links. Mobile edge computing (MEC) alleviates the problem by enabling mobile edge devices with cache storage to reduce network congestion and content delivery latency. In this paper, we study the problem of bandwidth minimization under Age of Information (AoI) constraint in mobile edge caching system with heterogeneous devices. We present a content refreshing mechanism, and propose an algorithm extended from the classical genetic algorithm to minimize average AoI. Specially, mobile users declare requests of the content service provision that are dynamically collected at base station (BS). Upon receiving these requests, the BS can decide how to allocate the bandwidth for updating the content, so that the average AoI in the network is minimized. Unlike existing work, this paper also takes into account the diverse QoS requirements of heterogeneous nodes in data transmission. Extensive simulations are conducted to validate the analytical results. Compared to other conventional algorithms, the results indicate that the proposed scheme can effectively reduce the average AoI.

Keywords: Age of information · Bandwidth scheduling · Genetic algorithm · Heterogeneous edge caching

1 Introduction

The past few decades have witnessed significant advances in the computing capabilities of mobile and sensing devices (e.g. smartphones), a variety of advanced real-time applications have been newly developed to meet the growing demand for high-quality of life and work. These emerging applications are commonly time-sensitive, leading to heavy transmission burden on resource-constrained mobile devices. To resolve this conflict, mobile edge computing (MEC) has emerged as an effective paradigm to support real-time application systems by providing communication and caching resources at the edge devices [1]. Mobile edge caching enables content service by using the storage resources of mobile devices, like MEC server, which benefits both for both network users and operators, but it may lead to staleness of dynamic sources whose content information changes over time and with the environment. To handle this situation, Age of Information

(AoI), which is the time elapsed since the generation of the current version, has received growing attention since it was initially conceived by Kaul et al. in [2]. Therefore, we consider devising effective cache refreshing schemes to optimize the AoI of the system.

Though the MEC servers are deployed close to mobile terminals for more frequent information updates, it still imposes a strict requirement on bandwidth resources of MEC servers. Particularly, due to heterogeneity of information in edge sources, the users may suffer from service quality caused by unpredictable network congestion and unreasonable bandwidth allocation [3]. Hence, it is still non-trivial to investigate bandwidth allocation mechanism in MEC-based networks.

In the existing literature, wireless network resource allocation has been widely discussed. For instance, Nguyen et al. in [4] proposed a market-based framework to allocate multiple types of resource in fog computing. Huang et al. in [5] developed an optimal algorithm to solve resource allocation problem in D2D communication. In [6], the authors leveraged a resource availability model, which is helpful for resource selection. Besides, Authors in [7–9] solved problems considering the costs and configuration jointly for different edge nodes in their work. However, most researchers focused on how to better allocate bandwidth to reduce system delay or improve MEC revenue, and rarely take the quality of delivered contents and experience of users into consideration.

Some works introduce AoI for a constraint of the model. For instance, the authors of [10–12] optimize the channel allocation within freshness requirements. But quite few people considered optimizing AoI through rationally allocating bandwidth of MEC server to heterogeneous nodes.

Therefore, in view of the shortcomings of the above researches and considering the heterogeneity of nodes in the process of bandwidth allocation, this paper proposes a bandwidth allocation scheme based on advanced genetic algorithm to minimize the system average AoI of edge caching. Firstly, we established a three-layer content-driven transmission model concluding end users, BS, and sources, and described the mechanisms for content transmitting and cache updating. Then, we emphasize the heterogeneity characteristic of the contents providers. We model the optimization problem using the queuing theory and propose an algorithm based on genetic algorithm to solve the problem. Simulation results show that the proposed scheme can effectively reduce the system average AoI compared with other reference schemes.

The rest of this paper is organized as follows: Sect. 2 provides the system model and Sect. 3 presents problem formulation of the transmission framework for the bandwidth distribution with AoI calculated by a queuing model. The proposed scheme is introduced in detail in Sect. 4, where efficient approaches based on classical genetic algorithm are proposed and analyzed. Simulation results are given in Sect. 5, followed by conclusions in Sect. 6.

2 System Model

Consider a mobile edge caching wireless network, as shown in Fig. 1, which consists of N IoT sources transmitting time-sensitive information to one Base Station (BS), and a number of mobile users running diverse applications. Each source collects content samples from environment and forwards them to BS through a wireless channel shared by all N sources. All mobile users can declare requests of obtaining specific content cached on BS for processing specific problems from applications.

The wireless content transmissions between content requesters (i.e. end users) and providers (i.e.BS) are achieved by cellular overlaying communications, where each user occupies an independent pre-allocated channel. In this paper, since our emphasis is on the transmission between BS and heterogeneous sources, the transmission scheduling at requester ends are omitted.

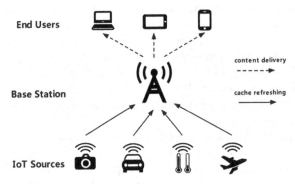

Fig. 1. Mobile edge caching with content refreshing.

Queueing Discipline. A source will transmit its most recent content (i.e. the freshest sample in their transmission queue) to the BS. This will help minimize the AoI of this source at the BS. When source $i \in \{1, 2, \cdots, N\}$ generates a new packet, older packets are discarded from its transmission queue to save its caching space.

Traffic Model. The randomly distributed IoT source nodes reflect the environmental content of specific area, which can be used by the users to handle the time-sensitive tasks generated by their applications, such bedroom temperature, the traffic congestion conditions, and so on. The content generation delay is considered to be relatively small compared with transmission, which is thus ignored to simplify the analysis.

Let the aggregate arrival of contents requests (proposed by all mobile users) at the BS be approximated as a Poisson process with an average rate λ total. For each source which delivers different content, we introduce p_i to represent the average probability of resource i being requested by users, to distinguish the popularity of users' requests for different content. Then we can know that,

$$\sum_{i=1}^{N} p_i = 1 \tag{1}$$

Accordingly, the requests of content from source i also follow Poisson process with arriving rate

$$\eta_i = p_i \lambda \qquad (2)$$

Transmission Model. Since this paper only emphasizes the transmission between BS and sources, we denote B as the available bandwidth of the BS for refreshing the content cache. Due to the heterogeneity of the resource nodes, we should allocate different bandwidth to those resources, so that the average AoI of the system could be minimized. We introduce a splitting ratio β for each resource node, so that $\beta_i B$ can describe the specific bandwidth value of the resource. The service rate of content delivery in source i is given by

$$\mu_i = \beta_i B \log_2 (1 + \gamma_R) \qquad (3)$$

where γ_R is the average received signal to interference and noise ratio (SINR) of the refreshing link.

Moreover, we simply assume that BS delivers contents to all users at same transmission speed, and represents it as μ_D.

Service Process. To better characterize the service process of BS, we introduce a variable ε_i to specify the threshold for content updating of source i. The BS provides service via the single delivery channel in a First-In-First-Out (FIFO) manner. If the AoI of source i is bigger than the threshold ε_i (given according to the importance of the information), the source should update it first before BS transmit it to the user. We use T_i and T_D to represent the time spent to refresh and deliver a content respectively. It is considered to follow independent exponential distributions to reflect the randomness of wireless transmission, which is given by

$$H_i = \begin{cases} T_D, & X = 0, \\ T_i + T_D, & X = 1, \end{cases} \qquad (4)$$

where X is a zero-one indicator showing whether the request is served with cache refreshing.

QoS Provisions. We assume that different kinds of contents have unequal size Z_i and diverse QoS provisions (expressed by transmission rate threshold τ_i). We list practical rate requirements of popular contents as shown in Table 1. So that $E[T_i] = Z_i/\mu_i$ and $E[T_D] = Z_i/\mu_D$.

3   Problem Formulation

In this section, we analyse the AoI performances by applying stochastic process and queuing theory. Then, we give the objectives of proposed scheme in detail.

Table 1. Typical QoS provision of contents.

Contents	Data rates [kbps]	Size [bits]
Short video	800	10 M
Audio file	320	2 M
Office file	200	1 M
Image file	100	500 k

3.1   Age of Information Analysis

The service model of the three-hierarchy centered on the BS can be analyzed independently as a M/M/1 queue since BS can store content and serve mobile users directly through one-hop transmission. In this M/M/1 queue, the customer arrival and service rates are set to η_i and $1/E[H_i]$, respectively. Besides, the cache refreshing process can be analyzed for the given refreshing cycle ε_i, since the arrival and the departure processes of an M/M/1 queue both follow Poisson process according to the Burke's Theorem [13].

Theorem 1. The average AoI of user-received contents from source i is given by.

$$A_i = \frac{1}{\mu_D} + \frac{1}{2}(\varepsilon_i + \frac{1}{\mu_i}) - \frac{1}{2\eta_i}(1 - e^{-\eta_i(\varepsilon_i - \frac{1}{\mu_i})}) \tag{5}$$

Proof. Previously, we artificially defined an refreshing cycle ε_i for source i, consider there are $M + 1$ requests are served in this cycle, and only the first request triggers cache refreshing. Denote by T_D the delivery time of the first request, so that only the first user who sent request received a content with AoI of $T_i + T_D$, while the other M requests are served during $[T_i + T_D, \varepsilon i + T_{D'}]$. As T_D and $T_{D'}$ are i.i.d. random variables, M follows Poisson distribution of mean $\eta_i(\varepsilon_i - T_i)$. So that the refreshing probability on average can be denoted as follows,

$$E[\frac{1}{M+1}] = \sum_{m=0}^{\infty} \frac{1}{m+1} \frac{[\eta_i(\varepsilon_i - \frac{1}{\mu_i})]^m}{m!} e^{-\eta_i(\varepsilon_i - \frac{1}{\mu_i})}$$

$$= \frac{1 - e^{-\eta_i(\varepsilon_i - \frac{1}{\mu_i})}}{\eta_i(\varepsilon_i - \frac{1}{\mu_i})} \tag{6}$$

Therefore, the average AoI of source i is

$$
\begin{aligned}
A_i &= E[\frac{1}{M+1}(T_i + T_D + M\frac{T_i + T_D + \varepsilon_i + T_{D'}}{2})] \\
&= E[\frac{1}{2}(T_i + \varepsilon_i + T_{D'} + T_D - \frac{\varepsilon_i - T_i - T_D + T_{D'}}{M+1})] \\
&= \frac{1}{\mu_D} + \frac{1}{2}(\varepsilon_i + \frac{1}{\mu_i}) - \frac{1}{2}(\varepsilon_i - \frac{1}{\mu_i})E[\frac{1}{M+1}] \\
&= \frac{1}{\mu_D} + \frac{1}{2}(\varepsilon_i + \frac{1}{\mu_i}) - \frac{1}{2\eta_i}(1 - e^{-\eta_i(\varepsilon_i - \frac{1}{\mu_i})})
\end{aligned}
\tag{7}
$$

The result is equal to Theorem 1.

Then, the average AoI and delay can be obtained, given by

$$
\bar{A} = \frac{1}{N}\sum_{i=1}^{N} A_i
\tag{8}
$$

3.2 Bandwidth Allocation Optimization

Based on the analysis upon the queuing model, we optimize the bandwidth allocation scheme to minimize the average AoI while meeting the QoS requirement of users. The problem can be formulated as follows.

$$
\min_{\{\beta_i\}} \bar{A}
\tag{9a}
$$

$$
\text{s.t.} \sum_{i=1}^{N} \beta_i = 1
\tag{9b}
$$

$$
0 \le \beta_i \le 1
\tag{9c}
$$

$$
\lambda < \sum_{i=1}^{N} \frac{1}{E[\frac{1}{M+1}]\frac{1}{\mu_i} + \frac{1}{\mu_D}}
\tag{9d}
$$

$$
\mu_i \ge \tau_i
\tag{9e}
$$

$$
\varepsilon_i \ge \frac{Z_i}{\mu_i}
\tag{9f}
$$

where constraint (9b) and (9c) are constrained descriptions of the bandwidth proportional allocation mechanism. And (9d) guarantees the system stability, while (9e) clarifies the constraints of each source on the user QoS. (9f) declares that refreshing cycle should not be less than the time required to update content.

(9a) is verified to be an NP-hard problem, and we omit the proof process due to space limitations. Accordingly, we propose a solution based on genetic algorithm in Sect. 4.

4   A Bandwidth Scheduling Scheme Based on Genetic Algorithm

In this section, a scheduling scheme based on genetic algorithm is proposed to optimize the scheduling ratio sequence of the BS refreshing bandwidth. Genetic algorithm [14] is invented to mimic some of the processes observed in natural evolution. Compared with the genetic algorithm, proposed algorithm embodies the unique constraints and transformation rules of bandwidth allocation. The specific steps of the BAGA algorithm are described in Algorithm 1.

4.1   Initialization of Population

We define the chromosome in this algorithm as a sequence of β, and encoding it to establish the mapping relationship from genotype to phenotype. The chromosome is composed of N bandwidth allocation ratios. Figure 2 describes a chromosome $\beta = \{\beta_1, \beta_2, \cdots, \beta_i, \cdots \beta_N\}$ of the population and shows the encoding process of β_i. In the figure, the allocation ratio of source i is 0.165.

The genes of each chromosome are composed of the randomly selected sequence of allocation ratio, and the mechanism is set to guarantee (9b) and (9e). The above process is repeated until all chromosomes are generated and encoded.

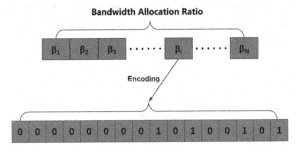

Fig. 2. A chromosome and encoding process of population.

4.2   Genetic Operation

Offspring solutions are generated by genetic operations including selection, crossover and mutation, and the solutions with low fitness are gradually eliminated through adaptive evaluation by referring to biological evolution, so that the optimal solution is generated through several iterations.

Fitness Function. The function we use to calculate the fitness of chromosomes is

$$F = G - \overline{A} \tag{10}$$

where G is a fairly large constant, which guarantees the fitness is positive. The larger fitness value means the smaller AoI of system, and the better quality of chromosomes.

Select Operation. We extract two chromosomes randomly from the initialized population, select the chromosome with the higher fitness, and repeat this operation until the required number of parent population is selected.

Cross Operation. In order to ensure the effective inheritance of features, we only adopt cross operations between the same β encoding sequence of adjacent chromosomes.

Mutation Operation. In the mutation operation, each gene has a certain probability of mutating from $\{0, 1\}$. To guarantee the QoS constraint, we will filter some undesirable mutation.

Generate New Populations. We combine the offspring population and parent population into the new population, arranging them in fitness descending order to optimize the population.

Repeat above operations until we reach the AoI value plateaus.

Algorithm 1 BAGA Algorithm

1: *Initialization:* Obtain K chromosomes to construct a population. For each chromosome, randomly allocate ratio from 0 to 1 for every β_i; Calculate μ_i.

2: **for** $i = 1$ to N **do**

3:    **while** $\mu_i < \tau_i$ **do**

4:       allocate another random ratio to β_i

5:    **end while**

6:    $\beta_i = \beta_i/(\beta_1 + \cdots + \beta_N)$

7: **end for**

8: Encode every β_i as a 16-bit binary sequence

9: *Genetic iteration:*

10: *Step 1: Calculate the Fitness F*

11: *Step 2: Selection:*

12: **for** $j = 1$ to M **do**

13:    Randomly select two chromosomes

14:    Add the one with higher F to selection pool

15: **end for**

16: *Step 2: Cross:*

17: Randomly select a breakpoint v_i for each β_i

18: **for** $j = 1,3,\ldots,$ M-1 **do**

19:       Compare randomly generated number $r \in$ $(0,1)$ with crossover probability cp

20:    **if** r < cp **do**

21:    **for** $i = 1$ to N **do**

22:    Exchange first v_i binary bits of j and j+1

23:    **end for**

24:    **end if**

25:    Add them to cross pool

26: **end for**

27: *Step 3: Mutation*

28: **for** $j = 1$ to M **do**

29:       Compare randomly generated number $r \in$ $(0,1)$ with mutation probability mp

30:    **if** r < mp **do**

31:    Randomly change one binary bit if the calculated μ still satisfies the QoS constraint

32:    **end if**

33: **end for**

34: Repeat *Step 1-4* until the F is steady

---

5 Performance Analysis

In our simulation, we conduct simulations on the open-source network simulator NS3 to validate the analytical results of AoI under the proposed scheme. The user locations and content requests are generated randomly by the Monte Carlo method. We set the BS's radius to be 100 m, and implement the queuing discipline for adjusting arriving rate λ.

The caching refreshing bandwidth of BS server is 10 MHz, and the average received signal to interference and noise ratio is set to 25. The size of the content follows Table 1. The BS serves the requests in a FIFO manner and implements the proposed cache refreshing scheme. In addition, the refreshing cycle is optimized in the scenario. The parameters of algorithm genetic algorithm are set as follows: crossover probability is 0.9, mutation probability is 0.05, population size N is 100.

The theoretical results of average AoI are obtained based on Theorem 1, which are compared with the simulation results in Figs. 3. The simulation and theoretical results are shown to be quite close in general, validating the approximated analysis.

It can be seen from the Fig. 3 that with the increase of the requests load, the average AoI is increasing, while our proposed scheme always keeps the best performance and has the optimal objective value under the same condition. Specifically, the average distribution means we assign the bandwidth averaged to each source, while we introduce the weighted values for the different types of contents in weighed mean distribution. GA refers to the traditional genetic algorithm that omits the special conditions of bandwidth allocation.

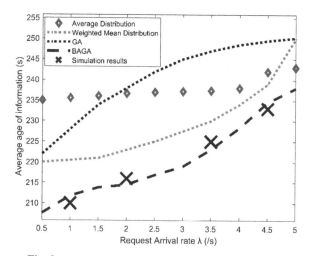

Fig. 3. Average AoI under different request arrival rate.

We also evaluate the part of heterogeneity constraints in our mechanism. As we can see from Fig. 4, even as the variety of content increases, our mechanism still ensures that the system reaches a relatively small AoI level within a smaller number of iterations. In addition, Fig. 5 proves the effectiveness of our endeavor on content heterogeneity. It shows that with the increase of the content type, proposed scheme could better guarantee the average AoI performance.

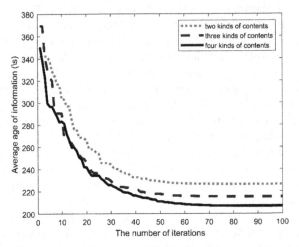

Fig. 4. The comparison of different size of the content type.

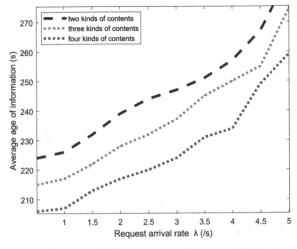

Fig. 5. The performance of different size of the content type under different request arrival rate.

We analyzed how the refreshing cycle ε affects the allocation ratio and came to the conclusion shown in Fig. 6. We ordered N sources in ascending order by the refreshing cycle and found their corresponding allocation proportions. As we expected, the refreshing cycle is approximately inversely proportional to the allocated bandwidth, as described in Theorem 1.

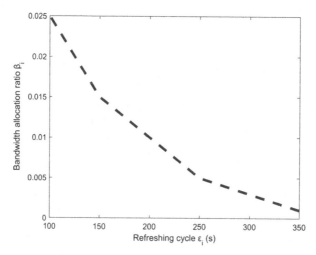

Fig. 6. Bandwidth allocation ratios of sources with different refreshing cycles.

6 Conclusions

In this paper, we study a bandwidth allocation problem with QoS constraints. We apply the queuing theory to analyzing the AoI performance in the BS-centered caching system. A novel scheduling scheme based on genetic algorithm that can always construct a scheduler to guarantee a low-level system AoI is proposed. Furthermore, we consider the heterogeneity of the source nodes, and generalize our scheme to the several sources that produce diverse types of contents. We showed that AoI could be optimized.

The results from this paper lay the foundation for future research of bandwidth allocation with AoI guarantee. Many issues could be further explored. For instance, it is worth studying the impact of the dependence between the arrival and service process. Moreover, the bandwidth competition with content delivery could also be taken into account.

Acknowledgements. This research was supported by the National Natural Science Foundation of China under Grant Nos. 62171413.

References

1. Ndikumana, A., et al.: Joint communication, computation, caching, and control in big data multi-access edge computing. IEEE Trans. Mob. Comput. **19**(6), 1359–1374 (2020). https://doi.org/10.1109/TMC.2019.2908403
2. Kaul, S., Yates, R., Gruteser, M.: Real-time status: how often should one update? In: Proceedings of IEEE INFOCOM, pp. 2731–2735, March 2012
3. Nath, S., Wu, J.: Deep reinforcement learning for dynamic computation offloading and resource allocation in cache-assisted mobile edge computing systems. Intell. Converged Networks **1**(2), 181–198 (2020). https://doi.org/10.23919/ICN.2020.0014

4. Nguyen, D.T., Le, L.B., Bhargava, V.K.: A market-based framework for multi-resource allocation in fog computing. IEEE/ACM Trans. Networking **27**(3), 1151–1164 (2019). https://doi.org/10.1109/TNET.2019.2912077
5. Yi, C., Huang, S., Cai, J.: Joint resource allocation for device-to-device communication assisted fog computing. IEEE Trans. Mob. Comput. **20**(3), 1076–1091 (2021). https://doi.org/10.1109/TMC.2019.2952354
6. Battula, S.K., O'Reilly, M.M., Garg, S., Montgomery, J.: A generic stochastic model for resource availability in fog computing environments. IEEE Trans. Parallel Distrib. Syst. **32**(4), 960–974 (2021). https://doi.org/10.1109/TPDS.2020.3037247
7. Wang, L., Jiao, L., Li, J., Gedeon, J., Mühlhäuser, M.: MOERA: mobility-agnostic online resource allocation for edge computing. IEEE Trans. Mob. Comput. **18**(8), 1843–1856 (2019). https://doi.org/10.1109/TMC.2018.2867520
8. Liu, B., Liu, C., Peng, M.: Resource allocation for energy-efficient MEC in NOMA-enabled massive IoT networks. IEEE J. Sel. Areas Commun. **39**(4), 1015–1027 (2021). https://doi.org/10.1109/JSAC.2020.3018809
9. Raveendran, N., Zhang, H., Song, L., Wang, L.-C., Hong, C.S., Han, Z.: Pricing and resource allocation optimization for IoT fog computing and NFV: an EPEC and matching based perspective. IEEE Trans. Mob. Comput. **21**(4), 1349–1361 (2022). https://doi.org/10.1109/TMC.2020.3025189
10. Ma, X., Zhou, A., Sun, Q., Wang, S.: Freshness-aware information update and computation offloading in mobile-edge computing. IEEE Internet Things J. **8**(16), 13115–13125 (2021). https://doi.org/10.1109/JIOT.2021.3082281
11. Liu, Q., Li, C., Hou, Y.T., Lou, W., Kompella, S.: Aion: a bandwidth optimized scheduler with AoI guarantee. In: IEEE INFOCOM 2021 - IEEE Conference on Computer Communications, 2021, pp. 1–10 (2021). https://doi.org/10.1109/INFOCOM42981.2021.9488781
12. Kadota, I., Modiano, E.: Age of information in random access networks with stochastic arrivals. In: IEEE INFOCOM 2021 - IEEE Conference on Computer Communications, 2021, pp. 1–10. https://doi.org/10.1109/INFOCOM42981.2021.948889
13. Guizani, M., Rayes, A., Khan, B., Al-Fuqaha, A.: Queuing theory. In: Network Modeling and Simulation: A Practical Perspective, Wiley, pp.197–233 (2010)
14. Choi, K., Jang, D., Kang, S., Lee, J., Chung, T., Kim, H.: Hybrid algorithm combing genetic algorithm with evolution strategy for antenna design. IEEE Trans. Mag. **52**(3), 1–4 (2016). Art no. 7209004, https://doi.org/10.1109/TMAG.2015.2486043

An Explainable Machine Learning Framework for Lower Limb Exoskeleton Robot System

Yifan Chen$^{(\boxtimes)}$, Xi Wang, Yili Ye, and Xuebo Sun

School of Mathematics and Computer Science, Zhejiang Normal University,
Jinhua 321004, China
2242155393@qq.com

Abstract. The lower limb exoskeleton robot system is one of the significant tools for the rehabilitation of patients with knee arthritis, which helps to enhance the health of patients and upgrade their quality of life. However, the unexplained gait recognition model decreases the prediction accuracy of the exoskeleton system. The existing explainable models are seldom used in the domain of gait recognition due to their high complexity and large computation. To strengthen the transparency of the model, SHapley Additive exPlanations (SHAP) is applied to gait recognition for the first time in this paper, and an interpretable model framework that can be applied to any lower limb exoskeleton is proposed. Compared with the existing methods, SHAP has a more solid theoretical basis and more efficient calculation methods. The proposed framework can find the relationship between input features and gait prediction, to identify the optimal sensor combination. Additionally, The structure of the gait recognition model can be optimized by adjusting the feature attention of the model with the feature crossover method, and the accuracy of the model can be upgraded by more than 7.12% on average.

Keywords: Interpretable model · Gait recognition model · Machine learning · Exoskeleton

1 Introduction

Knee osteoarthritis (KOA) is one of the major health threats in the world [1]. According to the China Health and Old-age Care Tracking Database (CHARLS) study, 8.1% of Chinese people suffer from KOA, which greatly reduces their quality of life. With the aging of the population, the incidence of the disease also shows a trend of gradual increase.

With the development of technology, wearable exoskeleton robot for lower limb rehabilitation has gradually become important instruments to help KOA patients recover [2,3]. The exoskeleton of lower limbs collects human signals from various parts of the body by placing different biosensors on hips and legs, etc. Machine learning technologies such as ANN, DNN, and CNN are applied to process the signals and provide corresponding assistance. Zexia et al. [4] and Chao

© The Author(s), under exclusive license to Springer Nature Singapore Pte Ltd. 2022
H. Ma et al. (Eds.): CWSN 2022, CCIS 1715, pp. 79–93, 2022.
https://doi.org/10.1007/978-981-19-8350-4_7

Wang et al. [5] developed a wearable sensing system to predict the knee adduction moment (KAM) during walking. Zhaoming Xie et al. used a strategy gradient algorithm to train new strategies, and mixed RL-based strategy gradient with gradient update defined by DASS tuple to propose a model based on iterative reinforcement learning to achieve gait prediction and walking assistance [6].

At present, although these algorithm models can show good estimation accuracy, very few algorithms can be explained. In the process of gait recognition, a large amount of data needs to be collected. The larger the data amount is, the more times the model addition and multiplication operation will be, and the system complexity will increase accordingly [7]. Different gait patterns will have a dependence on different data, but all the data collected are in a "black box", so it is impossible to understand the operation principle of the model. Therefore, the complexity and opacity of existing gait recognition algorithms bring new challenges. The failure of the model to provide any information behind the decision makes it impossible to further improve the predictive accuracy of the device, which is an important criterion for the performance of lower extremity exoskeleton devices. Therefore, it is important to propose an interpretable framework that can accommodate various complexities.

The main contributions of this paper are as follows:

- We propose an interpretation framework that can be applied to any lower-limb exoskeleton gait recognition model, providing local and global explanations for gait recognition, which is unique in the field of gait recognition. This framework helps to deepen the understanding of exoskeletal gait recognition, find the most important features that affect model prediction.
- We apply SHAP to the exoskeleton gait recognition model for the first time, which improves the transparency of the model, and the relationship between gait prediction and input features is discussed. Compared with other methods, SHAP has a better theoretical basis and the experimental results are in line with reality.
- We discuss the differences in machine learning interpretation between the two gait modes, find out the features that have the most influence on the model in different modes and improve the performance of the model by changing the feature attention of the model with the method of feature crossover. The results can provide guidance and reference for the structural design of the lower extremity exoskeleton model.

In the rest of the paper, We describe the related work in Sect. 2, establish the model structure in Sect. 3, and propose the interpretation framework in Sect. 4. In Sect. 5, experiments are carried out to prove that global interpretation can effectively improve the accuracy of the model. Section 6 is the conclusion and future work of this paper.

2   Related Works

In this section, we describe the concept of interpretability and review the work and contributions of interpretability techniques. An algorithm training produces predictive models that can be evaluated in terms of interpretability at each step. Interpretability has been studied by researchers in various fields, but there is no unified, official definition. This paper adopts the definition of Biran and Cotton [8], and interpretability refers to the level at which observers can understand the reasons for decisions. Lipton [9] also points out that the concept of interpretability is not a unified concept, but reflects concepts such as trust or transparency.

2.1 Sugeno-Type Fuzzy Inference

Keneni et al. established an interpretable model for the decision of unmanned aerial vehicle (UAV) [10], which can give the logic behind the decision of unmanned aerial vehicle (UAV) when it performs a predetermined mission and chooses to deviate from its designated path. This explicable model exists on a visual platform in the form of if-then rules derived from Sugeno-type fuzzy inference models. The high-order Sugeno model increases complexity but does not improve performance much, so it is rarely used.

2.2 Factor Analysis

Factor analysis is a technique that involves identifying important factors in a particular group (or cluster). The most commonly used factor analysis techniques include ANOVA analysis, principal component analysis (PCA), tree-based model, etc.

Amruthnath and Gupta et al. used Gaussian mixture clustering to divide the data into important groups and used spectral analysis to diagnose each cluster to a specific state of the machine [11]. Because the least square method is used to calculate factor scores, this method may sometimes fail.

2.3 Octave-Band Filtering

Lee et al. developed an interpretable deep learning model to estimate the remaining service life of rotating machinery [12]. The model uses an autoencoder to extract advanced features from the Fourier transform and uses them as input to a feedforward neural network to explain the behavior of the model by analyzing the composition of features and the relationship between features and estimated results. Octave filtering simplifies the model and improves its interpretability.

The interpretability of machine learning models is a very active and important research area in machine learning, but there are few interpretable models that can be applied to gait recognition.

3 Interpretable Machine Learning

The interpretability of models is divided into local interpretability and global interpretability [13]. Local interpretability can look at the impact of a single instance on the model's predictive behavior and explain why, while global interpretability helps users to understand the model directly from the overall structure of the model.

To improve the interpretability of the exoskeleton gait recognition system, this paper is based on LIME and Shapely values, using SHAP to explain the model from both local and global perspectives. SHAP connects LIME [14] and Shapley Values [15]. LIME and Shapely Values will be discussed first and then SHAP will be introduced.

3.1   Local Interpretable Model-Agnostic Explanations (LIME)

Local surrogate models are interpretable models that are trained to approximate the predictions of the underlying black-box model and used to interpret individual predictions of the black-box machine learning model.

LIME generates a new dataset consisting of perturbed samples and the corresponding predictions of the black-box model and then trains an interpretable model on this new dataset, which is weighted by the proximity of the sampled instances to the instance of interest. The local surrogate model can be calculated by the following expression:

$$\psi(x) = \underset{g \in G}{\mathrm{argmin}} \left\{ \mathcal{L}\left(f, g, w^x\right) + \Omega(g) \right\}, \tag{1}$$

where:

- $\mathcal{L}$ is a minimized loss function.
- f represents the original model.
- w^x defines the weight between the sampled data and the original data.
- g represents an explanation model of instance X.
- G is the family of possible explanations.
- Ω represents the complexity of model g.

Equation (1) shows that LIME wants to minimize the distance between the explained value and the predicted value of the original model by training weighted, explicable models on the variation's data set, thus explaining the prediction by explaining the local model.

3.2   Shapley Values

Based on game theory, predictions can be explained by assuming that every eigenvalue of an instance is a "player" in the game. The Shapley value is the average marginal contribution of a feature value across all possible coalitions [15]. In machine learning models, the Shapley value of each feature can be calculated, and using this method can tell us how to fairly distribute the "expenditure" between features.

The Shapley value of a feature value is its contribution to the payout, weighted and summed over all possible feature value combinations:

$$\phi_i(g, k) = \sum_{S \subseteq \{k_1, \ldots, k_n\} \setminus \{k_i\}} \frac{|S|!\,(P - |S| - 1)!}{P!}$$
$$* \left[g\left(S \cup k_i\right) - g\left(S\right) \right], \tag{2}$$

where:

- S is a subset of the features used in the model.
- p is the number of features.
- k is the vector of feature values of the instance to be explained. The k_i is explained in Eq. (2).
- $g(S)$ is the prediction for feature values in set S that are marginalized over features that are not included in set S:

$$g(S) = \int \hat{g}(k_1, \ldots, k_p)\, d\mathbb{P}_{k \notin S} - E_k(\hat{g}(k)).$$

Compared with other methods, Shapley value is considered the definition of fair payout, and it's the only attribution method that satisfies the properties of Efficiency, Symmetry, Dummy, and Additivity.

Unfortunately, Shapley values take a lot of computing time because there are 2^k possible coalitions of the feature values, which is unacceptable in the increasingly complex modern models.

3.3   SHapley Additive exPlanations (SHAP)

SHAP is a model-agnostic approach from the game theory proposed by Lundberg and Lee [16] to reverse-engineer the output of a predictive algorithm. The goal of SHAP is to explain a prediction $f(x)$ of an instance x by computing the contribution of each feature to the prediction. Figure 1 shows how SHAP is used to interpret the model and feedback on the results.

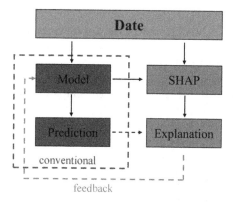

Fig. 1. How is SHAP used to explain models and feedback.

Given a explanation function $g(.)$ and a coalition vector $z' \in \{0,1\}^N$, SHAP specifies the explanation as:

$$g(z') = \phi_0 + \sum_{j=1}^{N} \phi_j z_j', \quad \phi_j \in \mathbb{R} \tag{3}$$

where:

- g is the explanation model.
- ϕ_j is the feature attribution for the feature j for instance x.
- N is the number of input features in x, the instance vector.
- $z' \in \{0,1\}^N$ is the coalition vector.

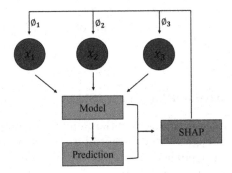

Fig. 2. Overview of the relationship between an input instance vector and the corresponding prediction.

According to Eq. (3), SHAP and LIME are both additive feature attribution methods, that is, attribute an effect ϕ_j to each feature. Figure 2 displays the relationship between an input vector and the corresponding prediction. SHAP weights the sampled instances based on the weight which the coalition would get in the Shapley value estimation. To achieve Shapley compliant weighting, the KernelSHAP is proposed:

$$\pi_x(z') = \frac{(N-1)}{\binom{N}{|z'|} |z'| (N - |z'|)}, \tag{4}$$

where N is the maximum coalition size and $|z'|$ is the number of present features in instance z'.

KernelSHAP can be estimated by five steps:

- Sample coalitions $z_k' \in \{0,1\}^N$, $k \in \{1, \ldots, K\}$, where $z_k' = 0$ means feature absent in coalition, $z_k' = 1$ meas feature present.
- Model $f(h_x(z_x'))$ is used to predict each z_k' by first converting z_k' to the original feature space, where $f(x)$ is the original model and $h_x(z') : \{0,1\}^N \to \mathbb{R}$.

- Compute the weight for each z_k' by Eq. (4).
- Train the linear model g by optimizing the following loss function L:

$$L\left(f, g, \pi_x\right) = \sum_{z' \in Z} \left[f\left(h_x\left(z'\right)\right) - g\left(z'\right)\right]^2 \pi_x\left(z'\right), \qquad (5)$$

where Z is the training data.

- Return the coefficients from function L, that is Shapley values ϕ_k.

SHAP takes the ideas behind LIME and Shapley Values as an approach to better understanding machine learning.

4   Methods

The interpretation framework proposed in this section can be used to improve the interpretability of any lower-limb exoskeleton gait recognition model. In the increasingly complex model system, a framework that can improve the transparency of gait prediction models is needed to select features with stronger model dependence. Figure 3 shows the interpretation framework for this article. Figure 3 is divided into two parts. The left side shows the structure of the traditional exoskeleton gait recognition model, and the right side is used to improve its interpretability.

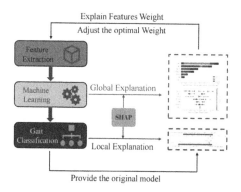

Fig. 3. A interpretation framework for the Exoskeleton gait prediction model.

Local and global interpretations of gait recognition models can be obtained by the proposed framework. Local interpretation can well explain the influence of features on every single sample, and show the positive and negative relationship, to judge whether features are good or bad. Global interpretation can explain the influence of different features of many samples from a macroscopic perspective and analyze the dependence of model output on different features.

4.1 Local Explanation

SHAP can be used to explain individual predictions. SHAP estimates the impact of each feature on a single sample based on the marginal contribution. The specific calculation method is shown in Eq. (2). For example, IMU_Z contributes the most to the Up prediction. At last, these values satisfy all of the properties in Sect. 3. Detailed results are shown in the experiment.

4.2 GLobal Explanation

SHAP values can be combined to explain global importance. Features with large absolute Shapley values are important, so average the absolute Shapley values for each feature in the data. By running SHAP on each instance, a matrix of Shapley values is generated. The matrix has one row per data instance and one column per feature. The entire model can be explained by analyzing the Shapley values in this matrix:

$$I_i = \frac{1}{n} \sum_{j=1}^{n} |\phi_i^{(j)}|, \tag{6}$$

where,

- I_i is the average Shapley values of the i-th feature.
- n is the number of samples in the dataset.
- $\phi_i^{(j)}$ is the Shapley values of the i-th feature for the j-th sample.

Therefore, SHAP can rank global feature importance by the magnitude of feature attributions. Identify the most important features for exoskeleton gait recognition models.

4.3 Tectonic New Feature

Based on SHAP and feature overlap, this paper proposes a new calculation method to adjust the characteristics of the optimal model, better train the gait model, and help scientists to interpret and understand model decisions.

The assumption is that through SHAP we get the two features that are most important to the model and get their contributions. Then, we can use these two features to cross, and construct a kind of brand-new characteristics, to achieve the nonlinear transformation of the sample space, making the model more focused on the features of the break-in in its favour, and improve model effect. The combination of features can be calculated by the following formula:

$$x_{new} = \sum_{i=1}^{n-1} \sum_{j=i+1}^{n} \phi_i x_i \phi_j x_j, \tag{7}$$

where, ϕ_i, ϕ_j represent global explanatory values of different features. Of course, we can focus on more than just the first two features, Specific experimental results will be given in Sect. 5.

5   Experiments

In this section, the experimental setup and the final results are discussed. Experimental results show that local interpretation and global interpretation can be used in the proposed framework under two gait modes. The purpose of this experiment is to understand the data dependence of the model and to provide an explanation for gait prediction.

5.1   Exoskeleton DataSet

Three different types of heterogeneous sensors, including IMU, SEMG and FSR sensor, were used to collect data in the laboratory environment based on the self-developed exoskeleton system. The IMU was placed on the femoris intermedius muscle of the thigh, and the three-axis attitude Angle of the joint was sampled 200 Hz. The SEMG was connected to the quadriceps femoris muscle of the user, and the sampling frequency is set 200 Hz to detect the changes in the muscles of the tester. The FSR was sampled 400 Hz and the pressure change was recorded.

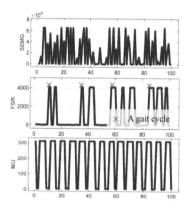

Fig. 4. Plots showing samples of the received data.

5.2   Data Preprocessing

Uniform Sampling Frequency. To ensure the consistency of different source data collected in the time domain, we need to perform a unified frequency operation on the data first.

According to the sampling time node of FSR as the benchmark time, the perception data of other sensors are represented on different time nodes. Then, the latest sensing data of sensors are used to fill the data so that the collected signals become continuous data of the same data length. Figure 4 shows some processed sample signals received from sensors.

Normalization Processing. Because features contain a value of 0, Min-Max Normalization is used for these features in this article:

$$x^* = \frac{x - x_{min}}{x_{max} - x_{min}}, \tag{8}$$

Based on this method, negative values can be well avoided and the data after linear transformation still satisfies the original distribution.

After standardized processing, All data can eliminate the original dimension in the range $[0, 1]$.

5.3 Data Analysis

In this study, we use the XGBoost model for gait classification. XGBoost is an efficient implementation of gradient boosting [17]. In recent years, its efficient computing speed and model performance has been sought after by the industry.

Given a dataset with n samples and m features, K additive functions are used in an XGBoost model to make an estimation,

$$\hat{y} = \phi(x_i) = \sum_{k=1}^{K} f_k(x_i), \tag{9}$$

where, $F = \{f(x) = w_{q(x)}\} \left(q : R^m \to T, w \in R^T\right)$ represents the space of regression tree, and $q(x)$ represents the number of leaf node, $w_{q(x)}$ is the weight of leaf node q. $f(x)$ is a regression tree in space, Each f_k corresponds to a tree which has independent tree structure q and leaf weight w. Following regularized objective is minimized to learn the set of functions,

$$L(\phi) = \sum_i l(\hat{y}_i - y_i) + \sum_k \Omega(f_k), \tag{10}$$

where, $\Omega(f) = \gamma T + \frac{1}{2}\lambda\|w\|^2$, $L(\phi)$ is the lost function of model and Ω is the regularized term, which makes the prediction of the final model more stable.

Table 1. Comparison results on the exoskeleton dataset

Mode	Performance			
	Accuracy	Precision	Recall	F1-score
Sit-updown	0.86	0.85	0.82	0.83
Stairs-updown	0.73	0.76	0.73	0.74

5.4 Performance in Different Modes

To evaluate the performance, the DataSet was subdivided into 70% training dataset, 10% validation dataset, and 20% testing dataset. To avoid randomness, we first train them ten times under the two gait modes, and the average overall performance of the model obtained is shown in Table 1.

As can be seen from the table above, the performance of the model is not very good. The underlying reasons behind poor model performance need to be understood and ways to improve its accuracy.

5.5   Local Explanation Result

This section discusses and visualizes the results of local interpretations of exoskeleton gait prediction models. At the same time, the differences in local interpretation by the XGBoost model under different gait modes are considered.

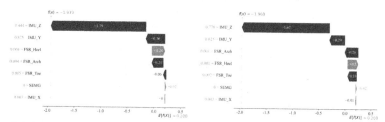

(a) Interpretation of *Stand* result from *sit* sample.   (b) Interpretation of *Stand* result from *up* sample.

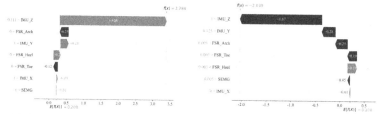

(c) Interpretation of *Stand* result from *stand* sample.   (d) Interpretation of *Stand* result from *down* sample.

Fig. 5. Interpretation of *Stand* results by different sample points.

Taking the *Stand* state as an example, the effect of each feature on a single *Stand* sample can be calculated. In order to avoid randomness, 200 vertical sample points were randomly selected and the average Shapley values of each feature were calculated. The relationship between each independent sample feature and SHAP is shown in Fig. 5. Figure 5 shows the interpretation of four different types of random sample points on *Stand* results, and $f(x)$ in the figure represents the predicted value that the random sample thinks this state is *Stand*. It can be seen from Fig. 5(a), 5(b) and 5(d) that IMU_Z plays a huge role in rejecting the Non-Stand state as the *Stand* state. Figure 5(c) also demonstrates this view, the effect of IMU_Z on *Stand* state is the most beneficial.

By comparing the local interpretation under different gait modes, Fig. 6 shows the interpretation of the *Stand* result under the two modes. It can be seen that although they have great confidence that the state is *Stand*, the interpretation results are different. As shown in Fig. 6(a), the first three features in the *Stand* state are IMU_Z, IMU_Y, and FSR_{Heel}. As shown in Fig. 6(b), XGBoost believes that FSR_{Arch}, IMU_Z, FSR_{Toe} and $SEMG$ play an important role in classification under the condition of *Stairs-updown*. Why the difference in interpretation? Because people need to provide kinetic energy with the above stairs, so the FSR, $SEMG$ has become a good important feature.

(a) Interpretation of *Stand* result from *Sit-updown* mode.

(b) Interpretation of *Stand* result from *Stairs-updown* mode.

Fig. 6. Interpretation of the same state in different modes.

5.6 Global Explanation Result

This section discusses the influence of different features on the overall model performance from a macro perspective. The global dependence of the model on different feature data is analyzed.

Taking the *Sit-updown* mode as an example, Fig. 7 shows the feature influence values of the four classification results, and the X-axis represents the average SHAP value of the feature. It can be seen from Fig. 7(a) and 7(d) that the *Down* state and the *Up* state have some similarities. In this state, the XGBoost model relies most on the change of FSR_{Toe}, because when a person stands up, toes unconsciously push to support the body. The changes of Fig. 7(b) and 7(c) can be explained in Fig. 5.

5.7 Tectonic New Feature

Based on the data dependence of XGBoost models in different modes, this paper constructs a new feature using feature crossover to improve the classification effect of XGBoost. Figure 8 shows the final dependence of the model on the dataset in both modes. Figure 8(a) shows that in the *Sit-updown* mode, the prediction results are most dependent on the change of IMU. Figure 8(b) shows that in the *Stairs-updown* mode, in addition to the change of IMU, the XGBoost

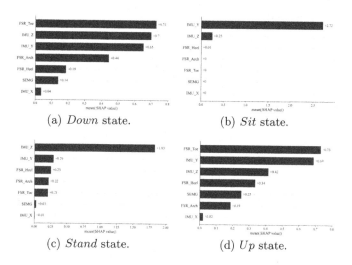

(a) *Down* state.　　　　　　(b) *Sit* state.

(c) *Stand* state.　　　　　　(d) *Up* state.

Fig. 7. The degree of data dependence of different classification results $(Sit-updown)$.

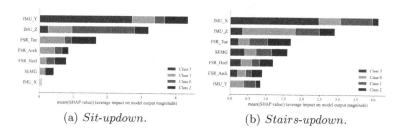

(a) *Sit-updown*.　　　　　　(b) *Stairs-updown*.

Fig. 8. The final dependence of the model on the dataset in both modes.

model is also more dependent on SEMG. The model's dependence on each feature is shown in Table 2.

We construct a list of features that are more dependent on models to assist model training and improve model performance. Considering the differences between heterogeneous sensors, we believe that it is meaningless to select the same sensor. Finally, in *Sit-updown* mode, we chose IMU_Y and FSR_{Toe} to build the new features, and in *Stairs-updown* mode, we chose IMU_Z and $SEMG$ to build the new features, again after ten rounds of training. Figure 9 shows the performance of the new dataset model compared to the original dataset. Compared with the original XGBoost model, the accuracy of the model after feature adjustment improved by 7.25% in *Sit-updown* mode and 7% in *Stairs-updown* mode on average.

In addition, we analyzed the classification effect of the model and found that the main reason for the low overall accuracy in *Stairs-updown* mode is that it is difficult to distinguish *up* state from *Down* state. Therefore, we hypothesized that if an additional IMU sensor was placed at the tibiae anterior muscle of the

Table 2. Specific feature weights of the XGBoost model

Feature	Mode	
	Sit-updown	*Stairs-updown*
IMU_X	0.62%	31.16%
IMU_Y	38.33%	6.38%
IMU_Z	28.19%	21.92%
$SEMG$	3.70%	12.02%
FSR_{Heel}	6.96%	9.00%
FSR_{Toe}	14.71%	12.76%
FSR_{Arch}	7.49%	6.76%

calf to distinguish *up* and *Down* states, the average overall model accuracy after adjustment could exceed 91% in the *Stairs-updown* mode.

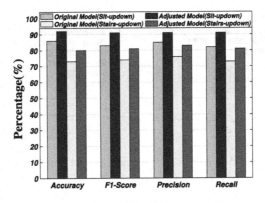

Fig. 9. The performance comparison between the model after feature adjustment and the original model.

6   Conclusion and Future Work

In this paper, SHAP is applied to propose an interpretation framework that can be applied to any lower-limb exoskeleton gait recognition model, which can help scientists to optimize the structure of the gait recognition model. The results of this experiment have been well verified in the lower extremity exoskeleton of knee arthritis, but there are still some deficiencies. In this paper, only two gait patterns are used. The significance can be further improved by increasing the number of data sets and features.

In future studies, we will adjust the data concentration of the model based on the experimental results, further improve the prediction accuracy of the exoskeleton device, and verify the system with KOA subjects. Another direction of future work is to try to build the data concentration of the real-time adjustment model for a dynamic environment.

References

1. Cross, M., et al.: The global burden of hip and knee osteoarthritis: estimates from the global burden of disease 2010 study. Ann. Rheum. Dis. **73**(7), 1323–1330 (2014)
2. Tsai, H.-R., et al.: iKneeBraces: knee adduction moment evaluation measured by motion sensors in gait detection. In: Proceedings of the ACM International Joint Conference on Pervasive and Ubiquitous Computing (UbiComp), pp. 386–391 (2016)
3. Shen, Y., et al.: A wearable sensor system for knee adduction moment measurement. In: Proceedings of IEEE International Conference on Real-Time Computing and Robotics (RCAR), pp. 7–12, June 2016
4. He, Z., Liu, T., Yi, J.: A wearable sensing and training system: towards gait rehabilitation for elderly patients with knee osteoarthritis. IEEE Sens. J. **19**(14), 5936–5945 (2019)
5. Wang, C., et al.: Real-time estimation of knee adduction moment for gait retraining in patients with knee osteoarthritis. IEEE Trans. Neural Syst. Rehabil. Eng. **28**(4), 888–894 (2020)
6. Heiden, E., et al.: NeuralSim: augmenting differentiable simulators with neural networks. arXiv:2011.04217, November 2020
7. Ming, Y., Qu, H., Bertini, E.: RuleMatrix: visualizing and understanding classifiers with rules. IEEE Trans. Vis. Comput. Graph. **25**(1), 342–352 (2019)
8. Biran, O., Cotton, C.V.: Explanation and justification in machine learning: a survey (2017)
9. Lipton, Z.C.: The mythos of model interpretability. Commun. ACM **61**(10) (2016)
10. Keneni, B.M., et al.: Evolving rule based explainable artificial intelligence for unmanned aerial vehicles. IEEE Access **7**, 17001–17016 (2019)
11. Amruthnath, N.: Factor analysis in fault diagnostics using random forest. arXiv:1904.13366, April 2019
12. Lee, N., Azarian, M.H., Pecht, M.G.: An explainable deep learning-based prognostic model for rotating machinery. arXiv e-prints (2020)
13. Du, M., Liu, N., Hu, X.: Techniques for interpretable machine learning. arXiv:1808.00033, May 2019
14. Ribeiro, M.T., Singh, S., Guestrin, C.: "Why should i trust you?": explaining the predictions of any classifier. In: The 22nd ACM SIGKDD International Conference ACM, pp. 1135–1144 (2016)
15. Shapley, L.S.: A value for n-person games. In: Contributions to Theory Games, vol. 2, no. 28, pp. 307–317 (1953)
16. Lundberg, S.M., Lee, S.-I.: A unified approach to interpreting model predictions. In: Proceedings of Advances in Neural Information Processing Systems, pp. 4765–4774 (2017)
17. Chen, T., Guestrin, C.: XGBoost: a scalable tree boosting system. In: Proceedings of the 22nd ACM SIGKDD International Conference on Knowledge Discovery Data Mining (KDD), pp. 785–794 (2016)

A Community Detection Algorithm Fusing Node Similarity and Label Propagation

Yuqi Liu, Jianyong Yu[✉], Zekun Liu, and Xue Han

School of Computer Science and Engineering, Hunan University of Science and Technology, Xiangtan 411201, China

yujyong@hnust.edu.cn

Abstract. As a scientific research method to reveal the intrinsic functional properties of complex network systems, Community Detection has already become one of the most popular research topics in complex networks. The typical label propagation algorithms are very suitable for large-scale networks due to their approximate linear time complexity. But too many random strategies in the algorithms make it not stable enough. For that reason, this paper proposes a Community Detection Algorithm Fusing Node Similarity and Label Propagation (FNSLP). First, the algorithm preprocesses the neighboring nodes of the seed nodes by node similarity to reduce the kinds of the initial label. Combined with nodes' influence, the label propagation ability is calculated. Then, the label selection of nodes is assisted by an improved label update strategy, which reduces the phenomenon of label oscillation and improves the accuracy and stability of label selection. Experimental results show that in four real networks, the algorithm achieves the maximum Modularity value on 75% of the datasets. In multiple artificial benchmark networks with different mixing parameters, the algorithm's Normalized Mutual Information value reaches the maximum value.

Keywords: Community detection · Complex networks · Label propagation · Node similarity

1 Introduction

In the real world, complex systems used to be abstracted as complex networks with certain structures. The complex network is divided into several clusters, where nodes in the same cluster are densely connected and nodes in different clusters are sparsely connected. These clusters are called communities. The process of dividing the network nodes into subgraphs according to their intrinsic topology of connectedness is called community detection [1–4]. Community detection algorithms are widely found in various domains in nature and society, such as transportation networks, protein networks, and online social networks [5–7].

Community detection as a technique for revealing the aggregation behavior of networks has become a major research method for extracting topological features of networks and understanding the evolutionary trends of nodes within communities [8]. However, the existing label propagation algorithms have problems such as strong randomness and poor robustness. Therefore, how to ensure the efficiency of the community detection algorithm and the accuracy of community detection are the main challenges of community discovery [9]. In recent years, researchers have proposed many community detection algorithms and improved them continuously. Raghavan et al. [10] proposed a label propagation-based community detection algorithm (LPA), which is simple and efficient, but the randomness and uncertainty in the iteration of the algorithm lead to unstable results of the algorithm delineation. Lin et al. [11] proposed a label propagation algorithm based on node importance and similarity. During the label update process, nodes update their labels based on the combined influence of their neighbor labels. Li et al. [12] proposed a new algorithm based on node similarities for community detection. The initialization process of node labels is carried out according to the node similarity to reduce the random selectivity in the propagation process. Zhao et al. [13] proposed the label entropy-based label propagation algorithm (LPA-E), which updates labels in the order from smallest to largest label entropy during iteration. Sun et al. [14] proposed an improved label propagation algorithm (KLPA) based on network preprocessing, which uses Kernel decomposition to preprocess the network and reduces the randomness of label updates. But the preprocessing stage removes some nodes in the network, which destroys the network structure to some extent. Zhang et al. [15] designed a stable label propagation association partitioning algorithm using an improved K-shell algorithm to calculate the node influence. Deng et al. [16] proposed an improved LPA algorithm based on label propagation ability to develop a new label update strategy by node importance ranking and label propagation ability, which makes the algorithm have high stability.

In this work, we combine the ideas of seed expansion [17] and label propagation [18] to propose a community detection algorithm fusing node similarity [19] and label propagation (FNSLP). First, the seed nodes are selected by the PageRank algorithm, and then the label preprocessing is applied to its neighboring nodes with node similarity so that the closely connected nodes have the same label. Label preprocessing can reduce the kinds of labels in the network and help subsequent label propagation. Then, nodes are updated in ascending sequence of PageRank values to reduce the randomness of the algorithm. The label propagation capability is calculated to assist label selection during label updates. The node labels are updated according to the label update strategy to improve the accuracy and stability of label selection. The experimental results show that the FNSLP algorithm not only reduces the randomness of the traditional label propagation algorithm but also improves the quality of community division.

Our contributions can be summarized as follows:

- A label preprocessing method that fuses node similarity is proposed. By calculating the similarity between the seed node and the neighbor nodes, the label of the seed node is assigned to the node that is closely connected with the seed node. After label preprocessing, the types of initial labels are reduced.
- In the label update phase, labels are updated in ascending order of PageRank value. The approach solves the issue of robustness in label propagation.
- Integrating node influence into the calculation formula of label propagation ability. A label update strategy is proposed to assist nodes in the step of selecting labels, which improves the accuracy of label selection.

2 Preliminaries

The network graph consists of nodes V and edges E. An undirected and unweighted network is represented by $G = (V, E)$, where $V = \{v_1, v_2, \ldots, v_n\}$ denotes the set of nodes in the network, $E = \{e_1, e_2, \ldots, e_m\}$ denotes the set of edges in the network. n is the number of nodes in the network, and m is the number of connected edges of the network. The set of neighboring nodes of node v_i is defined as $N_i = \{v_j | (v_i, v_j) \in E\}$, v_j is the neighboring node of v_i. The degree of v_i is noted as k_i. Since the preprocessing in Algorithm 1 may give multiple labels to nodes, the set of labels of v_i is denoted as $lb_i = \{l_{i1}, l_{i2}, \ldots, l_{in}\}$.

Definition 1 (Node Importance). We use the PageRank algorithm to calculate the node importance. The PR value corresponding to v_i indicates the importance of the node, which is noted as $PR(v_i)$ and calculated as follows:

$$PR(v_i) = d \left(\sum_{v_j \in M(v_i)} \frac{PR(v_j)}{L(v_j)} \right) + \frac{1-d}{n} \tag{1}$$

where $M(v_i)$ denotes the set of nodes pointing to node v_i. $L(v_j)$ denotes the out-degree of v_j. n denotes the total number of nodes in the network. d is the coefficient, called the damping factor, which is generally taken as $d = 0.85$. There are many studies applying the PageRank algorithm to the social network in the field of influence [20, 21], where the larger the PageRank value of a node in the network is, the greater the importance of that node has.

Definition 2 (Seed Node). The node with the largest PR from the pending node list V' is selected as the seed node. The node with the highest importance is recorded as the v_{cent}. The seed node v_{cent} is calculated as follows:

$$v_{cent} = argmax\{PR(v_i) | v_i \in V', PR(v_i) \in PR\} \tag{2}$$

where V' denotes the pending node list.

Definition 3 (Node Similarity). In this paper, node similarity is redefined from the perspective of community discovery. The node similarity formula is only used to calculate the similarity between a seed node and its neighbor nodes. The similarity is used to measure the degree of similarity between two nodes. The greater the similarity between two nodes is, the greater the probability of belonging to the same community is. For $v_i \in N_{cent}$, the similarity of v_i to v_{cent} is defined as follows:

$$Sim(v_i, v_{cent}) = \alpha \cdot \sum_{z \in N_{cent} \cap N_i} \frac{1}{k_z} + (1 - \alpha) \cdot \frac{\sum_{u \in N_i} \sum_{v \in N_{cent}} \delta(u,v)}{|N_i||N_{cent}|} \tag{3}$$

where z denotes the common neighbor nodes of v_i and v_{cent}. k_z denotes the degree of z. $|N_i|$ denotes the number of neighbor nodes of v_i. α is the coefficient, generally taken as $0.4 \sim 0.6$. $\delta(u, v)$ is used to determine whether there is a continuous edge between nodes u, v. If there is an edge between nodes u, v, then $\delta(u, v) = 1$, otherwise $\delta(u, v) = 0$. When $Sim(v_i, v_{cent}) \geq \delta$, v_i is said to be similar to v_{cent}. Otherwise, v_i is said to be dissimilar to seed v_{cent}.

Definition 4 (Node Residual Similarity). In the label preprocessing process, when $Sim(v_i, v_{cent}) \geq \delta$, the label of v_{cent} is added to the set of labels of v_i. Then calculate the residual similarity R_sim_i of v_i. The residual similarity R_sim_i of nodes is calculated as follows:

$$R\_sim_i = R\_sim_i - Sim(v_i, v_{cent}) \tag{4}$$

where R_sim_i has an initial value of 1; β is a parameter controlling the number of labels a node can have. When $R\_sim_i < \beta$, it indicates that one or more labels have been added to the label set of v_i. So, the probability that v_i can still belong to other communities is small, then v_i is removed from V'. On the contrary, if $R\_sim_i \geq \beta$, it indicates that v_i may still belong to other communities, and keep v_i in V'.

Definition 5 (Label Propagation Ability). The label propagation capability represents the probability that the label of v_i to be updated at the t th iteration is l, denoted as $P_i^t(l)$. The $P_i^t(l)$ is defined as follows:

$$P_i^t(l) = \frac{\sum_{u \in N_i \cap l \in lb_u^{t-1}} \frac{k_u}{\sum_{q \in N_i} k_q}}{\sum_{u \in N_i} \left(\frac{k_u}{\sum_{q \in N_i} k_q} \cdot \left| lb_u^{t-1} \right| \right)} \tag{5}$$

where lb_u^{t-1} denotes the set of labels of node u at the $t-1$ th iteration. The LPA algorithm only considers the number of label occurrences in neighboring nodes during label updating and updates the label with the most occurrences as the node's label. The FNSLP algorithm incorporates the influence of nodes into the influence of labels. The formula $\frac{k_u}{\sum_{q \in N_i} k_q}$ is expressed as the ratio of the degree of u to the sum of the degrees of all neighboring nodes of v_i, and the influence of neighboring u among all neighbors of v_i is measured by this formula. The denominator in the formula is expressed as the sum of the influence of all neighbor nodes of v_i multiplied by the total number of labels of that neighbor node, i.e., the sum of the influence of all labels of all neighbor nodes of v_i. And the numerator is the sum of the influence of u with l labels in the neighbors of v_i.

Definition 6 (Label Update Strategy). The list LB_i^t denotes the set of labels of all neighboring nodes of v_i at the t th iteration. For $l \in LB_i^t$, if $P_i^t(l) > \gamma$, add l to the lb_i^t of v_i. If the label propagation capacity of all labels in the list LB_i^t is less than γ, the label $maxl^t$ with the largest $P_i^t(l)$ is selected and added to the label set lb_i^t. $maxl^t$ is defined as follows:

$$maxl^t = argmax \sum_{l \in LB_i^t} P_i^t(l) \tag{6}$$

where γ is a parameter used to control the number of labels. In the first iteration, γ is a parameter as the reciprocal of the average degree of the network. And γ increases by 0.1 for each iteration until $\gamma \geq 0.5$, the value of γ remains unchanged. Because of $\sum_{l \in LB_i^t} P_i^t(l) = 1$, each node will only retain one label in the end. There are two label update methods in the label propagation process, one is a synchronous update and the other is an asynchronous update [22]. Synchronous update means that in the t th iteration of label propagation, the label of the node to be updated is determined by the labels of its neighbor nodes at the $t - 1$ th iteration. In general, the use of synchronous updates is more conducive to the stability and convergence of the algorithm. The FNSLP algorithm adopts the synchronous update method.

3   FNSLP Algorithm Design

The FNSLP algorithm is divided into two steps: label preprocessing and label updating.

1) Label preprocessing stage. Different from the LPA algorithm, the initial stage of the FNSLP algorithm does not assign unique labels to all nodes. In the label propagation algorithm, the labels of weakly influential nodes will be eliminated in the iterative process. The labels of large influential nodes are usually reserved, and these nodes are often in the center of each community. Therefore, the FNSLP algorithm pre-finds the nodes that may be in the center of the community. Then calculate the node similarity on its neighbor nodes, so that the nodes with high similarity have the same label before the label is propagated. Meanwhile, some nodes in the network may have multiple labels after label preprocessing. But the types of labels in the network are decreased, which reduces the randomness of subsequent label propagation. The pseudo-code in the label preprocessing stage is shown in Algorithm 1.

Algorithm 1. Preprocessing of Labels

Input: $G = (V, E)$, R_sim_i, α, δ, β;

Output: $L = \{lb_1, lb_2, ... lb_n\}$.

  1: $PR \leftarrow nx.pagerank(G)$;

  2: $V' \leftarrow V$;

  3: **while** $V' \neq \emptyset$ **do**

  4:      $v_{cent} \leftarrow argmax\{PR(v_i)|v_i \in V'\}$;

  5:      $lb_{cent} \leftarrow cent$, $cent = 1, 2, 3, ..., |V|$;

  6:      **for** v_i in $N_{cent} \cap V'$ **do**

  7:          calculate $Sim(v_i, v_{cent})$;

  8:          **if** $Sim(v_i, v_{cent}) \geq \delta$ **then**

  9:              $lb_i \leftarrow lb_i \cup lb_{cent}$;

  10:         calculate R_sim_i;

  11:         **if** $R\_sim_i < \beta$ **then**

  12:             $V'.remove(v_i)$;

  13:      $V'.remove(v_{cent})$;

---

2) Update of labels phase. The FNSLP algorithm uses the method of label propagation to detect the community. Considering that the label of a node with a large degree is more easily propagated to its neighboring nodes. And the propagation ability of a label is related to the influence of the node with the label. Therefore, the FNSLP algorithm proposed combines the influence of neighbor nodes with the number of times the label appears in the neighbor node to represent the influence of the label. After label pre-processing, there may be multiple labels in the label set of some nodes. In the iterative process of the FNSLP algorithm, the γ value is continuously increased, and the final γ value is kept as 0.5 to ensure that each node only retains one label at the end of the algorithm. After many iterations of the algorithm, when the labels of all nodes no longer change, the nodes with the same label are divided into a community. The pseudo-code in the label update stage is shown in Algorithm 2.

Algorithm 2. Update of Labels

Input: $G = (V, E)$, $L = \{lb_1, lb_2, \dots lb_n\}$, γ, PR;

Output: $C = \{C_1, C_2, \dots, C_k\}$.

  1: $PR\_sort \leftarrow sorted(PR)$;

  2: while $True$ do

  3:    for v_i in PR_sort do

  4:      $LB_i \leftarrow \{L(v_j⊠|v_j \in N_i\}$;

  5:      for l in LB_i do

  6:        calculate $P_i(l)$;

  7:        if $P_i(l) > \gamma$ then

  8:          $L'(v_i).append(l)$;

  9:      if $L'(v_i) == \emptyset$ then

10:        $maxl \leftarrow argmax\{P_i(l)|l \in LB_i\}$;

11:        $L'(v_i).append(maxl)$;

12:    if $L' == L$ then

13:      break;

14: else

15:    $L \leftarrow L'$;

16:    if $\gamma < 0.5$ then

17:      $\gamma \leftarrow \gamma + 0.1$;

---

4 Experiments

To evaluate the effectiveness of the FNSLP algorithm, we choose three comparison algorithms and conduct experiments on four real networks and two artificial benchmark networks, respectively. The comparison algorithms include LPA, LPA-E, and KLPA. Both LPA-E and KLPA algorithms are improved LPA algorithms. The LPA-E algorithm proposed the concept of label entropy, which updates the labels in the order from smallest to largest label entropy. The KLPA algorithm preprocesses the network using the K-Shell indices of the nodes. The label propagation is then performed on the preprocessing network by an improved algorithm. As far as we know, the above three algorithms are typical and are often used as comparison algorithms.

4.1 Evaluation Criterions

In this paper, Modularity (Q) [23] is used to judge the quality of the algorithm's community detection results. Q is a common evaluation index to measure the structural strength of a community structure. Q is defined as follows:

$$Q = \sum_{c=1}^{n_c} \left[\frac{l_c}{m} - \left(\frac{d_c}{2m} \right)^2 \right]$$ (7)

where n_c represents the number of communities. l_c represents the number of connected edges within the community. d_c represents the sum of the degree values of all nodes in the community. m represents the total number of connected edges in the network. Q is between 0 and 1. The closer the Q is to 1, the better the quality of the community division.

For the network with a known real community structure, the standardized mutual information (NMI) [24] can be used to evaluate the community results of the algorithm. The NMI represents the degree of matching between the community results divided by the community discovery algorithm and the real community structure of the network. NMI is defined as follows:

$$NMI(A, B) = \frac{-2 \sum_{i=1}^{C_A} \sum_{j=1}^{C_B} N_{ij} log \left(\frac{N_{ij} \cdot N}{N_{i \cdot} \cdot N_{\cdot j}} \right)}{\sum_{i=1}^{C_A} N_{i \cdot} log \left(\frac{N_{i \cdot}}{N} \right) + \sum_{j=1}^{C_B} N_{\cdot j} log \left(\frac{N_{\cdot j}}{N} \right)}$$ (8)

where C_A represents the number of real communities. C_B represents the number of communities divided by the algorithm. A represents the real community structure. B represents the community result divided by the algorithm. N represents the number of nodes. $N_{i \cdot}$ represents the number of nodes in the i th community in A. $N_{\cdot j}$ represents the number of nodes in the j th community in B. N_{ij} represents the number of nodes in the real community i that appear in the community j divided by the algorithm. NMI ranges from 0 to 1. The closer NMI is to 1, the more similar the community structure divided by the algorithm is to the real community structure. When $NMI = 1$, it means that the community structure divided by the algorithm is exactly the same as the real community structure.

4.2 Experimental Data Set

The four real network datasets [25] used in the experiments are the Karate Club Network (Karate), the American College Football League Network (Football), the Dolphins Social

Table 1. Information on real networks

Network	Node	Edge	Community
Karate	34	78	2
Football	115	616	12
Dolphins	62	159	2
Polbooks	105	441	3

Network (Dolphins), and the American Political Books Network (Polbooks). The basic information of the four real networks is shown in Table 1.

The LFR artificial benchmark network is often used to test the performance of the community discovery algorithm [26]. The artificial synthetic network used in the experiments in this paper is generated by the LFR artificial benchmark network generation tool proposed by Lancichinetti et al. [27]. The specific parameter settings are shown in Table 2.

Table 2. LFR benchmark network parameters

Network	N	k	$maxk$	$minc$	$maxc$	mu
N1	1000	20	50	50	200	0.1 ~ 0.5
N2	2000	20	50	50	200	0.1 ~ 0.5

where N represents the number of nodes in the network. k Represents the average degree value of the network. $maxk$ Represents the maximum degree value of the network. $minc$ And $maxc$ represent the minimum and the maximum number of nodes in a community respectively. mu is a mixing parameter, which measures the stability of the algorithm an important indicator of the degree of confusion in the community structure. The smaller the mu is, the clearer the community structures are. The larger the mu is, the more difficult it is to find the community.

4.3 Analysis of Experimental Results in Real Networks

The experimental results of the FNSLP and three comparison algorithms on four real network datasets are shown in Table 3. It can be seen from the experimental data in the table that the FNSLP algorithm is generally better than the comparison algorithms in terms of Q and NMI. Among them, in the Karate network, the community result of the FNSLP algorithm is consistent with the real community structure of the network. After the Karate network is divided by this algorithm, the remaining labels 0 and 33 correspond to the two communities headed by the club manager and the principal. The Q and NMI of this algorithm in Karate and Football networks are higher than other algorithms, only in Polbooks network are slightly lower than those of LPA-E and KLPA.

Table 3. Experiment results on real networks

Network	Algorithm	Q	NMI
Karate	LPA	0.362	0.586
	LPA-E	0.368	0.754
	KLPA	0.367	0.83
	FNSLP	0.372	1
Football	LPA	0.459	0.753
	LPA-E	0.477	0.767
	KLPA	0.60	0.89
	FNSLP	0.603	0.909
Dolphins	LPA	0.425	0.376
	LPA-E	0.446	0.382
	KLPA	0.406	0.730
	FNSLP	0.483	0.671
Polbooks	LPA	0.405	0.470
	LPA-E	0.495	0.563
	KLPA	0.48	0.72
	FNSLP	0.451	0.544

4.4 Influence of Parameter δ

In the label preprocessing stage of Algorithm 1, the similarity between v_i and its adjacent v_{cent} needs to be calculated. If $Sim(v_i, v_{cent}) \geq \delta$, the label of the v_{cent} is added to the label set of v_i. Therefore, the parameter δ is a key parameter that controls which communities the v_i can belong to. Since the degree of closeness between nodes is also related to the network's mixing parameter. The experiment is carried out on LFR networks with different *mu*. The experimental results are shown in Fig. 1 and Fig. 2.

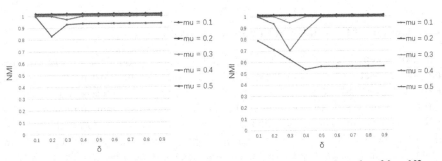

Fig. 1. Experimental results of δ on N1.   **Fig. 2.** Experimental results of δ on N2.

It can be seen from the experimental results that when $mu \leq 0.3$, δ has little effect on the results of community division. In the N1 network, when $mu <= 0.2$, no matter how the δ changes, the value of *NMI* is equal to 1. It means that the community divided by the algorithm is consistent with the actual community structure. In the N2 network, when $mu < 0.3$, the *NMI* is 1 at any δ. It can be seen that in networks where mu is small, the nodes in the same community are closely related, and the δ has little effect on community detection. The FNSLP algorithm has extremely high accuracy and stability. When $\delta > 0.1$, the *NMI* decreased with the increase of the δ. When $mu = 0.5$, the *NMI* drops obviously. When $\delta > 0.5$, the *NMI* remains unchanged. However, due to the large scale of the network, the similarity value between nodes is relatively small. When δ is large, similar nodes cannot be identified. The algorithm fails to achieve the purpose of label preprocessing, resulting in the node label no longer changing with the δ in preprocessing. Therefore, when $\delta \geq 0.5$, the community result divided by the algorithm no longer changes. The label propagation ability calculation formula and label propagation strategy proposed by the FNSLP algorithm can still maintain a high accuracy of the algorithm. To sum up, it is recommended that when $mu \geq 0.3$, $\delta = 0.1$, the community result divided by the algorithm is the best at this time. When $mu < 0.3$, δ can takes any value.

4.5 Compare the Results with or Without Fusing Node Similarity

To verify the effectiveness and feasibility of the label preprocessing process of fusing node similarities, an experiment for comparison is set up in this paper. The FNSLP algorithm is compared with the algorithm in this paper which does not fuse the label preprocessing process of node similarity on four real networks. Compare the Q and NMI values of the community detection results of the two algorithms. The FLP algorithm is used to represent the algorithm of this paper without the label preprocessing process. The experimental results are shown in Fig. 3 and Fig. 4.

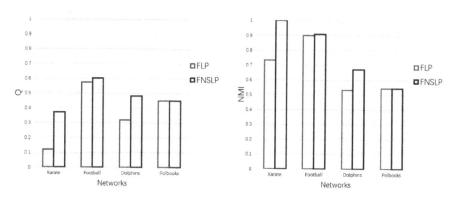

Fig. 3. Experimental results of Q.   **Fig. 4.** Experimental results of NMI.

The Q and NMI values of the FLP algorithm are lower than the FNSLP algorithm in the three real networks of Karate, Football, and Dolphins. Since the FLP algorithm has no label preprocessing process for fusing node similarities, it gives unique labels to all nodes in the network. So, it leads to a wide variety of labels in the network, which is not conducive to label propagation. However, the label preprocessing phase of the FNSLP algorithm incorporates the calculation of node similarity. The label preprocessing is performed on similar nodes in the network so that closely related nodes are given the same label. It also eliminates the less influential labels in the network and retains the labels that play a decisive role in the network. To sum up, the strategy of label preprocessing fused with node similarity improves the quality of community detection.

4.6 Analysis of Experimental Results in LFR Networks

To further test the performance of the FNSLP algorithm. The FNSLP algorithm and the three comparison algorithms are tested on LFR artificial benchmark networks with different *mu*. When *mu* = 0.1, the community detection results by the algorithm in the N1 and N2 networks are shown in Fig. 5 and Fig. 6. The communities in the figure are represented by nodes of different colors, and the clusters of nodes with the same color clustered together represent a community. As shown in Fig. 5 and Fig. 6, the N1 network is divided into 8 communities and the N2 network is divided into 16 communities. The results of the community detection by the FNSLP algorithm are consistent with the real community structure.

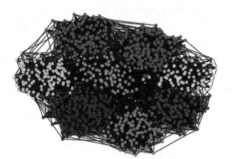 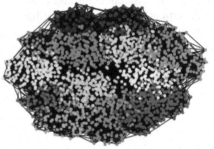

Fig. 5. Community Division Result on N1.   **Fig. 6.** Community Division Result on N2.

For the N1 and N2 artificial benchmark networks, the *NMI* by each algorithm are shown in Fig. 7 and Fig. 8. It can be seen from Fig. 7 and Fig. 8 that the *NMI* of the FNSLP algorithm on the two LFR networks with different mu values re higher than comparison algorithms. In the N1 network, when *mu* = 0.1, the community structure in the network is obvious. And the *NMI* of the FNSLP algorithm is comparable to the three comparison algorithms. When *mu* gradually increases, the difficulty of community detection gradually increases, and the *NMI* of the three comparison algorithms in the N1 network show a significant downward trend. While the FNSLP algorithm only degrades when *mu* is greater than 0.4. In the N2 network, with the increase of the *mu*, the LPA and the LPA-E algorithms still show an obvious downward trend. The *NMI* of the FNSLP algorithm is 1 when *mu* < 0.4, and the *NMI* is 0.9973 when *mu* = 0.5. The experimental results show that the FNSLP algorithm has high accuracy and stability. The label preprocessing in the FNSLP algorithm weakens the randomness of label propagation so that the algorithm can still divide high-quality communities in the network with higher mixing parameters. Secondly, by adjusting the update order of node labels according to the ascending sequence of PageRank values, the label influence of weakly influential nodes is minimized. The effectiveness of label propagation of large-influenced nodes is ensured, and the quality of community division is improved.

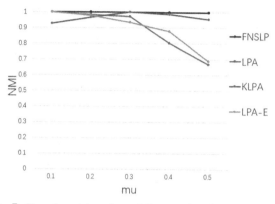

Fig. 7. Experimental results on N1 networks with different *mu*.

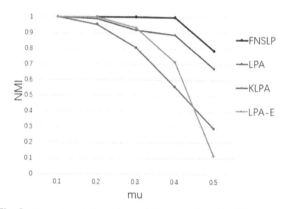

Fig. 8. Experimental results on N2 networks with different *mu*.

5 Conclusion

The traditional label propagation algorithms have too many random strategies for label updating, which make them not stable enough. To solve this problem, this paper proposes a community detection algorithm fusing node similarity and label propagation. Aiming at the problem of scattered node labels in the initial stage of the LPA, this paper solves the problem by label preprocessing. The PageRank algorithm is used to identify seed nodes, and label preprocessing is performed on neighbor nodes of seed nodes by calculating node similarity. After preprocessing, the seed node and its neighbor nodes with high similarity have the same label. Preprocessing avoids the appearance of trivial and fragmented communities, while also reducing the randomness of subsequent label propagation. During the label update, the order of nodes in the label propagation process of LPA is random, however, the random update order can seriously affect the stability of the algorithm. Considering the difference in importance of nodes, this paper updates the node labels in the ascending order of node PR values. In the process of label updating, the label propagation ability is calculated by combining the influence of nodes. And the label selection of nodes is assisted by the label updating strategy. This reduces the phenomenon of label oscillation and improves the accuracy of node label selection. Thereby the algorithm improves the quality of community detection. Finally, compared with the experimental results of other algorithms, the stability and effectiveness of the FNSLP algorithm are verified.

Since the FNSLP algorithm requires label preprocessing, the running time increases when the network size increases. In the future, we will make further efforts to improve the efficiency of the algorithm by simplifying the algorithm calculation process to adapt to larger-scale networks. Another research direction is to apply the algorithm to the findings of overlapping communities [28, 29] by adjusting the threshold and calculation formula.

Acknowledgment. This work was supported by R&D projects in key areas of Guangdong Province under Grant 2021B0101200003, and the Scientific Research Project of Hunan Education Department under Grant 19C0766.

References

1. Barabási, A.L.: Network science. Philos. Trans. R. Soc. A Math. Phys. Eng. Sci. 371(1987), 20120375 (2013)
2. Khan, B.S., Niazi, M.A.: Network community detection: a review and visual survey. arXiv preprint arXiv:1708.00977 (2017)
3. Ma, L., Li, N., Guo, Y., et al.: Learning to optimize: reference vector reinforcement learning adaption to constrained many-objective optimization of industrial copper burdening system. IEEE Trans. Cybern. (2021)
4. Ma, L., Wang, X., Wang, X., et al.: TCDA: truthful combinatorial double auctions for mobile edge computing in industrial Internet of Things. IEEE Trans. Mob. Comput. **PP**(99) (2021)
5. Shirazi, S., Albadvi, A., Akhondzadeh, E., et al.: A new application of community detection for identifying the real specialty of physicians. Int. J. Med. Informatics **140**, 104161 (2020)
6. Javed, M.A., Younis, M.S., Latif, S., et al.: Community detection in networks: a multidisciplinary review. J. Netw. Comput. Appl. **108**, 87–111 (2018)
7. Huang, X., Chen, D., Ren, T., et al.: A survey of community detection methods in multilayer networks. Data Min. Knowl. Disc. **35**(1), 1–45 (2021)
8. Jin, D., Yu, Z., Jiao, P., et al.: A survey of community detection approaches: from statistical modeling to deep learning. IEEE Trans. Knowl. Data Eng. (2021)
9. Yulin, T.: A community detection algorithm based on label propagation. J. Lanzhou Univ. Arts Sci. (Natural Science Edition) (2021)

10. Raghavan, U.N., Albert, R., Kumara, S.: Near linear time algorithm to detect community structures in large-scale networks. Phys. Rev. E **76**(3), 036106 (2007)

11. Lin, T.-S., Sun, F.-X.: Label propagation algorithm based on node importance and similarity. Comput. Syst. Appl. **30**(10), 218–223 (2021)

12. Li, W., Xie, Z., Yu, Z.: A new algorithm based on node similarities for community detection. Softw. Guide **17**(2), 63–67 (2018)

13. Zhao, Y., Li, S., Chen, X.: Community detection using label propagation in entropic order. In: 2012 IEEE 12th International Conference on Computer and Information Technology. IEEE, pp. 18–24 (2012)

14. Sun, S., Fan, J., Qu, J., et al.: Improved label propagation algorithm based on network preprocessing. Comput. Syst. Appl. **27**(4), 173–177 (2018)

15. Zhang, M., Li, L.: Research on stable label propagation community division algorithm. Comput. Technol. Dev. **30**(1), 129–134 (2020)

16. Deng, K., Chen, H., Huang, R.: Improved LPA algorithm based on label propagation ability. Comput. Eng. **44**(3), 60–64 (2018)

17. Qi, J., Xun, L., Yi, W.: Overlapping community detection algorithm based on the selection of seed nodes. Appl. Res. Comput. **34**(12), 3534–3537 (2017)

18. Laassem, B., Idarrou, A., Boujlaleb, L.: Label propagation algorithm for community detection based on Coulomb's law. Phys. A **593**, 126881 (2022)

19. Yang, H., Cheng, J., Yang, Z., et al.: A node similarity and community link strength-based community discovery algorithm. Complexity **2021**(22), 1–17 (2021)

20. Gao, Y., Yu, X., Zhang, H.: Overlapping community detection by constrained personalized PageRank. Expert Syst. Appl. **173**, 114682 (2021)

21. Zhang, Y., Xia, X., Xu, X., et al.: Robust hierarchical overlapping community detection with personalized PageRank. IEEE Access **8**, 102867–102882 (2020)

22. Brahim, L., Loubna, B., Ali, I.: A literature survey on label propagation for community detection. In: 2021 Fifth International Conference on Intelligent Computing in Data Sciences (ICDS), pp. 1–7. IEEE (2021)

23. Newman, M.E.J., Girvan, M.: Finding and evaluating community structure in networks. Phys. Rev. E **69**(2), 026113 (2004)

24. Fortunato, S.: Community detection in graphs. Phys. Rep. **486**(3–5), 75–174 (2010)

25. Qui, X., Cheng, Y.: An improved particle-swarm-optimization algorithm for community discovery in social networks. J. Chin. Comput. Syst. **35**(6), 1422–1426 (2014)

26. Lancichinetti, A., Fortunato, S., Kertész, J.: Detecting the overlapping and hierarchical community structure in complex networks. New J. Phys. **11**(3), 033015 (2009)

27. Lancichinetti, A., Fortunato, S., Radicchi, F.: Benchmark graphs for testing community detection algorithms. Phys. Rev. E **78**(4), 046110 (2008)

28. Wu, Q., Chen, R., Yu, W., et al.: Overlapping community detection algorithm fusing label preprocessing and node influence. J. Comput. Appl. **40**(12), 3578 (2020)

29. Wu, Q., Chen, R., Yu, W., Liu, G.: Overlapping community detection algorithm fusing label preprocessing and node influence. J. Comput. Appl. **40**(12), 3578 (2020)

Cooperative Edge Caching Strategy Based on Mobile Prediction and Social-Aware in Internet of Vehicles

Kan Chaonan[✉], Wu Honghai, Xing Ling, and Ma Huahong

Henan University of Science and Technology, Luoyang 471000, China
kancn158@163.com

Abstract. The explosion of traffic caused by the rapid growth of multimedia services of Internet of Vehicles (IoV) has brought heavy load to mobile networks. The edge caching of the Internet of vehicles is considered as a promising technology. When the existing content caching strategy is used in the vehicle network, it faces the challenge of high content caching delay caused by the high-speed mobility of vehicle users and insufficient social relations. To address these challenges, this paper proposes a Cooperative Edge Caching Scheme based on Mobility Prediction and Society Aware (CCMPSA). In this strategy, the Long Short-Term Memory (LSTM) network is used to predict the location of the vehicle at the next moment, the vehicle cache nodes are selected according to the social relationship reflected by the similarity of interest and communication probability between the vehicles, and the dynamic decision of the content cache problem is realized by deep reinforcement learning. The simulation results show that the performance of the proposed strategy is better than random caching and non-cooperative caching algorithms, and it not only reduces the content transmission delay and improves the cache hit ratio, but also improves the experience quality of the whole system.

Keywords: Caching decisions · Deep reinforcement learning · The edge caching · The long short-term memory network · Internet of Vehicles

1 Introduction

With the development of IoV, vehicular applications such as vehicular intelligent terminals, autonomous driving and vehicle entertainment continue to emerge, which have a positive impact on the development of vehicular roads. However, the emergence of these intelligent applications may require large computing and storage resources, high network bandwidth and strict response time bring heavy traffic load to the core network. Mobile edge caching technology [1] is considered to be an effective method to solve the problem of high content requirements in IoV. By caching highly frequently requested content close to users, such as vehicles and RSUs, requested content can be obtained directly from vehicles or RSUs via wireless transmission, rather than through remote core network, thus reducing the delay of content access and improving the quality of user experience.

© The Author(s), under exclusive license to Springer Nature Singapore Pte Ltd. 2022
H. Ma et al. (Eds.): CWSN 2022, CCIS 1715, pp. 108–119, 2022.
https://doi.org/10.1007/978-981-19-8350-4_9

The existing research on edge caching strategy in Internet of vehicles focuses on optimizing network utility, including cost [2], cache hit ratio [3] and delay [4]. In order to provide better service for content requesters, cooperative caching between vehicles and RSUs has been studied by scholars at home and abroad [5, 6]. In the Vehicle-to-Vehicle (V2V) content sharing scenario, the mobility of vehicles can provide content for more request vehicles, but it also causes frequent request interruptions and higher delay. To solve this problem, Reference [7, 8] proposed a cooperative caching scheme based on mobility prediction. Considering the complexity of social relations between vehicles, the social relations between vehicles were studied in References [9, 10] and applied to the selection of vehicle cache nodes. In addition, machine learning method [11, 12], as an effective method to improve the cognitive ability and intelligence of Internet of Vehicles, has been widely used in content caching in Internet of Vehicles. However, the randomness of vehicle movement and the complexity of social relations between vehicles still face challenges in using cooperative caching strategies in the scenario of Internet of vehicles.

In view of the above problems, this paper makes four major contributions:

(1) We propose a mobile prediction and social-aware edge caching cooperation scheme, which can improve cache hit ratio and reduce transmission delay. The scheme includes three parts: trajectory prediction, cache vehicle selection and cache decision.
(2) We use recursive neural network to predict the movement trajectory of vehicles. According to the mobility characteristics of the vehicle, the RSU of the vehicle at the next moment is found by using recursive neural network. The contact rate and interest similarity between vehicles within the coverage range of RSU are used to calculate the strength of social relations between vehicles and find the cached vehicles.
(3) We design a cache decision strategy with mobility and sociality. Deep reinforcement learning is used to solve the objective function of minimizing the content acquisition delay, and the optimal cache decision is obtained.
(4) We use drive simulation to evaluate the performance of our scheme. CCMPSA has higher cache hit ratio and lower content access delay compared with random cache strategy and strategy that does not consider cache vehicle nodes.

2 System Model

In this section, the proposed system model of cooperative caching strategy is introduced, including network scenario, caching model, communication model, and the problem is formulated. For convenience, the main notations used are summarized in Table 1.

2.1 Network System

In the urban vehicle Network cache system, there are multiple RSUs and multiple vehicles in the coverage range of remote cloud. Assuming that the coverage range of different RSUs does not overlap, the communication range of RSUs and vehicles are represented by D_R and D_V respectively, as shown in Fig. 1. Vehicles can serve as either content requester or content provider for requesting users. Vehicle carriers with Cache space are called Cache Vehicles (CVs). A set of $RSUs = \{S_1, ..., S_n, ..., S_N\}$ equidistant distributed on both sides of the road for communication with vehicles, where N is the number of RSUs. RSUs collaborate with each other over fiber optic connections. Assume that the set of vehicles within the coverage of RSU S_n is $V = \{1, 2, ..., m, ..., M\}$, where M is the number of vehicles within the coverage of RSU S_n. Where, the set of vehicles that can be used as cache is $CV = \{1, 2, ..., c, ..., C_i\}$, and $|C_i|$ is the number of CVs. The content set of a vehicle request is defined as $\mathbb{Q} = \{1, 2, ..., q, ..., Q\}$, and Q indicates the amount of content that can be requested by the vehicles, each request content size vector is $s_Q = \{s_1, ..., s_q, ..., s_Q\}$, C_{CV} shows the cache capacity of CV, the cache capacity of RSU is denoted as C_{RSU}, and the remote content provider has all content. In order to better capture the moving track of the vehicle, the service time is divided into $T = \{1, 2, ... t, ..., T\}$ discrete time slot index, and the duration of each time is τ.

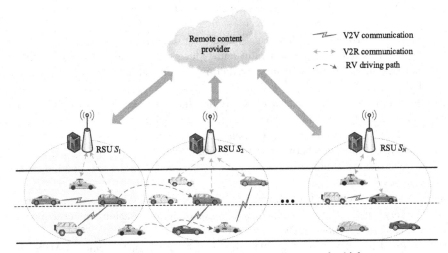

Fig. 1. Cooperative cache architecture for Internet of vehicles

2.2   Caching Model

We will determine the content distribution based on the popularity of the content, considering the different frequency of requests for each content, assuming that the popularity of the content follows the Zipf distribution. At this point, content popularity changes slowly and remains constant during slot t. The probability of all vehicles requesting content q in slot t is

$$p_q(t) = \frac{1/i_q^{k_t}}{\sum_{q=1}^{Q} 1/i_q^{k_t}} \quad \forall q = 1, 2, ..., Q \tag{1}$$

where i_q is the sorted index of the number of requests of content q in the whole content library; k_t $(0 < k_t < 1)$ represents the slope of distribution of content popularity in time slot t. The larger the k_t, the higher the demand for hot content. According to the above formula, the probability vector of vehicle m requesting all contents in time t can be figured out

$$p_Q = (p_1, \ldots, p_q, \ldots, p_Q) \tag{2}$$

Table 1. Major Notations

Notation	Explanation
N	Number of RSUs
M	Number of vehicles within the coverage of RSU S_n
$|C_i|$	Number of CVs within the coverage of RSU S_n
Q	The amount of content the vehicles can request
s_q	Size of request content q
$C_{CV}(C_{RSU})$	Cache capacity of CV (RSU)
p_q	Probability of all vehicles requesting content q
k_t	Slope of distribution of content popularity in time slot t
$r_{m,S_n}(t)(r_{m,S_n}(t))$	Data transmission rate between RV m and CV c (RSU S_n)
B	Transmission bandwidth
$p_c(p_{S_n})$	Transmitting power of V2V CV c (RSU S_n)
σ^2	Additive White Gaussian noise
$h_{m,c}(h_{m,S_n})$	Channel gain between RV m and CV c (RSU S_n)
$T_{m,c}(T_{m,S_n})$	Delay of RV m obtaining content q from vehicle c (RSU S_n)
$x_{t,m}$	Current position of vehicle m

In addition, we use binary matrix $A_{Q \times (|C_i|+1)}$ to represent the cache decision. When $a_{q,c} = 1$, it means that the requested content q is cached in CV and $a_{q,c} = 0$ otherwise. If $a_{q,|C_i|+1} = 1$, q is cached in RSU, otherwise $a_{q,|C_i|+1} = 0$. Define $A_{Q \times (|C_i|+1)}$ as 0 or 1 to improve cache hit ratio

$$a_{q,c}, a_{q,|C_i|+1} \in \{0, 1\} \tag{3}$$

2.3 Communicating Model

In the cooperative caching strategy proposed in this paper, the delay for vehicles to acquire content from CVs or RSU is different. Therefore, it is necessary to model the delay of obtaining content in different ways. To prevent signaling overhead caused by frequent switching, the RVs select only the transmission link (V2V/V2R) with the lowest delay to obtain content, and assumes that the RV can obtain all content within the coverage range of the RSU. Vehicle users are requested to obtain content in the following two ways:

(1) **Obtaining content through V2V link**: When RV m sends a content request, first checks whether it has cached the content, and there is no delay at this time. Otherwise, RV m checks whether the CVs of the content is cached in the communication range. If there is and all content can be obtained from CVs within the V2V communication range ($D_{V2V} \leq D_V$), the content is obtained through V2V communication. According to Shannon's theorem, the data transmission rate between RV m and CV c is:

$$r_{m,c}(t) = B \log_2(1 + \frac{p_c h_{m,c}}{\sigma^2 + \sum_{m' \neq m} p_c h_{m',c}})$$
(4)

where B is the transmission bandwidth and σ^2 is the additive White Gaussian noise. p_c is the transmitting power of CV c, $h_{m,c}$ is the channel gain between RV m and CV c. $\sum_{m' \neq m} p_c h_{m',c}$ is the interference of other vehicles on the communication link between CV c and RV m. The delay of RV m obtaining content q from CV c of V2V in time t is

$$T_{m,c} = \frac{s_q}{r_{m,c}(t)}$$
(5)

(2) **Obtaining content through V2I link**: If RV m cannot obtain content from CVs through V2V communication, the RV m sends content request to its RSU S_n, and if there is requested content in RSU S_n, it sends content to vehicle m. Interference from other RSUs is not considered here because RSUs use a different frequency band. Similarly, the data transmission rate between RSU S_n and RV m is:

$$r_{m,S_n}(t) = B \log_2(1 + \frac{p_{S_n} h_{m,S_n}}{\sigma^2})$$
(6)

where p_{S_n} is the transmitting power of S_n, h_{m,S_n} is the channel gain between vehicle m and RSU S_n. The delay of vehicle m acquiring content q from RSU S_n in time t is

$$T_{m,S_n} = \frac{s_q}{r_{m,S_n}(t)}$$
(7)

2.4 Problem Formulation

Content acquisition delay is an important performance index in the cache system, which can reflect the communication quality between the RVs and the CVs. Assuming that the content request of each vehicle follows the Poisson process, the content request set of vehicle m at slot t is $Q_m(t) \subseteq Q$. In order to minimize the content acquisition delay, vehicle m will choose to obtain content from RSU S_n or CV c with the lowest delay. According to the above analysis, the objective function for considering the limited cache capacity is

$$\min_{A_{Q \times (|C_i|+1)}} \sum_{m \in V} \sum_{q \in \mathbb{Q}} \left(\sum_{c \in CV} a_{q,c} \times T_{m,c}(t) + a_{q,|C_i|+1} \times T_{m,S_n}(t) \right)$$

$$C1 : a_{q,c}, a_{q,|C_i|+1} \in \{0, 1\}$$

$$C2 : \sum_{c=1}^{|C_i|} a_{q,c} + a_{q,|C_i|+1} \le 1$$

$$C3 : \sum_{c \in CV} s_Q \times a_{:,c} \le C_{CV}$$

$$C4 : \sum_{S_n \in RSU} s_Q \times a_{:,|C_i|+1} \le C_{RSU}$$

$$(8)$$

where C1 and C2 are constraints on the values of elements in the cache decision matrix, C1 is the content that can be cached or not cached in CVs and RSUs, and is represented by 0 or 1. For reasonable utilization of storage capacity and reduce the cache delay, C2 is used to ensure that each content caching to only RSU within range of a CV. C3 and C4 ensure that contents cached in CVs and RSUs do not exceed their total storage capacity.

The above optimization problem is solved to obtain the caching decision matrix, which determines the collaborative caching scheme.

3   CCMPSA Caching Strategy

This section proposes a DRL-based CCMPSA caching strategy. It includes vehicle mobility prediction, cache vehicle selection and deep reinforcement learning algorithm based on CCMPSA.

3.1   Vehicle Mobility Prediction

The moving trajectory of the vehicles is a standard time series in RSU. LSTM network is often used to process the time series data. It can effectively memorize the relevant information of the historical trajectory of the vehicle, and predict the next RSU of the vehicle when only the current position information is known. Each neural network layer of LSTM is composed of weight, bias and activation function. The core part is the unit state, which stores the information hidden in the historical trajectory of the vehicle that can be used to speculate the future movement mode of the vehicle. The unit states are as follows:

$$f_t = \sigma(W_f.[h_{t-1}, x_t] + b_f)$$

$$(9)$$

$$i_t = \sigma(W_i.[h_{t-1}, x_t] + b_i)$$

$$(10)$$

$$\tilde{C}_t = \tanh(W_C.[h_{t-1}, x_t] + b_C) \tag{11}$$

$$C_t = f_t \times C_{t-1} + i_t \times \tilde{C}_t \tag{12}$$

$$o_t = \sigma(W_0.[h_{t-1}, x_t] + b_o) \tag{13}$$

$$h_t = o_t * \tanh(C_t) \tag{14}$$

where f_t is the forgetting gate, indicating which features of C_{t-1} are used to calculate C_t; sigmoid is usually used as the activation function, and the output of sigmoid is a value in the range of $[0, 1]$; $\tilde{C}_t$ represents the update value of unit state, which is obtained by the input data and hidden points through a neural network, and the activation function is usually expressed by tanh; i_t is the input gate, calculated by x_t and h_{t-1} through sigmoid activation function; o_t is the output gate, h_t is the hidden layer output vector.

LSTM can predict the location of the next moment based on the location data generated by V2V vehicles over a historical period. The vector $X_{t,m} = [x_{t-M',m}, x_{t-M'+1,m}, \ldots, x_{t,m}]$ formed by the historical position information of the previous t slots is used as input. $x_{t,m}$ is the current position of V2V vehicle m, M' represents the number of historical data that can be recorded by deep neural network. The probability distribution $h_{tm} = [h_{tm1}, h_{tm2}, \ldots, h_{tmL}]$ of vehicle m accessing each location is used as the output of LSTM, and L is the total number of accessible locations. This paper assumes that the position of the highest probability is the real position of the vehicle at the next moment.

3.2 Caching Vehicles Selection

The choice of cached vehicles can be determined according to the social relations between vehicles. When the demand between vehicles is consistent and the communication link of data transmission can be established, we call vehicles socially relevant. Social relations have two characteristics: one is the similarity of interests between vehicles; the other is the contact rate between vehicles.

(1) **Interest similarity**: In this paper, the interest similarity between the requested RV m and m' is calculated by the interest similarity between the requested vehicle m and m'. The interest similarity between vehicles m and m' in time slot t is expressed as

$$s^w_{m,m'}(t) = \frac{\sum_{q \in L_{m,m',t}} \frac{1}{\log M_{q,t}}}{\sqrt{l_{m,t}} \cdot \sqrt{l_{m',t}}} \tag{15}$$

where $M_{q,t}$ is the number of vehicles interested in content q in time slot t. $\frac{1}{\log M_{q,t}}$ is the weight of each content in time slot t, which is used to measure the importance of each content in calculating the similarity of interest. $L_{m,m',t}$ is a set of contents of interest to both vehicle m and m' in slot t. $l_{m,t}$ is the number of contents of interest to vehicle m in time slot t.

(2) **Communication contact rate**: The number of vehicles that can be associated with each other in the process of driving per unit time is defined as communication contact rate, and the contact rate between vehicles within the coverage area of a given RSU S_n is $l_{M,n} = \{l_{1,n}, ..., l_{m,n}, ..., l_{M,n}\}$.

Therefore, the social relationship intensity between vehicle m and m' in time t is

$$o_{m,m'} = l_{M,n}.s^w_{m,m'}(t) \tag{16}$$

where $o_{m,m'} \in [0, 1]$, if and only if $m = m', a_{m,m'} = 1$. Similarly, the strength matrix of social relationship among all vehicles in vehicle set V can be given

$$O = \begin{bmatrix} o_{1,1} & \cdots & o_{1,|M|} \\ \vdots & \ddots & \vdots \\ o_{|M|,1} & \cdots & o_{|M|,|M|} \end{bmatrix} \tag{17}$$

3.3 Cooperative Caching Strategy Based on DRL

Deep Reinforcement Learning (DRL) is an improved strategy of reinforcement learning, which uses deep neural network to automatically learn low-dimensional features and effectively solves the problem of dimension disaster. DQN is one of the most commonly used methods in DRL. For the content request of RV m, DQN can be used to calculate the Q value (reward) corresponding to the action of establishing V2V link with RV m. DQN only needs to sample part of the state, and then further uses the neural network to train the accurate enough value function, so as to effectively deal with the high dimensional problem in the state space. The Q value is trained by minimizing the loss function during DQN iteration to approximate the objective function, where the loss function can be expressed as

$$L(\theta) = E\left[\left(R + \gamma \max_{a'} Q(s', a'; \hat{\theta}) - Q(s, a; \theta)^2\right)\right] \tag{18}$$

where θ is the network parameter.

We use the DQN method to solve the optimization problem of cooperative caching, where the state s is set as $S = (|C_i|+1, |C_i| \times C_{CV} + C_{RSU})$, the action a is set as the cache decision vector $A_{Q \times (|C_i|+1)}$, and the reward function R is the delay corresponding to the cache decision vector, that is, $R = \sum_{m \in V} \sum_{q \in Q} (\sum_{c \in CV} a_{q,c} \times T_{m,c}(t) + a_{q,|C_i|+1} \times T_{m,S_n}(t))$.

In DQN algorithm, by updating the neural network parameters to calculate the target Q value, DQN algorithm is updated as follows:

$$Q(s, a; \theta) \leftarrow Q(s, a; \theta) + \alpha(R + \lambda \max_{a'} Q(s', a'; \hat{\theta}) - Q(s, a; \theta)) \tag{19}$$

s' and a' represent the state and action at the next moment respectively, and R and λ represent the behavior reward and discount factor, respectively. After training, according to the position of the maximum Q value in the Q matrix, the optimal cache decision matrix is obtained.

As shown in Algorithm 1, the detailed processes of Cooperative cache strategy for Internet of Vehicles based on DQN are described as follows.

Algorithm1 Cooperative cache strategy based on DQN

1: **Phase 1**: Initialization
2: (1) RSUs deployment, number of vehicles m, content library and content size
3: (2) Cache decision matrix: $A_{Q \times (|C_i|+1)}$, R, Q matrix, $Q(s,a;\theta)$ and $\hat{Q}(s',a';\hat{\theta})$

4: **Phase 2**: Trajectory prediction
5: for each vehicle do
6:    Calculate the position probability distribution in time t
7:    Select the position with the highest probability as the next position of the vehicle
8: end for
9: **Phase 3**: Cache vehicle selection
10: for each vehicle do
11:    Calculate the social relationship between vehicles
12:    Determine the cached vehicles according to the social relationship matrix
13: end for
14: **Phase 4**: Obtain the Optimal Caching Decision
15: repeat
16: for each iteration do
17:    for every RSU do
18:       Get the next moment of the requested vehicle set V
19:       p_Q is obtained by Zipf distribution
20:    end for
21:    Randomly select an action a from all possible actions of state S
22:    Calculate the delay based on the cache decision vector of action a
23:    $R = \sum\limits_{m \in V} \sum\limits_{q \in Q} (\sum\limits_{c \in CV} a_{q,c} \times T_{m,c}(t) + a_{q,|C_i|+1} \times T_{m,s_n}(t))$
24:    This experience (s,a,R,s') is stored in the experience playback unit
25:    $Q(s,a;\theta) \leftarrow Q(s,a;\theta) + \alpha(R + \lambda \max\limits_{a'} Q(s',a';\hat{\theta}) - Q(s,a;\theta))$
26:    $L(\theta) = E\left[(R + \gamma \max\limits_{a'} Q(s',a';\hat{\theta}) - Q(s,a;\theta))^2 \right]$
27:    $s' \leftarrow s$
28: end for
29: until Q matrix stability
30: return Q matrix
31: Get the final cache decision by $A^* = \arg\max\limits_{a} Q(s,a;\theta)$

---

4   Simulation Results

This section will evaluate the performance of the proposed CCMPSA in the edge caching of the Internet of vehicles. In this simulation, the number of vehicles follows the increasing distribution of [10,20,30,40,50]. For simplicity, the probability of vehicle requesting service is subject to uniform distribution [0,1], the Zipf parameter is 0.6, the bandwidth is set to 10 MHz, and the transmission power of vehicles and RSU are 1M/s and 2M/s respectively. The number of contents in the content library is 10, and the size of each content follows the uniform distribution of [10,20,30,40,50] MB. The buffer capacity of the vehicle and RSU is set to 50 MB and 100 MB respectively. The number of units of LSTM network is 128, and the learning rate is 0.001. The number of predicted vehicle location information used in this paper is 1100. In mobility prediction, the training data set is 800 and the test data set is 300.

Figure 2 shows the results of the predicted mobility patterns. The blue line segment represents the real position of the vehicle, and the red line represents the position predicted by the LSTM method. It can be seen from the figure that the predicted position is almost consistent with the real position, indicating that the effect of LSTM in predicting the vehicle trajectory is very accurate.

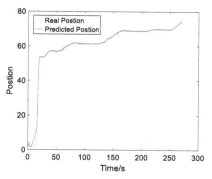

Fig. 2. Real position and predicted position as the time interval varies

In this simulation, the number of times to set the training Q matrix is 20000. When evaluating the performance of the hit rate and content acquisition delay, four cache strategies are used to compare with CCMPSA. (1) RL-based cooperative caching (RL) [5]: only mobility is considered, not social relationships. (2) DAC [13]: a cooperative cache that does not predict the future trajectory of the vehicle and considers social relationships. (3) Random caching (RC): RSU and caching vehicles cache all contents with the same probability, and RVs randomly select caching devices. (4) Non-Cooperative Caching (NCC): the vehicle is not considered as the cache node, and only the content is cached on the RSU.

Figure 3 depicts the content caching latency for five caching policies with different total caching capacity, namely CCMPSA, RL, DAC, RC and NCC. As can be seen from the figure, with the increase of the total cache capacity, the content caching delay gradually decreases, but the proposed algorithm has greater advantages in terms of delay. When does not take into account the mobility of vehicles, or social relationships between vehicles or collaborative caching, the two vehicles are less likely to share content, leading to performance degradation. When vehicle caching nodes are not considered, the demand of all vehicles puts a huge load on the RSU, which degrades the cache performance.

Figure 4 shows that the total caching capacity has an impact on the cache hit rate of the five strategies, and the cache hit rate increases with the increase of the total caching capacity. This is because larger caching capacity means more content can be cached so that CVs and RSU can meet more requests from vehicle users. The CCMPSA strategy proposed in this paper predicts the trajectory of the vehicle and the social relationship between vehicle users. The vehicle with more accurate selection as the cache has obvious advantages compared with other strategies, and also obtains a better cache hit rate.

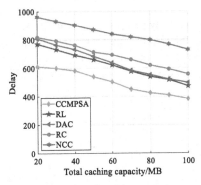

Fig. 3. Impact of total caching capacity on delay

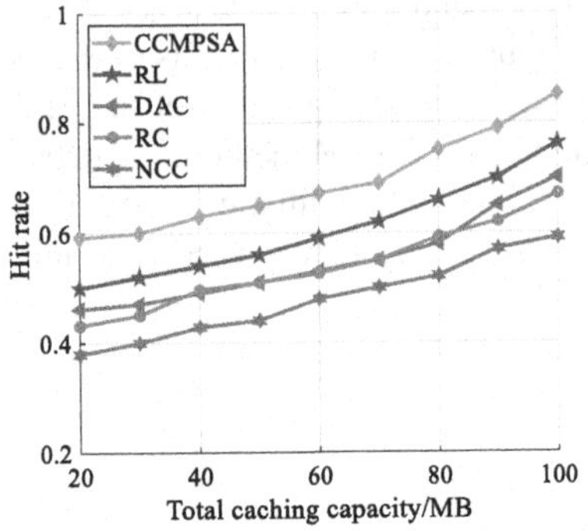

Fig. 4. Impact of total caching capacity on the hit ratio

5   Conclusion

This paper has proposed a DQN based cooperative caching strategy for the Internet of vehicles to solve the transmission delay caused by the complexity of vehicle mobility and social relations. Specifically, it includes three stages: trajectory prediction, cache vehicle selection and cache decision. Simulation results have showed that the proposed mechanism can effectively improve the cache hit rate and reduce the transmission delay. The future work will consider the cooperative caching problem between multiple RSUs and multiple cached vehicles.

6   Funding Statement

This work is fully supported by the National Natural Science Foundation of China (62071170, 62171180, 62072158), the Program for Innovative Research Team in University of Henan Province (21IRTSTHN015), in part by the Key Science and the Research Program in University of Henan Province (21A510001), Henan Province Science Fund for Distinguished Young Scholars (222300420006), and the Science and Technology Research Project of Henan Province under Grant (222102210001).

References

1. Liu, M., Yu, F.R., Teng, Y., Leung, V., Song, M.: Computation offloading and content caching in wireless blockchain networks with mobile edge computing. IEEE Trans. Veh. Technol. **67**(11), 11008–11021 (2018)

2. Chen, J., Wu, H., Yang, P., Feng, L., Shen, X.: Cooperative edge caching with location-based and popular contents for vehicular networks. IEEE Trans. Veh. Technol. **69**(9), 10291–10305 (2020)

3. Wang, R., Kan, Z., Cui, Y., Wu, D., Zhen, Y.: Cooperative caching strategy with content request prediction in Internet of vehicles. IEEE Internet Things J. **8**(11), 8964–8975 (2021)

4. Gupta, D., Rani, S., Ahmed, S.H., Garg, S., JalilPiran, M., Alrashoud, M.: ICN-based enhanced cooperative caching for multimedia streaming in resource constrained vehicular environment. IEEE Trans. Intell. Transp. Syst. **22**(7), 4588–4600 (2021)

5. Bang, J., Nam, Y., Choi, H., Lee, E., Oh, S.: Cooperative content downloading protocol based on the mobility Information of vehicles in Intermittently connected Vehicular Networks. In: 34th International Conference on Information Networking (ICOIN), pp. 271–275(2020)

6. Huang, X., Xu, K., Chen, Q., Zhang, J.: Delay-aware caching in Internet-of-vehicles networks. IEEE Internet Things J. **8**(13), 10911–10921 (2021)

7. Lin, Y., Chen, A., Jing, D., Wang, J., Wu, G.: A cooperative caching scheme based on mobility prediction in vehicular content centric networks. IEEE Trans. Veh. Technol. **67**(6), 5435–5444 (2018)

8. Qin, Z., Leng, S., Zhou, J., Mao, S.: Collaborative edge computing and caching in vehicular networks. In: 2020 IEEE Wireless Communications and Networking Conference (WCNC) (2020)

9. Yao, L., Wang, Y., Wang, X., Wu, G.: Cooperative caching in vehicular content centric network based on social attributes and mobility. IEEE Trans. Mob. Comput. **20**(2), 391–402 (2021)

10. Zhang, Y., Zhang, K., Cao, J., Liu, H., Maharjan, S.: Deep reinforcement learning for social-aware edge computing and caching in urban informatics. IEEE Trans. Industr. Inf. **16**(8), 5467–5477 (2020)

11. He, Y., Zhao, N., Yin, H.: Integrated networking, caching, and computing for connected vehicles: a deep reinforcement learning approach. IEEE Trans. Veh. Technol. **67**(1), 44–55 (2018)

12. Lin, P., Song, Q., Song, J., Jamalipour, A., Yu, F.R.: Cooperative caching and transmission in CoMP-integrated cellular networks using reinforcement learning. IEEE Trans. Veh. Technol. **69**(5), 5508–5520 (2020)

13. Zhuo, X., Li, Q., Cao, G., Dai, Y., Porta, T.L.: Social-based cooperative caching in DTNs: a contact duration aware approach. In 2011 IEEE Eighth International Conference on Mobile Ad-Hoc and Sensor Systems, pp. 92–101 (2011)

A Graph Neural Network Based Model for IoT Binary Components Similarity Detection

Zhiyu Wang[1,2], Xulun Hu[3,4], Fang Zuo[2,5]($\boxtimes$), Hong Li[3], Yiran Zhang[6], and Weifeng Wang[1,2]

[1] Henan International Joint Laboratory of Intelligent Network Theory and Key Technology, Henan University, Kaifeng 475000, China
[2] School of Software, Henan University, Kaifeng 475000, China
zuofang@henu.edu.cn
[3] Institute of Information Engineering, Chinese Academy of Sciences, Beijing 100000, China
[4] School of Software and Microelectronics, Peking University, Beijing 100000, China
[5] Subject Innovation and Intelligence Introduction Base of Henan Higher Educational Institution-Software Engineering Intelligent Information Processing Innovation and Intelligence Introduction Base of Henan University, Kaifeng 475000, China
[6] School of Computer Science and Engineering Northeastern University, Shenyang 110000, China

Abstract. IoT binary similarity detection is a way to determine whether two IoT components have a homology relationship. It is used to address security concerns arising from the reuse of open source components in the IoT software supply chain. In order to solve the problems caused by different architectures and different optimization levels during compilation, we propose a graph neural network based similarity assessment model for IoT binary components. We introduce an attention mechanism to get graph-level embedding based on GraphSAGE node-level embedding extraction, witch considers the importance of function nodes. Through comparative experiments with other models, this model shows better performance with 96.96% accuracy.

Keywords: IoT security · Binary similarity detection · Binary feature encoding · Graph neural network

1 Introduction

With the development of IoT technology, the number of IoT devices is increasing year by year. It has brought a lot of security issues since IoT software uses a lot of open source components in the development process to improve efficiency and reduce expenses. As mentioned by Black Duck in OSSRA 2022, 100% of codebases in the IoT sector contain an open source, and 64% of the IoT codebases contain security risk. [6] In order to detect and analyze the security threats brought by the reuse of such components in the IoT software supply chain, it

H. Ma et al. (Eds.): CWSN 2022, CCIS 1715, pp. 120–131, 2022.
https://doi.org/10.1007/978-981-19-8350-4_10

is necessary to build a homology relationship analysis model between components. Its goal is to analyze whether different components are compiled from the same source code, and then compare the differences between the open source component binaries in the IoT software and the officially released open source component binaries.

However, iot binary components are compiled with different architectures and different optimization levels, witch causes binaries from the same source code to be compiled differently and makes similarity analysis difficult. In order to solve this problem, we propose a similarity detection model for IoT binary files based on GraphSAGE and attention mechanism. Since every AFCG of the binary files compiled with the same source code in different architectures and different optimization levels is basically the same, we use it as the original feature. Then we introduce attention mechanism to get graph-level embedding based on GraphSAGE node-level embedding extraction, witch considers the importance of function nodes. Finally, the similarity of features can be calculated through the module based on NTN.

To summarize, the key contributions of this article are the following:

1) Propose an AFCG feature embedding method bases on GraphSAGE and Attention which considers the importance of function nodes and its results can be used for similarity calculation, which is the innovation of the proposed method in this paper.
2) Prepare a dataset of IoT binary components with different architectures and different optimization levels.
3) Design and conduct sufficient experiments to prove that this model has better performance in binary similarity detection than other models.

2   Related Work

With the development of artificial intelligence technology, more and more binary homology analysis methods use artificial intelligence related technologies.

IHB. [4] IHB uses the readable strings in binary files as binary file features to calculate the homology relationship of two different components. However, many binary files contain few or no readable strings, so this method is difficult to extract features for homologous comparison of such binary files.

B2V. [3] The B2V method uses the same function attributes of different architectures and the calling relationship between functions as graph features to realize the similarity comparison of binary files of different architectures and different compilation options. However, the structure2vec used by B2V ignores the order of function nodes and their importance, and uses a simple cosine algorithm for similarity calculation, so it will adversely affect the similarity evaluation.

Safe. [12] Safe is a method based on natural language processing. The semantics of binary functions are obtained through natural language processing, and the similarity of binary functions is compared by comparing semantics. Although this method can extract the semantic information of the function, it ignores the structural features of the program.

SimGnn. [1] Since AFCG is used as the original feature in this paper, the method of graph neural network can be used as the scheme of feature extraction. For example, SimGnn uses attention mechanism to emphasize the influence of key nodes on graph similarity judgment, and designs a pairwise node comparison method. This comparison method uses fine-grained node-level information to support graph-level embedding, which enables it to effectively detect the similarity of two graph structures.

3 Architecture

3.1 Overview

The overall architecture of the model is shown in the Fig. 1. The model first uses IDA Pro to extract the Attributed Function Call Graph (AFCG) of the two binary components to be compared, and takes it as the original feature of the two binary components. The second step is to perform graph convolution on the original features of the two components obtained in the previous step through the graph neural network GraphSAGE to obtain the respective node-level embeddings of each layer of the network. The third step is to embed the respective nodes of the three layers through the attention unit to obtain the node feature vector of each layer, and then convert the graph embedding of each layer into a single graph vector of the whole graph through MLP. The fourth step uses the NTN network to predict the similarity between the two graph vectors, and then obtains the similarity score set. The similarity score of the two binary components is finally obtained after the dimensionality reduction operation of the set is carried out through a fully connected network.

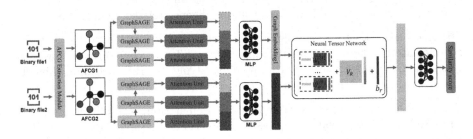

Fig. 1. The architecture of the model

3.2 Module Description

AFCG Extraction Module. Attributed Function Call Graph (AFCG) is proposed by B2V [3], which represents a binary file by using a directed graph with a node attribute. AFCG can be represented by the set $G(V, E \subseteq V \times V)$, where V represents the set of each function node in the binary file, and each function node v_i has some attribute values representing the function. Assuming that the function v_i calls v_j, the directed edge between the two functions v_i and v_j of the function is represented by $(v_i, v_j) \in E$.

For the attribute value representing the function, the attribute of each node v_i in the graph, we refer to the cross-architecture function attributes selected by B2V [3] and the cross-architecture basic block attributes used in other works [7,14]. Finally, 9 attributes are selected as the attribute set representing the function in the AFCG graph. The selected attributes include three categories. The first category is the number feature of function code blocks. The second category is the number features in the function code block, including the number of instructions, the number of strings, and the number of constants, which can describe the function code block from the data level of the code. The third category is the number features of the logical structure in the function code block, including the number of basic blocks contained in the function control flow graph CFG, the number of times the function calls other functions, and the number of times the function is called. These properties can describe the graph structure information of the function in the AFCG and the structure information inside the function basic block.

Node-level Embedding Module. This module uses the graph neural network to aggregate the graph structure data of the AFCG to obtain the node-level embedding of the AFCG. Here we choose GraphSAGE [9] as the feature extraction model in this module. In the process of learning and training, GraphSAGE will aggregate the neighbor nodes of the target node to represent the embedding of the target node, so in the node embedding of the graph, the neighbor relationship of the node can be better preserved and extracted.

In this module, we use the three-layer GraphSAGE [9] to extract the node embedding of the graph. For each node x_i of the graph data input by Graph-SAGE, the representation result h_j^k of the node h_i of the kth layer is calculated as shown in the formula:

$$
\begin{aligned}
A_k &= Aggregate_k(h_v^{k-1}, \forall v \in N_i) \\
h_j^k &= \sigma(W^k \cdot Cat(h_j^{k-1}, A_k))
\end{aligned}
\tag{1}
$$

The h_v^{k-1} in the formula represents the embedded representation of the node h_v of the $(k-1)$th layer, N_i represents the set of neighbor nodes of the node h_i, and $Aggregate_k$ represents the aggregation operation on the neighbor nodes. Cat represents the splicing operation. This step is to splice the embedding of the $(k-1)$th layer of the node h_i and the neighbor aggregation representation obtained by the previous layer.W_k represents a learnable parameter weight matrix, σ represents an activation function. In this model, the $mean$ function is used as the aggregation function and $ReLU$ function is used as the activation function

Graph-level Embedding Module. Graph-level embedding module uses attention to fuse the node-level embeddings into a graph-level embedding.

Attention models were first used by Bahdanau [2,5] for machine translation. Later, the attention mechanism gradually popularized and evolved, and was widely used in the field of artificial intelligence. The purpose of using the attention mechanism in this model is to more effectively generate graph-level embeddings from node-level embeddings in the graph. By using the attention mechanism and training the weight parameters in the attention mechanism, the more important nodes in the graph can have greater weights in the graph-level embedding, so as to obtain a more accurate graph-level embedding of the graph. Its calculation consists of four parts, as shown in the following formula:

$$c_i = ReLU((\frac{1}{N}\sum_{n=1}^{N} z_{i,n}) \cdot W_i) \tag{2}$$

$$\alpha_i = LeakyReLU(Z_i \cdot c_i^T) \tag{3}$$

$$r_i = Z_i^T \cdot \alpha_i \tag{4}$$

$$E = MLP(Cat(r_1, r_2, r_3)) \tag{5}$$

First, we need to get a global graph context representation $c_i \in \mathbb{R}^{1 \times D_i}$ of an embedding vector by formula 2. In the formula, $z_{i,m} \in \mathbb{R}^{D_i}$ represents the embedding of the mth node in the GraphSAGE output of the ith layer, and $W_i \in \mathbb{R}^{D_i \times D_i}$ represents the learnable weight matrix of c_i. By training the learned parameters W_i, c_i can describe the structure and feature information of the graph from the perspective of the whole graph.

Second, we calculate the attention weight $\alpha_i \in \mathbb{R}^{D_i}$ of each node embedding $z_{i,m}$ in the entire node embedding set Z_i. In the formula 3, $Z_i \in \mathbb{R}^{D_i \times N_i}$ represents the node-level embedding output by the ith layer GraphSAGE, N denotes the number of nodes, and D_i denote the dimension of the embedding representation output by the ith layer GraphSAGE. The nonlinear activation function here is $LeakyReLU$. [8]$LeakyReLU$ also outputs a minimum value when the input is less than 0, so it can avoid the situation that the gradient is 0 and cannot be trained.

Next, Multiply the obtained graph attention weight matrix with the entire node embedding set to obtain the graph embedding $r_i \in \mathbb{R}^{D \times 1}$ of the entire graph.

Finally, we fuse the graph embedding of each layer through an MLP unit for dimension reduction, and obtain the final graph-level embedding $E \in \mathbb{R}^{D_G \times 1}$ of the graph, and D_G represents the vector dimension of the obtained graph-level embedding ($D_G = \sum_{i=1}^{3} D_i$). The graph-level embedding calculation method is shown in formula 5. Cat represents the splicing operation, and the obtained three-layer AttentionUnit output is spliced. For the MLP network, we use a two-layer fully connected network, and the activation function uses ReLU.

Graph Embedding Similarity Calculation Module. After obtaining the graph-level embeddings E_1 and E_2 of the input two components, this module uses an NTN to calculate the similarity between E_1 and E_2, and then obtain the similarity scores for the two input binary components through a fully connected network.

Neural Tensor Network [13] was proposed by Richard to calculate how likely it is that there is a relationship between two entities. NTN is also widely used in the calculation of similarity in later development. For example, DeepRan [11] uses NTN to calculate the similarity of two commodity entities to rank users' queries, and ABiRCNN [10] uses NTN to measure the similarity between questions and answers.

For the input E_1 and E_2, NTN calculates the similarity relationship $S(E_1, E_2)$ between E_1 and E_2 by formula 6 ($S(E_i, E_j) \in \mathbb{R}^k$), where $W_2^{[1:k]} \in \mathbb{R}^{D_G \times D_G \times k}$ and $V_R \in \mathbb{R}^{k \times D_G}$ are two weight matrices, $b_R \in \mathbb{R}^k$ is the bias term, and the f function is a nonlinear activation function, here we choose the ReLU function.

$$S(E_i, E_j) = f(E_j \cdot W_2^{[1:k]} + V_R \cdot [E_i, E_j]^T + b_r) \qquad (6)$$

After obtaining the k-dimensional graph similarity relationship vector $S(E_i, E_j)$, we input it into a fully connected neural network for fusion dimensionality reduction, and obtain a score $\widehat{Sim(E_i, E_j)}$ representing the similarity of the two binary components. For the output of the last layer of neural network, The activation function we chose is $tanh$, which is used to map the similarity score between $(-1, 1)$.

In the training part, the loss function set by the model is mean square error function. Assuming that the similarity score of the two binary components of the standard training set is $Sim(E_i, E_j)$, the loss function can be expressed as formula 7, where B represents the training set, and $|B|$ is the number of binary component pairs included in the training set during training.

$$Loss = \frac{1}{|B|} \sum_{(i,j) \in B} (Sim(E_i, E_j) - \widehat{Sim(E_i, E_j)})^2 \qquad (7)$$

4 Experiment

4.1 Experiment Setup

Dataset. Since there is no publicly available homology diagram dataset for cross-architecture and cross-optimization-level binary components, we have collected the source code of 462 open source Iot related component projects, and compiled the project in the source code on different architectures and different optimization levels with the buildroot tool. The architectures include MIPS, ARM, X86 and X64, while the optimization options are O0 and O1 respectively. We can get 279,029 executable binaries based on different architectures through the above steps. Then we extracted the graph data files corresponding to all binary files through the AFCG extraction tool. However, we need to filter out the graph files of binary files in the two cases after analyzing the node data and edge data of the above data files, In the first case, since some source files are library files, the compiled binary files and graph data files only contain the node data of the function, not edges representing function calls. The second case is that the graph data files obtained by some binary files contain less information, such as only two node data and one edge data. After obtaining 113,590 original binary graph data files, we made statistics according to the number of nodes in the graph. It can be found the proportion of the two is 8:13 through statistics that the number of binary graph data nodes is 43,396 when the number is less than 10, while the number is 70,194 when the number is greater than or equal to 10.

Due to the large proportion of the obtained original graph data with less than 10 nodes, in order to generate the training set, verification set and test set of model, we divided the original graph data into three parts according to the scale of graph nodes: Small node datasets (between 3 and 10 nodes), large node datasets (10 or more nodes), and mixed node datasets (all graph data). Then, we can generate a corresponding training set, validation set and test set respectively for the three kinds of original graph data sets. First of all, we can ignore the architecture of figure data difference between the data, then randomly select two figure data g_i and g_j from each original data set. If the two graph data correspond to the same source program, we generate a graph data pair $< g_i, g_j, 1 >$, where 1 means that the two graphs come from the same source program. Otherwise, we generate another graph data pair $< g_i, g_j, -1 >$, where -1 indicates that the two programs are from different sources. We pre-set the ratio of postive to negative as 1:1, and the ratio of training set, verification set and test set as 9:0.5:0.5. According to this generation method, the dataset as shown in the Table 1 can be generated.

Table 1. Training dataset scale

Node scale	Training	Validation	Test
(3, 10)	78112	4340	4340
(10, 1000)	126350	7020	7020
(3, 1000)	204462	11360	11360

Performance Indicators. The indicators of model experiment include accuracy, precision, recall rate and MSE (Mean Squared Error). Among them, accuracy refers to the probability that the model predicts correctly, precision refers to the probability that the model predicts correctly for positive samples, recall rate refers to the probability that the model predicts correctly in positive samples, and MSE refers to the average square error between the prediction result and the true similarity.

4.2 Experiment Results

Hyperparameter Selection Experiment. We adjusted the dimensions of graph embedding of hyperparametric model into four different dimensions, and conducted network training in graph data sets with the number of nodes between 10 and 1000 in different dimensions respectively. As shown in the Figs. 2 and 3, the training performance of model in 50 Epochs was obtained. It can be seen from the figure that AUC and LOSS curves of the model can reach a relatively stable state when the model at the status of about 30 epochs under different graph embedding representation dimensions. When the embedding dimension is 64, the LOSS value in the training process is significantly lower than that of the training model in other dimensions.

Table 2 shows the test results of different graph embeded-dimension models in three data sets. In the small-scale AFCG data set with a number of nodes between 3 and 10, the embeded-dimension model with a dimension of 36 is significantly higher than other embeded-dimension models in the three test indicators. In the other two data sets, the performance of the embedded model representing dimension 36 is close to that of the best model. For example, in the AFCG data set with the number of nodes ranging from 3 to 1000, the accuracy of the model representing dimension 36 is only 0.33% lower than that of the model representing dimension 32, and the recall rate is only 0.17% lower than that of the model representing dimension 64. Therefore, the dimension of embedding representation of the model can be selected as 36 to be suitable for graph similarity analysis of different scales.

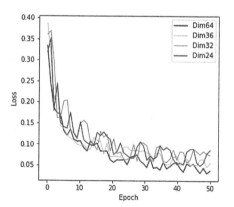

Fig. 2. Loss of different Graph Dim

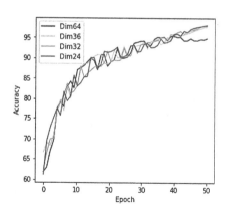

Fig. 3. Accuracy of different Graph Dim

Attention Module Selection Experiment. In the second part of the experiment, we tested the number of attention unit modules used by the node embedding module. We set up three groups for comparative experiments. The first group only used the node representation output of the last layer GraphSAGE

Table 2. Results for different scale datasets

Dataset	Dim	Accuracy	Precision	Recall	MSE
3–1000	Dim64	95.21%	94.50%	**93.69%**	0.0691
	Dim36	**96.41%**	97.76%	93.51%	**0.0685**
	Dim32	95.39%	**98.09%**	93.60%	0.0785
	Dim24	95.75%	98.06%	93.15%	0.0737
10–1000	Dim64	**98.31%**	98.40%	**98.69%**	**0.0215**
	Dim36	97.46%	**98.52%**	96.70%	0.0357
	Dim32	97.69%	97.09%	98.00%	0.0481
	Dim24	97.27%	98.18%	97.42%	0.0435
3–10	Dim64	94.56%	97.18%	91.77%	0.0883
	Dim36	**96.42%**	98.27%	**94.55%**	**0.0694**
	Dim32	95.90%	98.09%	93.61%	0.0769
	Dim24	95.95%	**98.68%**	93.15%	0.0738

to represent the input data as the graph embedding module, the second group used the node embedding representation output of the second and third layer GraphSAGE to represent the input module data as the graph embedding, and the third group uses the node embedding output by the three-layer GraphSAGE in SimCAC as a graph to represent the data of the input module. After training, the result as shown in the figure can be obtained. As shown in the Figs. 4 and 5, when the attention module consists of one layer or three layers, the training effect of network accuracy and LOSS value is relatively stable. However, using the three-layer attention module can achieve relatively stable and optimal effect more quickly. Therefore, the multi-layer attention fusion method used by the model has achieved relatively good results.

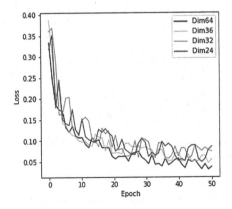

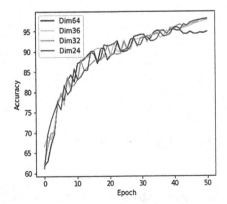

Fig. 4. Loss of different Attention layers

Fig. 5. Accuracy of different Attention layers

Comparison Experiment of Different Models. In this experiment, we have compared the performance of other three models with our model in different datasets. We have implemented the cross-architecture binary component similarity analysis model used in B2V [3], which is most suitable for our experimental scenarios and targets. In addition, we also implement a comparison model that uses Cosine to replace NTN network as the similarity score calculation module in our model and graph similarity detection model Simgnn [1]. After completing the training and testing process, we got the results as shown in Table 3. It can be found from the table that our model and Simgnn have better performance in small node dataset and mixed node dataset, while our model has better test results than the other three models in large node dataset.

Table 3. Experimental results of different models

Dataset	Dim	Accuracy	Precision	Recall	MSE
3–1000	Model(NTN)	**98.57%**	99.04%	97.93%	**0.019**
	Model(cos)	66.34%	70.81%	89.16%	0.266
	Simgnn	97.63%	**99.15%**	**98.19%**	0.022
	B2V	57.65%	68.37%	72.21%	0.310
10–1000	Model(NTN)	**98.45%**	**98.93%**	**98.03%**	**0.019**
	Model(cos)	63.24%	67.29%	87.86%	0.257
	Simgnn	85.26%	87.97%	82.86%	0.115
	B2V	53.29%	63.58%	73.68%	0.322
3–10	Model(NTN)	**94.57%**	94.39%	**94.07%**	0.071
	Model(cos)	65.32%	75.61%	82.76%	0.278
	Simgnn	73.68%	**95.97%**	71.67%	**0.062**
	B2V	56.42%	73.01%	71.68%	0.252

5   Conclusion

This paper mainly introduces the research and design of Iot binary component similarity assessment model based on graph neural network, as well as the comparison experiment with other models. The advantage of this model is that it can ignore the effects of architecture and optimization level during compilation. It includes AFCG extraction module, node-level embedding module, graph-level embedding module and graph embedding similarity calculation module. The process of the model proposed in this paper is as follows: firstly, we extracted AFCG of IoT binary component as the original graph features, then used graph neural network to transform graph features into node-level embeddings, and used attention to fuse node-level embeddings into a graph-level embedding. Finally, we calculated the similarity of two graph embeddings by NTN as the similarity of components. Through experiments, our model can achieve 96.41% accuracy,

98.09% precision and 93.69% recall in the mixed dataset. Compared with other models, it can also show better performance. But from the perspective of feature selection, there are still many features for model selection. For the attribute representation of functions, statistical features will ignore the order of instructions in the function, so in the future work, we will consider using new features from the perspective of instruction flow for further research.

Acknowledgements. This work is supported by Graduate Education Innovation and Quality Improvement Action Plan project of Henan University (No. SYLJD2022008 and No. SYLKC2022028), 2022 Discipline Innovation Introduction Base cultivation project of Henan University and Key Technology Research and Development Project of Henan Province under Grant 222102210055.

References

1. Bai, Y., Ding, H., Bian, S., Chen, T., Sun, Y., Wang, W.: SimGNN: a neural network approach to fast graph similarity computation. In: Proceedings of the Twelfth ACM International Conference on Web Search and Data Mining, pp. 384–392 (2019)
2. Chaudhari, S., Mithal, V., Polatkan, G., Ramanath, R.: An attentive survey of attention models. ACM Trans. Intell. Syst. Technol. (TIST) **12**(5), 1–32 (2021)
3. Chen, Yu., Li, H., Ma, Y., Shi, Z., Sun, L.: Robust network-based binary-to-vector encoding for scalable IoT binary file retrieval. In: Chellappan, S., Cheng, W., Li, W. (eds.) WASA 2018. LNCS, vol. 10874, pp. 53–65. Springer, Cham (2018). https://doi.org/10.1007/978-3-319-94268-1_5
4. Chen, Y., Li, H., Zhao, W., Zhang, L., Liu, Z., Shi, Z.: IHB: a scalable and efficient scheme to identify homologous binaries in IoT FirmWares. In: 2017 IEEE 36th International Performance Computing and Communications Conference (IPCCC), pp. 1–8. IEEE (2017)
5. Cho, K., Van Merriënboer, B., Bahdanau, D., Bengio, Y.: On the properties of neural machine translation: Encoder-decoder approaches. arXiv preprint arXiv:1409.1259 (2014)
6. Duck, B.: Open source security and risk analysis (OSSRA) - 7th. Technical report, Synopsys (2022)
7. Feng, Q., Zhou, R., Xu, C., Cheng, Y., Testa, B., Yin, H.: Scalable graph-based bug search for firmware images. In: Proceedings of the 2016 ACM SIGSAC Conference on Computer and Communications Security, pp. 480–491 (2016)
8. Gu, J., et al.: Recent advances in convolutional neural networks. Pattern Recogn. **77**, 354–377 (2018)
9. Hamilton, W., Ying, Z., Leskovec, J.: Inductive representation learning on large graphs. Adv. Neural Inf. Process. Syst. **30**, 1–11 (2017)
10. He, X., Xu, H., Sun, X., Deng, J., Li, J.: ABiRCNN with neural tensor network for answer selection. In: 2017 International Joint Conference on Neural Networks (IJCNN), pp. 2582–2589. IEEE (2017)
11. Kabir, R.H., Pervaiz, B., Khan, T.M., Ul-Hasan, A., Nawaz, R., Shafait, F.: DeepRank: adapting neural tensor networks for ranking the recommendations. In: Djeddi, C., Jamil, A., Siddiqi, I. (eds.) MedPRAI 2019. CCIS, vol. 1144, pp. 162–176. Springer, Cham (2020). https://doi.org/10.1007/978-3-030-37548-5_13

12. Massarelli, L., Di Luna, G.A., Petroni, F., Baldoni, R., Querzoni, L.: SAFE: self-attentive function embeddings for binary similarity. In: Perdisci, R., Maurice, C., Giacinto, G., Almgren, M. (eds.) DIMVA 2019. LNCS, vol. 11543, pp. 309–329. Springer, Cham (2019). https://doi.org/10.1007/978-3-030-22038-9_15
13. Socher, R., Chen, D., Manning, C.D., Ng, A.: Reasoning with neural tensor networks for knowledge base completion. Adv. Neural Inf. Process. Syst. **26**, 1–10 (2013)
14. Xu, X., Liu, C., Feng, Q., Yin, H., Song, L., Song, D.: Neural network-based graph embedding for cross-platform binary code similarity detection. In: Proceedings of the 2017 ACM SIGSAC Conference on Computer and Communications Security, pp. 363–376 (2017)

Multi-scale Temporal Feature Fusion for Time-Limited Order Prediction*

Jun Wang[1], Xiaolei Zhou[2(⊠)], Yaochang Liu[1], Xinrui Zhang[1], and Shuai Wang[1]

[1] Southeast University, Nanjing, China
{junwang19,213181431,xinrui_zhang,shuaiwang}@seu.edu.cn
[2] National University of Defense Technology, Nanjing, China
zhouxiaolei@nudt.edu.cn

Abstract. The time-limited order is a new type of real-time delivery service that platforms need to complete the order delivery with different time granularity (e.g. one day, two days, or three days). Predicting the number of time-limited orders plays an important role for real-time order delivery allocation and anomaly detection in logistics IoT scenarios. However, the impact between orders of different time granularity is complex and the contribution of the static order features is unknown. Previous order predicting methods are not suitable for time-limited orders because they do not fully consider the dependencies among orders with different time granularity. In this paper, we propose a spatial-temporal framework based on stacked long short-term memory networks (LSTM) and deep & cross network (DCN) to take the dependencies of multi-scale temporal features into account and fuse cross-domain static features effectively. In addition, we utilize a multi-head attention mechanism to model the heterogeneous strengths of different dependencies. We evaluate our model on a real-world dataset with about 400,000 orders from one of the largest logistics companies in China. The evaluation results show that the Mean Absolute Error and R2 score of our method achieve 9.407 and 0.948, outperforming state-of-the-art solutions.

Keywords: Delivery order prediction · Multi-temporal granularity fusion · Multi-head attention mechanism · Deep&Cross network

1 Introduction

Time-limited orders delivery service is a new real-time delivery service model born in response to customers' different needs for order delivery timeliness. Couriers deliver the time-limited orders from warehouses to customers within a time limit (e.g. one day, two days, or three days) [1,2]. Among all of the time-limited orders, one-day delivery orders are the most important part. This type of

This work was supported in part by Science and Technology Innovation 2030 - Major Project 2021ZD0114202, National Natural Science Foundation of China under Grant No. 61902066 and Natural Science Foundation of Jiangsu Province under Grant No. BK20190336.

order is more likely to be favored by customers and has higher requirements for transportation, and its sudden surge may lead to the collapse of logistics companies resulting in extensive order delays. With the continuous development of current logistics IoT systems, real-time order dispatching is becoming more and more important. It is essential for the logistics platform to know the number of one-day delivery orders to help the platform monitor the abnormal situation of time-limited order quantity and achieve better allocation of logistics resources.

There are many existing works related to demand prediction using the technology of artificial neural networks. In Shabani's work [5] on water demand forecasting, the authors consider the impact of multiple scales on the time series, but the authors make the process of forecasting each scale independently, ignoring the correlation between different time granularity. Also, their framework does not exploit static features.

While the spatial-temporal model of Yao et al. [11] on taxi demand prediction considers static features such as geographic location and crowd distribution, it only considers the future impact of orders at near time points and does not consider the impact of temporal fluctuations at higher scales such as weekends and holidays

In this paper, we aim to model the temporal dependencies among different time-limited order types and effectively combine the cross-domain static features to predict the one-day delivery orders. Accordingly, there are the following challenges: (i) The impact of orders with different time limits on one-day delivery orders is not explicit. We find complex interactions between orders that need to be completed with different time granularity. How to model the temporal dependencies among these orders for the prediction of the number of time-limited orders is challenging; (ii) Static order features and order temporal features with different time granularity contribute to one-day delivery order quantity prediction differently. It is not straightforward to distinguish spatial-temporal features with heterogeneous strengths.

To address these challenges, we propose a spatial-temporal framework based on stacked long short-term memory networks (LSTM) and deep & cross network(DCN), which effectively fuses multi-scale temporal features and cross-domain static features. We first design a multi-scale time series model to learn the temporal dependencies between orders with different time granularity. Then, we design a static feature extraction module based on depth and crossover network to effectively fuse cross-domain static features. In summary, our key contributions are as follows:

- To the best of our knowledge, we are the first to combine multi-time-order features for one-day delivery order predicting. We effectively mine the temporal dependencies between orders with different time granularity and combine cross-domain spatial features to predict the one-day delivery orders.
- To address the temporal dependencies ambiguity, we design the multi-scale time series module based on stacked LSTM to capture the orders' temporal dependencies with different time granularity. Then, we design the multi-head attention mechanism to model the heterogeneous strengths of different

temporal features. Meanwhile, we design a static feature enhancement module to effectively combines the temporal and spatial features to predict the number of one-day delivery orders.

- We evaluate our model on a real-world delivery dataset with about 400,000 orders from one of China's largest logistics companies. Experiments show that we outperform the RMSE, MAE, and R2 score of state-of-the-art methods based on LSTM by 12.715, 9.407 and 0.948, respectively.

2   Motivation

2.1   Data

Our work is based on one of the largest online sales platforms, who provides data with temporal and static features. Table 1 shows an example of each feature.

Table 1. An example of order record

Temporal	No. of one-day Delivery order 58	No. of Two-day Delivery order 327	No. of three-day Delivery order 7
	Number of order 968	Weight of items 1142.96	Volume of items 5875345.087
Static	Item categories		
	Mobile Communication	Digital	Stationery

Temporal Features. A record contains the number of orders placed by a user in an hour that should be delivered on the same day, as well as those delivered on the next day and the third day. In addition, it also contains the total number of orders placed during that time, the total weight and volume of the items ordered.

Static Features. The goods in each order belong to different categories, and these categories greatly affect the timeliness of order delivery.

2.2   Temporal Dependencies and Static Order Features

Figure 1 shows the Pearson product-moment correlation coefficient matrix between the timing features. The closer the value is to 1, the higher the correlation between these two variables. However, we can see that the correlation between one-day and two-day delivery orders is much greater than the correlation between one-day and three-day. In fact, orders delivered on the fourth day and later have very little correlation with the first day of delivery. So we only model the dependencies among orders with these three time limits.

For static features, we found that the category of time-limited orders has a non-negligible impact on the granularity of the time it takes to deliver, for example, food delivery tends to take one day, while more expensive items take longer. To capture the effects of static features, we utilize the DCN model.

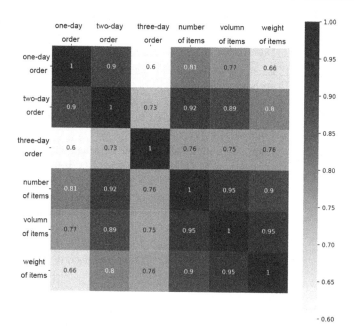

Fig. 1. Heat map of time series characteristics

3 Model Framework

In this section, we first introduce the problem definitions and notions. Then we detail each model component and outline the proposed framework.

3.1 Definitions and Notations

Let's assume we have n hours of order data now. The meaning of each notation is given in Table 2.

Our input is the number of one-day delivery orders X for the first n moments, the number of two-day delivery orders Y, the number of three-day delivery orders Z, other temporal features A and static discrete features B. Our goal is to predict the number of one-day delivery orders at $n + 1$th moment x_{n+1}.

3.2 Time-Series Mixing Module

For timing-dependent inputs, our model is based on the stacked LSTM model. We put three time-limited orders into each of the three parallel LSTM networks at the same time. As shown in Fig. 2. This way the three layers can take different

Table 2. Notation description

Notation	Description
$X = \{x_1, \ldots x_i \ldots, x_n\}$	Each x denotes the number of one-day delivery orders in an hour, and the length of the time series is n
$Y = \{y_1, \ldots y_i \ldots, y_n\}$	Each y represents the number of orders within one hour that should be delivered tomorrow, and The length of the time series is n
$Z = \{z_1, \ldots z_i \ldots, z_n\}$	Each z represents the number of orders within one hour that should be delivered the day after Tomorrow, and the length of the time series is n
$A = \{\alpha_1, \ldots \alpha_i \ldots, \alpha_n\}$	$\alpha_i \in \mathbb{R}^m$ denotes the set of m temporal features at moment i. Let $A \in \mathbb{R}^{m \times n}$ be these temporal features of the First n time steps
$B = \{\beta_1, \ldots \beta_i \ldots, \beta_n\}$	$\beta_i \in \mathbb{R}^r$ denotes the set of r static discrete features at moment i. Let $B \in \mathbb{R}^{r \times n}$ be these discrete features of The first n time steps

time granularity. The input of the next layer is connected to the hidden layer of the previous layer and used as the input of the next unit.

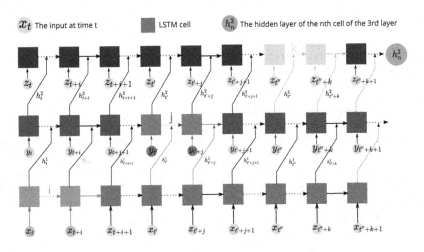

Fig. 2. Multi-grain Mixing LSTM

Suppose we are at time t, and the time granularity of one-day, two-day and three-day delivery orders is i, j, and k, respectively. The three-layer LSTM network function is simply defined as f, g, p, then each hidden layer h of the first layer can be expressed by the following equation:

$$h_1^{t+i} = f(x_t, ..., x_{t+i}) \tag{1}$$

The output of the first layer is connected to the output of each cell of the second layer to obtain the output of the second layer.

$$h_2^{t+j} = g([y_t : y_{t+j}], [h_1^t : h_1^{t+j}]) \tag{2}$$

Finally, we utilize the same method to connect the second layer to the third layer to obtain the third hidden layer we want.

$$h_3^{t+k} = g([z_t : z_{t+k}], [h_2^t : h_2^{t+k}]) \tag{3}$$

For the other temporal features, we put them as a tensor, the whole into an LSTM network. Take the hidden layer h_o^n of the last cell of this network and connect it with the output h_3^n of the last cell of the last layer in the above Eq. (3). This is the output of our timing module Out_{time}. It incorporates the information of primary temporal features with different temporal granularity and links the secondary temporal features.

$$Out_{time} = concat(h_o^n, h_3^n) \tag{4}$$

After that we introduce a multi-headed attention mechanism for the $Out_{time} \in \mathbb{R}^n$. First, for the inputs in the sequence, we multiply them with three random weight matrices W^Q, W^K, W^V (representing the key matrix, value matrix and query matrix respectively) to get three sets: $q_i, k_i, v_i, i \in [1, n]$.

$$\begin{cases} q_i = W^Q Out_{time_i} \\ k_i = W^K Out_{time_i} \\ v_i = W^V Out_{time_i} \end{cases} \tag{5}$$

Then we use these vectors to compute the attention matrix α. For example, for the first row of the matrix, we compute the vector dot product of q_1 with $k_1, ..., k_n$ to obtain all through $\alpha[1:1], ..., \alpha[1:n]$.

$$\alpha[i:j] = \frac{q_i^T k_j}{d_{qk}} \tag{6}$$

Then we normalize them to all through $\alpha[1:1], ..., \alpha[1:n]$ by the softmax function. Finally, we multiply them with the corresponding $v_1, ..., v_n$ and sum them to obtain the output λ_1 corresponding to Out_{time_1}.

To extract the multidimensional features, we utilize six randomly initialized matrices and let these variables pass through them. As for the input Out_{time_t}, the $\lambda_1, ..., \lambda_n$ obtained by the first attention mechanism is noted as λ^1, we get $\lambda^1, ..., \lambda^6$, and then we concatenate them together and pass them through a linear layer to get the corresponding output $Out_{attention}[t]$. Finally we get all the vectors of the temporal fusion.

3.3   Static Features Enhancement Module

For static discrete features, such as the variety of items in an order. Assume that the probability of one-day order is 0.6 for electronic goods, 0.8 for valuables, and 0.3 for low-priced goods; and a computer belongs to both electronic goods and valuables, its probability of one-day order should be higher than the average value of the probability of one-day order of these two categories, or even higher than 0.8; and if it is just a USB cable, its probability of one-day order should be lower than 0.3. To make our features have this capability, we utilize the DCN model.

For these product categories β_t at hour t, we often use one-hot codes to represent them. The one-hot code b for each hourly feature with the weight matrix W_{embed} yields the dense vector b_{embed}. Then they are put into the DCN.

$$b_{embed,i} = W_{embed,i} b_i \tag{7}$$

$$\beta_{embed,t} = [b_{embed,1}, ..., b_{embed,r}] \tag{8}$$

For the l-th layer of the crossover network, the input crossover vector β_l is multiplied with the original vectors β_0 of the first layer to obtain a crossover matrix of dimension r^2. This matrix is then multiplied with the weight vector w_l and added with the offset b_l and input β_l to obtain the crossover vector of the next layer β_{l+1}. Each layer having the following formula:

$$\beta_{l+1} = \beta_0 \beta_l^T w_l + b_l + \beta_l \tag{9}$$

where β_l is the l-th layer. w_l, b_l are the weight matrix and bias parameters of th l-th layer.

For the deep neural network, we set up three layers. The activation function of each layer is $ReLu$. Due to the characteristics of deep neural networks, it can capture higher-order nonlinear features.

After all the inputs go into two different modules, we need to combine them efficiently. We concat the output of the two modules together and obtain the final prediction after passing it through two linear layers.

3.4   System Overview

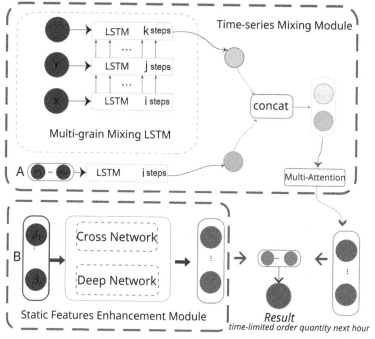

Fig. 3. The overview of the model

The Fig. 3 above shows our overall structure. We put the input X, Y and Z with strong temporal correlation into each of the three simultaneous LSTM networks and fuse them efficiently. Meanwhile, the other temporal features that do not require consideration of time granularity are passed as a whole as a vector A through one layer of the LSTM network. We aggregate these temporal features and pass them through a layer of multi-headed attention mechanisms. At the same time, we pass the static discrete features through the DCN network, and then we fuse the static features with the temporal features to get the next hour's one-day delivery order quantity.

4   Experiments

4.1   Experiment Setup

Dataset. The real dataset contains 399415 real-time order records in three months from JD (one of China's largest logistics companies), which are detected by the IoT system of warehousing and logistics. According to the user's expectations, order records are classified into three categories: the order expected to arrive in one day, two days and three days. Additionally, each order contains the information of delivery warehouse ID, purchase item type and actual completion time of order. We count the three types of order records separately. The number of one-day delivery orders in the next hour is our predicted target.

Metrics. We denote that $\hat{y}_i$ and y_i are the prediction value from model and ground truth at t_i respectively and $\bar{y}$ is the average of the true values. Four metrics are utilized in our evaluation.

Root Mean Square Error(RMSE):

$$RMSE = \sqrt{\frac{1}{n} \sum_{i=1}^{n} (\hat{y}_i - y_i)^2}$$

Mean Absolute Error(MAE):

$$MAE = \frac{1}{n} \sum_{i=1}^{n} |\hat{y}_i - y_i|$$

Mean Absolute Percentage Error(MAPE):

$$MAPE = \frac{100\%}{n} \sum_{i=1}^{n} \left| \frac{\hat{y}_i - y_i}{y_i} \right|$$

R^2 score

$$R^2 = 1 - \frac{\sum_{i}^{n} (\hat{y}_i - y_i)^2}{\sum_{i}^{n} (\bar{y} - y_i)^2}$$

Both RMSE and MAE evaluate errors between the model predicted value and real value. RMSE penalizes the errors larger than the real value while MAE gives the same weight to the errors. R^2 score utilize the mean value of the real value as a reference to evaluate whether the prediction error of the model is greater than or less than the error caused by only using the mean value to predict. The larger the R^2 score, the better the fitting ability of the model.

4.2   Performance Comparison

Baselines. To verify the effectiveness of our model, we compared it with the following state-of-the-art methods.

- **ARIMA**: A regression model often used for univariate short time series forecasting.
- **SVR**: Support vector regression(SVR) utilizes the same basic idea as Support Vector Machine (SVM).

- **RF** [9]: Random Forest(RF) is an ensemble of decision trees algorithms that are used for regression predictive modeling.
- **LSTNet** [3]: LSTNet leverages the strengths of both the convolutional layer and the recurrent layer to capture different temporal dependencies.
- **Informer** [12]: The Informer model is an improvement of the Transformer, which has good performance for long series prediction.
- **Attention-LSTM**: LSTM is a common deep learning model for temporal prediction, and its combination with the attention mechanism is the mainstream temporal prediction method nowadays.

Ablation Experiment. To validate the effectiveness of two components we proposed for multi-scale temporal features extraction and cross-domain static features fusion, we test the effect of each component from this ablation experiment.

- **Single-Scale LSTM**: We set the output time steps of three separate LSTM networks to the same. This model is used to reflect whether it is effective to handle different time-limit delivery by setting different time steps of each LSTM layer.
- **Multi-Scale LSTM**: Our model removes the DCN part. This model is used to reflect whether it is effective to process static features with the DCN module.

4.3 Experiment Results

I. Model Setting and Experimental Results Comparison
We set the hidden layer size of the LSTM network to 32, six heads for the multi-headed attention mechanism, and dropout to 0.1. There are 99 features passed into the DCN model, the number of cross network layers is 2, and the number of deep network layers is 3. Our network uses MSE as the loss function, and the optimizer uses adaptive moment estimation with cosine annealing whose maximum number of iterations is set 5. The maximum epoch is set to 50, and converges at $33(\pm 4)$ epochs in 5 experiments with an average time of 11,784 s.

The optimal time steps of our model are set to [36,24,12] by minimizing validation errors, which indicates that we utilize the last 36 h, 24 h and 12 h of three types of order records to predict one-day delivery orders in the next hour.

The time steps of LSTM and Attention-LSTM are set to 24 h. As described in Table 3, our model achieves the best results compared with other models on most evaluation metrics, RMSE, R^2 score. The RMSE of Informer is very low, second only to our model, but none of its other metrics are excellent, which we believe is related to its loss function being MSE, and its optimization direction is to reduce MSE in training.

As a variant based on LSTM, LSTM is our main comparison object. It is clearly observed from Table 3 that our model achieves better results on all the metrics compared to LSTM.

Table 3. Performance evaluation of different models

Model	RMSE	MAPE	MAE	R^2 score
ARIMA	44.60 ± 0.35	1.571 ± 0.021	37.61 ± 0.34	0.334 ± 0.004
SVR	16.79 ± 0.18	1.294 ± 0.011	13.22 ± 0.11	0.866 ± 0.010
RF	14.80 ± 0.12	0.253 ± 0.002	9.75 ± 0.09	0.896 ± 0.010
LSTNet	22.47 ± 0.27	0.390 ± 0.004	17.26 ± 0.22	0.838 ± 0.011
Informer	14.36 ± 0.10	0.720 ± 0.007	12.91 ± 0.12	0.913 ± 0.007
Attention-LSTM	14.56 ± 0.19	0.188 ± 0.002	10.72 ± 0.13	0.932 ± 0.010
Single-Scale LSTM	14.97 ± 0.13	0.188 ± 0.002	11.19 ± 0.09	0.928 ± 0.006
Multi-Scale LSTM	13.95 ± 0.08	0.255 ± 0.002	10.42 ± 0.07	0.938 ± 0.007
Multi-Scale LSTM & DCN	**12.72 ± 0.08**	**0.231 ± 0.002**	**9.41 ± 0.06**	**0.948 ± 0.007**

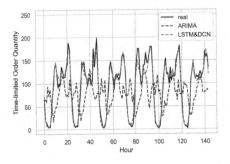

Fig. 4. Predict results of Multi-Scale LSTM&DCN and ARIMA

Fig. 5. Comparison results of Single-Scale and Multi-Scale LSTM

As can be seen from Fig. 4, LSTM and our model predict periodic fluctuations. However, for LSTM, its prediction at the peak point of orders is generally low, which may mislead logistics companies in resource scheduling.

II. The effect of different designed components

We keep our multi-scale LSTM's time steps consistent and choose [24,24,24] by minimizing validation errors. This model is denoted as Single-scale LSTM.

Multi-scale LSTM makes greater improvement compared to Single-scale LSTM, which reveals the diversity of time dependence of temporal features from the dataset and the effective extraction of different time granularity features by our model. Moreover, implemented with a deep feature crossing module, our model obtains more effective information from cross-domain static features fusion. As shown in Table 3 and Fig. 5, the prediction effect of multi-scale LSTM '&' DCN is closer to the real value than that of Multi-scale LSTM by static features extraction.

5   Related Work

Time-series forecasting is an extremely valuable problem. People previously used simple mathematical models such as ARIMA, and machine learning models LSTM. In recent years, deep learning methods have also been widely used in demand forecasting [10]. Before 2018, the mainstream temporal prediction models revolved around RNN. With the work on attention mechanism in the Transformer [7], which was supposed to be a breakthrough in Natural Language Processing, but inspired by this, a large number of researchers introduced attention mechanism into the work of temporal prediction [4]. This is also one of the approaches taken by our model.

Another major problem of time-series prediction is the extraction of features, especially static ones(e.g.: spatial information, types of goods, etc.), and they often need to be processed before they can be put into the RNN network. Previous works mostly utilize CNN [3] to extract spatial features, and there are also novel works to learn spatial static features by Graph Neural Networks [6]. As for the scenario we encountered, the most important static features are the categories of items, we refer to google's practice about click-through rate prediction [8] and introduce their work on DCN to order feature enhancement.

6   Conclusion

In this paper, we propose a new framework for fusing temporal and static features in a new scenario of predicting the number of time-limited orders. We innovatively propose a multi-temporal granularity fusion LSTM network and introduce a multi-headed attention mechanism to improve its global memory capability. We also introduce DCN to enhance a large number of sparse discrete features. Experimental results show that: the fusion of different temporal granularity and static cross-domain features helps to further improve the predictive power of LSTM networks.

References

1. Guo, B., et al.: Concurrent order dispatch for instant delivery with time-constrained actor-critic reinforcement learning. In: 2021 IEEE Real-Time Systems Symposium (RTSS), pp. 176–187 (2021). https://doi.org/10.1109/RTSS52674.2021.00026
2. Hu, S., Guo, B., Wang, S., Zhou, X.: Effective cross-region courier-displacement for instant delivery via reinforcement learning. In: Liu, Z., Wu, F., Das, S.K. (eds.) WASA 2021. LNCS, vol. 12937, pp. 288–300. Springer, Cham (2021). https://doi.org/10.1007/978-3-030-85928-2_23
3. Lai, G., Chang: modeling long-and short-term temporal patterns with deep neural networks. In: The 41st International ACM SIGIR Conference on Research & Development in Information Retrieval, pp. 95–104 (2018)
4. Ran, X.S.: An LSTM-based method with attention mechanism for travel time prediction. Sensors 19(4), 861 (2019)

5. Shabani, S., Candelieri, A.: Gene expression programming coupled with unsupervised learning: a two-stage learning process in multi-scale, short-term water demand forecasts. Water **10**(2), 142 (2018)
6. Si, C., Chen, W.: An attention enhanced graph convolutional LSTM network for skeleton-based action recognition. In: Proceedings of the IEEE/CVF Conference on Computer Vision and Pattern Recognition, pp. 1227–1236 (2019)
7. Vaswani, A., et al.: Attention is all you need. In: Advances in Neural Information Processing Systems, vol. 30 (2017)
8. Wang, R., Fu, B.: Deep & cross network for ad click predictions. In: Proceedings of the ADKDD 2017, pp. 1–7 (2017)
9. Wang, Z., Wang, Y.: Random forest based hourly building energy prediction. Energy Build. **171**, 11–25 (2018)
10. Yan, H., Wang, S., Yang, Y., Guo, B., He, T., Zhang, D.: o^2-siterec: store site recommendation under the o2o model via multi-graph attention networks. In: 2022 IEEE 38th International Conference on Data Engineering (ICDE), pp. 525–538 (2022). https://doi.org/10.1109/ICDE53745.2022.00044
11. Yao, H., Wu: Deep multi-view spatial-temporal network for taxi demand prediction. In: Proceedings of the AAAI Conference on Artificial Intelligence, vol. 32 (2018)
12. Zhou, H., Zhang, S., Peng, J.: Informer: beyond efficient transformer for long sequence time-series forecasting. In: Proceedings of AAAI (2021)

Dynamics Modeling of Knowledge Dissemination Process in Online Social Networks

Yumeng Hao, Xiaoming Wang$^{(\boxtimes)}$, Yaguang Lin, and Chengxin Zhang

Shaanxi Normal University, Xi'an 710119, China
wangxm@snnu.edu.cn

Abstract. In the process of individuals acquiring and sharing knowledge in online social networks, the difference of knowledge internalization ability, the lack of trust and incentive mechanism hinder the effective dissemination and prediction of knowledge. Therefore, it is significant to find effective ways to predict and promote knowledge dissemination in online social networks. In this paper, we establish a novel dynamics model, which considers the complex psychological cognition and behavior of individuals, and adds two new states to describe the dynamic process of knowledge dissemination more accurately compared with the classical infectious disease model. Besides, we investigate the trend of knowledge dissemination and the stability of the proposed model. Our theoretical analysis shows the proposed model can effectively judge and predict the trend of knowledge dissemination through a threshold, and simulation experiments verify the proposed knowledge dissemination dynamics model is reasonable, and it can effectively promote knowledge dissemination.

Keywords: Online social networks · Knowledge dissemination · Dynamics modeling · Stability analysis

1 Introduction

Knowledge plays an inestimable role in the fields of economy, politics and culture. And the progress of society and human civilization are inseparable from knowledge dissemination [1]. Only through dissemination can we maximize the value of knowledge [2]. Besides, with the development of information technology, online social networks have become an indispensable way to obtain information, express emotions and communicate with each other [3–7], and have become an important platform for knowledge dissemination [8, 9]. Therefore, it is significant to find effective ways to predict and promote knowledge dissemination in online social networks.

Previously, Liu et al. [10] proposed ILSFI model on scale-free networks considering the heterogeneity of interest, benefit and social networks. Wang et al. [11] established a VEA model considering the correlation between the ratio of recipients to receive knowledge in the process of knowledge dissemination and whether they had the knowledge before. Liao et al. [12] put forward RHS model considering the internalization mechanism of knowledge dissemination process in complex networks.

However, most of these knowledge dissemination models considered the psychology of individuals in specific situations, or studied knowledge dissemination for a certain scene. They ignored the redivision of individual states in knowledge dissemination and the universality of model application. Moreover, when individuals receive knowledge, they often experience confusion, thinking, hesitation, etc., and they may receive knowledge but do not master it. Similarly, they will consider whether to share knowledge according to the relationship with the recipient and their own interests. Therefore, if a model can take into account the above new traits of knowledge dissemination, it can accurately and effectively describe the dynamic process of knowledge dissemination.

To sum up, the main contributions of this paper are summarized as follows: 1) We propose a novel dynamics model called UBGSLF based on the individual's psychological cognition and behavior in the process of knowledge dissemination. It can accurately describe the dynamic process of knowledge dissemination in online social networks. 2) We theoretically derive the boundary conditions for the existence or extinction of knowledge, and analyze the stability and trend of UBGSLF model in knowledge dissemination. 3) We carry out simulation experiments based on the theoretical derivation results of UBGSLF model. The results show that the UBGSLF model proposed in this paper can effectively predict the dynamic process of knowledge dissemination.

The rest chapters of this paper are organized as follows. In section two, we establish a novel dynamics model to describe the dynamic process of knowledge dissemination in online social networks. In section three, we mainly analyze and prove the stability of the proposed model. In section four, we conduct simulation experiments, evaluate the proposed model by adjusting parameters, and give the corresponding strategies according to the evaluation results. In section five, we conclude this paper.

2   System Model

According to individual's psychological cognition and behavior in the process of knowledge dissemination, when individuals acquire knowledge, there are two situations after thinking: 1) Individuals are in a state of half knowledge. 2) Individuals internalize knowledge. In addition, considering the trust and interests among individuals, there will be two situations: willing and unwilling to share knowledge. Besides, according to the research of Ebbinghaus, the brain of an individual has the law of forgetting things, so there exists a situation of forgetting knowledge.

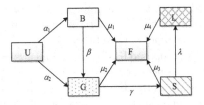

Fig.1. UBGSLF knowledge dissemination model.

Based on the above, we assume that there are N nodes in the network region, and each node can interact and communicate with each other. When knowledge disseminates in the network region, nodes can be divided into the following six states, and the details of the states are shown in Table 1. Among them, state L is elected from state S, and it has more reliable knowledge, stronger willingness to share, and is willing to unconditionally help other individuals. The node states transition relationships of the proposed UBGSLF model are shown in Fig. 1.

Table 1. Classification of node states

Node state	Whether learned knowledge	Whether mastered knowledge	Whether shared knowledge	Whether shared knowledge unconditionally	Whether forgot knowledge
U	No	No	No	No	Uncertainty
B	Yes	No	No	No	No
G	Yes	Yes	No	No	No
S	Yes	Yes	Yes	No	No
L	Yes	Yes	Yes	Yes	No
F	No	No	No	No	Yes

Each node in the network region belongs to one of the six states defined at any time, and they can be transformed over time. We define the transition relationship of node states in knowledge dissemination as shown in Table 2.

In this paper, we use $p(k)$ to represent the degree distribution under the heterogeneous network framework, where the degree k of each individual represents the number of neighbors that each individual can contact. In addition, we use $U_k(t)$, $B_k(t)$, $G_k(t)$, $S_k(t)$, $L_k(t)$, $F_k(t)$ to represent the number of nodes in states U, B, G, S, L, F at any time t. According to the transition relationship of node states proposed above, we establish the system dynamics equation, which is as follows:

$$\begin{cases} \frac{dU_k(t)}{dt} = -\alpha_1 U_k(t)(\Theta_{S_k} + \Theta_{L_k}) - \alpha_2 U_k(t)(\Theta_{S_k} + \Theta_{L_k}) \\ \frac{dB_k(t)}{dt} = \alpha_1 U_k(t)(\Theta_{S_k} + \Theta_{L_k}) - \beta B_k(t)(\Theta_{S_k} + \Theta_{L_k}) - \mu_1 B_k(t) \\ \frac{dG_k(t)}{dt} = \alpha_2 U_k(t)(\Theta_{S_k} + \Theta_{L_k}) + \beta B_k(t)(\Theta_{S_k} + \Theta_{L_k}) - \gamma G_k(t) - \mu_2 G_k(t) \\ \frac{dS_k(t)}{dt} = \gamma G_k(t) - \lambda S_k(t) - \mu_3 S_k(t) \\ \frac{dL_k(t)}{dt} = \lambda S_k(t) - \mu_4 L_k(t) \\ \frac{dF_k(t)}{dt} = \mu_1 B_k(t) + \mu_2 G_k(t) + \mu_3 S_k(t) + \mu_4 L_k(t) \end{cases} \quad (1)$$

where

$$\Theta(S_k(t)) = \langle k \rangle^{-1} \sum_{k=1}^{n} kp(k)S_k(t), k = 1, 2, ...n, \Theta(L_k(t)) = \langle k \rangle^{-1} \sum_{k=1}^{n} kp(k)L_k(t), k = $$

$1, 2, ...n$. $\langle k \rangle := \sum_{k=1}^{n} kp(k)$ represents the average degree of the network, $\Theta(S_k(t))$ and $\Theta(L_k(t))$ represent the probability of the selected node contacting the nodes in state S and

L respectively. It can be abbreviated as Θ_{Sk} and Θ_{Lk}. System (1) constitutes a nonlinear UBGSLF system d-ynamics model, which satisfies the initial value conditions:

$$U_k(0) \geq 0, B_k(0) \geq 0, G_k(0) \geq 0, S_k(0) \geq 0, L_k(0) \geq 0, \Theta(S_k(0)) + \Theta(L_k(0)) > 0, \Theta_{L_k} > \Theta_{S_k} \quad (2)$$

Table 2. Transition relationship of node states

Parameter	Definition
α_1	The probability of U tranferring to B and need to continue learning
α_2	The probability of U turning to G
β	The probability of B transferring to G after learning again
γ	The probability of G turning to S when G have ideas to share knowledge
λ	The probability that S are elected and tranfer to L
$\mu_1, \mu_2, \mu_3, \mu_4$	The probability that B, G, S, L forget their existing knowledge and turn to F, respectively

3 Theoretical Analysis

First we calculate basic regeneration number R_0 by using next generation matrix [13]. In order to simplify the calculation, we express $(<k>^{-1}\alpha_1 jp(j))_{ij}$, $(<k>^{-1}\alpha_2 jp(j))_{ij}$, $(<k>^{-1}\beta jp(j))_{ij}$, $(-<k>^{-1}\beta jp(j))_{ij}$ with α_1, α_2, β_1, $-\beta_1$ respectively. And R_0 is defined as follows:

$$R_0 = \frac{\alpha_2 \gamma C_2}{\beta_1 M} + \frac{(\alpha_1 + \alpha_2)(A_3 + A_4)}{M} \quad (3)$$

where $M, A_1, A_2, B_1, B_2, B_3, B_4, C_1, C_2, C_3, C_4, D_1, D_2, D_3, D_4$ are defined as follows:

$M = \beta\mu_2\mu_3\mu_4 - \beta_1\mu_1\mu_4\gamma + \beta\mu_3\mu_4\gamma + \lambda\mu_1\mu_2\mu_4 + \lambda\mu_1\mu_4\gamma + \mu_1\mu_2\mu_3\mu_4 + \mu_1\mu_3\mu_4\gamma + \beta\lambda\mu_2\mu_4 - \beta_1\lambda\mu_1\gamma + \beta\lambda\mu_4\gamma,$

$A_1 = \lambda\mu_2\mu_4 - \beta_1\mu_4\gamma - \beta_1\lambda\gamma + \lambda\mu_4\gamma + \mu_2\mu_3\mu_4 + \mu_3\mu_4\gamma, A_2 = \beta\lambda\mu_4 + \beta\mu_3\mu_4, A_3 = \beta\mu_4\gamma, A_4 = \beta\lambda\gamma, B_1 = -\gamma(\beta_1\lambda + \beta_1\mu_4),$

$B_2 = \beta\lambda\mu_4 + \beta\mu_3\mu_4 + \lambda\mu_1\mu_4 + \mu_1\mu_3\mu_4, B_3 = \mu_4\gamma(\beta + \mu_1), B_4 = \lambda\gamma(\beta + \mu_1), C_1 = -(\beta_1\lambda\mu_2 + \beta_1\lambda\gamma + \beta_1\mu_2\mu_4 + \beta_1\mu_4\gamma),$

$C_2 = \beta_1\lambda\mu_1 + \beta_1\mu_1\mu_4, C_3 = \mu_4(\beta + \mu_1)(\mu_2 + \gamma), C_4 = \lambda(\beta + \mu_1)(\mu_2 + \gamma), D_1 = -(\beta_1\lambda\mu_2 + \beta_1\lambda\gamma + \beta_1\mu_2\mu_3 + \beta_1\mu_3\gamma),$

$D_2 = \beta_1\lambda\mu_1 + \beta_1\mu_1\mu_3, D_3 = \beta_1\mu_1\gamma, D_4 = \beta_1\lambda\mu_2 + \beta\lambda\gamma + \beta\mu_2\mu_3 - \beta_1\mu_1\gamma + \beta\mu_3\gamma + \lambda\mu_1\mu_2 + \lambda\mu_1\gamma + \mu_1\mu_2\mu_3 + \mu_1\mu_3\gamma.$

Then we analyze and determine the stability of system (1). We can easily get knowledge-free equilibrium point $E^0 = (0, B_1{}^0,...,B_n{}^0, G_1{}^0,...,G_n{}^0, S_1{}^0,...,S_n{}^0, L_1{}^0,...,L_n{}^0), B_k{}^0 = 0, G_k{}^0 = 0, S_k{}^0 = 0, L_k{}^0 = 0$. And we get the following two theorems.

Theorem 1. *If $R_0 < 1$, knowledge-free equilibrium point E^0 is locally and globally asymptotically stable, and is unstable if $R_0 > 1$.*

Theorem 2. *If $R_0 > 1$, knowledge-bound equilibrium point E^* is globally asymptotically stable.*

Proof. We can obtain knowledge-bound equilibrium point $E^* = (U_1{}^*,...,U_n{}^*, B_1{}^*,...B_n{}^*, G_1{}^*,..., G_n{}^*, S_1{}^*,...,S_n{}^*, L_1{}^*,...L_n{}^*, F_1{}^*,...,F_n{}^*)$, $B_k{}^* > 0$, $G_k{}^* > 0$, $S_k{}^* > 0$, $L_k{}^* > 0$. Then we construct a Lyapunov function as follows: $V = V_U + V_B + V_G + V_S + V_L$.

$$V_U = \sum_{k=1}^{n} a(k) \int_{U_k^*}^{U_k} \frac{\xi - U_k^*}{\xi} d\xi, \ V_B = \sum_{k=1}^{n} a(k) \int_{B_k^*}^{B_k} \frac{\xi - B_k^*}{\xi} d\xi, \ V_G = \sum_{k=1}^{n} a(k) \int_{G_k^*}^{G_k} \frac{\xi - G_k^*}{\xi} d\xi,$$

$$V_S = \sum_{k=1}^{n} a(k) \int_{S_k^*}^{S_k} \frac{\xi - S_k^*}{\xi} d\xi, \ V_L = \sum_{k=1}^{n} a(k) \int_{L_k^*}^{L_k} \frac{\xi - L_k^*}{\xi} d\xi$$

where $a(k)$ is a positive constant. Then the sum of their derivatives V' are as follows:

$$V' = V_U' + V_B' + V_G' + V_S' + V_L' = \sum_{k=1}^{n} a(k)\alpha_1 U_k^*(S_j^* + L_j^*)\langle k\rangle^{-1} \sum_{j=1}^{n} jp(j)V_1 + \sum_{k=1}^{n} a(k)\alpha_2 U_k^*(S_j^* + L_j^*)\langle k\rangle^{-1} \sum_{j=1}^{n} jp(j)V_2$$

$$+ \sum_{k=1}^{n} a(k)\beta B_k^*(S_j^* + L_j^*)\langle k\rangle^{-1} \sum_{j=1}^{n} jp(j)V_3 + \sum_{k=1}^{n} a(k)\gamma G_k^* V_4 + \sum_{k=1}^{n} a(k)\lambda S_k^* V_5$$

We set function $\Gamma(x) = x - 1 - \ln x$, and can easily conclude that $\Gamma(x) \geq \Gamma(1) = 0$ is always true when $x > 0$. Therefore, we can determine the value range of V_1, V_2, V_3, V_4, V_5.

$$V_1 = 2 - \frac{U_k^*}{U_k} + \frac{S_j + L_j}{S_j^* + L_j^*} - \frac{B_k}{B_k^*} - \frac{U_k(S_j + L_j)}{U_k^*(S_j^* + L_j^*)} \cdot \frac{B_k^*}{B_k} \leq \frac{S_j + L_j}{S_j^* + L_j^*} - \frac{B_k}{B_k^*} - \ln \frac{S_j + L_j}{S_j^* + L_j^*} + \ln \frac{B_k}{B_k^*} = W_1,$$

$$V_2 = 2 - \frac{U_k^*}{U_k} + \frac{S_j + L_j}{S_j^* + L_j^*} - \frac{G_k}{G_k^*} - \frac{U_k(S_j + L_j)}{U_k^*(S_j^* + L_j^*)} \cdot \frac{G_k^*}{G_k} \leq \frac{S_j + L_j}{S_j^* + L_j^*} - \frac{G_k}{G_k^*} - \ln \frac{S_j + L_j}{S_j^* + L_j^*} + \ln \frac{G_k}{G_k^*} = W_2,$$

$$V_3 = \frac{B_k(S_j + L_j)}{B_k^*(S_j^* + L_j^*)} - \frac{B_k(S_j + L_j)}{B_k^*(S_j^* + L_j^*)} \cdot \frac{G_k^*}{G_k} - \frac{G_k}{G_k^*} + 1 \leq -\frac{G_k}{G_k^*} - \ln \frac{S_j + L_j}{S_j^* + L_j^*} + \ln \frac{G_k}{G_k^* - G_k} = W_3,$$

$$V_4 = \frac{G_k}{G_k^*} - \frac{S_k}{S_k^*} - \frac{S_k^*}{S_k} \cdot \frac{G_k}{G_k^*} + 1 \leq \frac{G_k}{G_k^*} - \frac{S_k}{S_k^*} - \ln \frac{S_k}{S_k^*} + \ln \frac{G_k}{G_k^*} = W_4, \ V_5 = \frac{S_k}{S_k^*} - \frac{L_k}{L_k^*} - \frac{L_k^*}{L_k} \cdot \frac{S_k}{S_k^*} + 1 \leq \frac{S_k}{S_k^*} - \frac{L_k}{L_k^*} - \ln \frac{L_k}{L_k^*} + \ln \frac{S_k}{S_k^*} = W_5$$

Then we can obtain $V' \leq W$, where the definition of W is as follows:

$$W = \sum_{k=1}^{n} a(k)\alpha_1 U_k^*(S_j^* + L_j^*)\langle k\rangle^{-1} \sum_{j=1}^{n} jp(j)W_1 + \ln \frac{B_k}{B_k^*} + \sum_{k=1}^{n} a(k)\alpha_2 U_k^*(S_j^* + L_j^*)\langle k\rangle^{-1} \sum_{j=1}^{n} jp(j)W_2 + \sum_{k=1}^{n} a(k)$$

$$\beta B_k^*(S_j^* + L_j^*)\langle k\rangle^{-1} \sum_{j=1}^{n} jp(j)W_3 + \sum_{k=1}^{n} a(k)\gamma G_k^* W_4 + \sum_{k=1}^{n} a(k)\lambda S_k^* W_5$$

According to the characteristics of $\Gamma(x)$ and the formula shown above, we can get the following equation:

$$\frac{S_k^*}{S_k} = \frac{L_k^*}{L_k} = \frac{U_k(S_j + L_j)}{U_k^*(S_j^* + L_j^*)} \cdot \frac{G_k^*}{G_k} = \frac{U_k(S_j + L_j)}{U_k^*(S_j^* + L_j^*)} \cdot \frac{B_k^*}{B_k} = \frac{B_k(S_j + L_j)}{B_k^*(S_j^* + L_j^*)}(\frac{G_k^*}{G_k} - 1) = 1 \tag{4}$$

Next, we need to choose an appropriate value of $a(k)$ to make $W = 0$. We define a weight matrix $G = (m_{kj})_{(n+1) \times (n+1)}$ as follows:

$$m_{kj} = \begin{cases} \alpha_1 U_k^*(S_j^* + L_j^*)\langle k \rangle^{-1} j p(j), 1 \leq k, j \leq n \\ \alpha_2 U_k^*(S_j^* + L_j^*)\langle k \rangle^{-1} j p(j), 1 \leq k \leq n, j = n+j, 1 \leq i \leq n \\ \beta B_k^*(S_j^* + L_j^*)\langle k \rangle^{-1} j p(j), 1 \leq k \leq n, j = n+p, 1 \leq p \leq n \\ \gamma G_k^*, k = n+q, 1 \leq q \leq n \\ \lambda S_k^*, k = n+j, 1 \leq j \leq n \\ 0, \text{otherwise} \end{cases} \quad (5)$$

We can easily know that G is irreducible. Then we consider a Laplacian matrix $L(G)$ with c_k as the algebraic cofactor of $L(G)$, where $c_k > 0$, $1 \leq k \leq n$. We define $c_k = a(k)$, then we obtain $W = \sum_{k=1}^{2n} \sum_{j=1}^{2n} c_k m_{kj} \varphi_{kj}$, and the definition of φ_{kj} is as follows:

$$\varphi_{kj} = \begin{cases} W_1, 1 \leq k, j \leq n \\ W_2, 1 \leq k \leq n, j = n+j, 1 \leq i \leq n \\ W_3, 1 \leq k \leq n, j = n+p, 1 \leq p \leq n \\ W_4, k = n+q, 1 \leq q \leq n \\ W_5, k = n+j, 1 \leq j \leq n \end{cases} \quad (6)$$

Referring to [14], we can get $\sum_{k=1}^{2n} \sum_{j=1}^{2n} c_k m_{kj} \varphi_{kj} = \sum_{k=1}^{2n} \sum_{j=1}^{2n} c_k m_{kj} \varphi_{jk}$, and $W = \sum_{k=1}^{2n} \sum_{j=1}^{2n} c_k m_{kj} \varphi_{kj} = 0$. Then through formula (4), we can get $\frac{U_k^*}{U_k} = \frac{B_k^*}{B_k} = \frac{G_k^*}{G_k} = \frac{S_k^*}{S_k} = \frac{L_k^*}{L_k} = 1$. Finally, according to LaSalle invariance theorem, we prove the global asymptotic stability of E^*.

To sum up, we clearly draw a conclusion: when $R_0 < 1$, knowledge dissemination will die out; when $R_0 > 1$, knowledge dissemination will be active.

4   Numerical Simulations

Refer to [15], in this experiment, we set the network as $p(k) = 2m^2 k^{-3}$. Among them, the minimum degree is defined as $m = 3$ and the network size is defined as $N = 1000$.

Table 3. Parameter setting of model

	α_1	α_2	β	γ	λ	μ_1	μ_2	μ_3	μ_4
(a)	0.01	0.02	0.11	0.15	0.11	0.07	0.06	0.05	0.04
(b)	0.0008	0.0008	0.0008	0.04	0.04	0.07	0.06	0.05	0.04

We simulate the process of knowledge dissemination in the case of $R_0 > 1$ and $R_0 < 1$. The reasonable node states transition probability and parameter values we set are shown in Table 3, and the simulation results are shown in Fig. 2. Besides, in the case of setting interference, we set five different initial state values for simulation in the dynamic process of knowledge dissemination, as shown in Fig. 3.

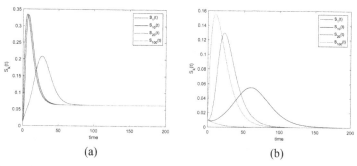

(a)   (b)

Fig. 2. Dynamic evolution of the proportions of individuals in case of (a) $R_0>1$ and (b) $R_0<1$.

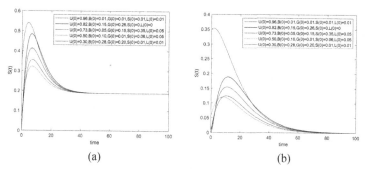

(a)   (b)

Fig. 3. Dynamic evolution of the proportions of individuals under different initial values in case of (a) $R_0>1$ and (b) $R_0<1$.

As can be seen from Fig. 2 and Fig. 3, knowledge dissemination in each state node is closely related to R_0, which is consistent with the theoretical analysis conclusion of the dynamics model we propose. When $R_0 > 1$, knowledge begins to show a trend of growth and dissemination, gradually decreases after the peak, and finally tends to stabilize. At this point, knowledge will continue to disseminate. When $R_0 < 1$, knowledge gradually decreases after rapid increase, there are only nodes without knowledge in the system finally, and knowledge is no longer disseminated.

On the basis that knowledge can be continuously disseminated (i.e. $R_0 > 1$), we simulate the dynamic dissemination of knowledge under different parameter settings of the model, as shown in Fig. 4. The default parameter setting is as follows: $\alpha_1 = 0.01$, $\alpha_2 = 0.02$, $\beta = 0.11$, $\gamma = 0.15$, $\lambda = 0.02$, $\mu_1 = 0.07$, $\mu_2 = 0.06$, $\mu_3 = 0.05$, $\mu_4 = 0.01$. We keep the values of other parameters unchanged, and observe the influence of α_1 when $\alpha_1 \in \{0.01, 0.05, 0.08\}$. Similarly, we observe the influence of α_2, β, γ when $\alpha_2 \in \{0.02, 0.06, 0.09\}$, $\beta \in \{0.11, 0.26, 0.30\}$, $\gamma \in \{0.15, 0.28, 0.40\}$ respectively.

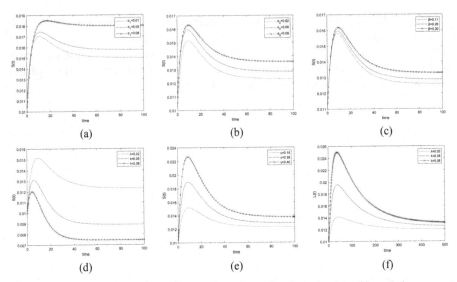

Fig. 4. The influence of parameters in the dynamic dissemination of knowledge

From Fig. 4, we can conclude that parameters α_1, α_2, β, γ, λ can promote the dissemination of knowledge. Therefore, in order to strengthen knowledge dissemination, we should take measures to increase the contact probability among individuals, set up incentive mechanism to enhance individuals' willingness to share knowledge, and increase the selection rate of nodes L.

5   Conclusion

This paper mainly studies how to establish an appropriate knowledge dissemination dynamics model, so as to effectively simulate and predict the dynamic process of knowledge dissemination. Firstly, we propose a novel UBGSLF knowledge dissemination dynamics model. On this basis, we derive and prove the stability of the model. Finally, we verify the accuracy of the derived results and the effectiveness of the model through simulation experiments, and give the corresponding strategies to promote knowledge dissemination. This paper provides theoretical basis and feasible methods for the prediction and application of knowledge dissemination in online social networks. Besides, the proposed model can also be applied to many real scenes. In the future work, we will further study the dynamics model, influencing factors, strategies to promote the efficient dissemination of knowledge.

References

1. Yang, C., Fu, L., Gan, X.: Evolving knowledge graph-based knowledge diffusion model. In: 2021 IEEE Wieless Communications and Networking Conference. IEEE, Nanjing, China (2021)
2. Wang, Y., Cai, Z., Zhan, Z., et al.: An optimization and auction-based incentive mechanism to maximize social welfare for mobile crowdsourcing. IEEE Trans. Comput. Soc. Syst. **6**(3), 414–429 (2019)
3. Banez, R., Gao, H., Li, L., et al.: Modeling and Analysis of opinion dynamics in social networks using mutiple-population mean field games. IEEE Trans. Signal Inf. Process. Netw. **8**, 301–316 (2022)
4. Kar, P., et al.: Are fake images bothering you on social network? Let us detect them using recurrent neural network. IEEE Trans. Comput. Soc. Syst. Early access, 1–12 (2022)
5. Wang, X., Wang, X., Min, G., et al.: An efficient feedback control mechanism for positive/negative information spread in online social networks. IEEE Trans. Cybern. **52**(1), 87–100 (2022)
6. Jagadishwari, V.: Talkative Friend algorithm for inferring ties in social networks. 2021 Third International Conference on Intelligent Communication Technologies and Virtual Mobile Networks, pp. 181–184 (2021)
7. Qiu, T., Chen, B., Arun, K., et al.: A survey of mobile social networks: applications, social characteristics, and challenges. IEEE Syst. J. **12**(4), 414–429 (2018)
8. Cai, Z., He, Z., Guan, X., et al.: collective data-sanitization for preventing sensitive information inference attacks in social networks. IEEE Trans. Depend. Sec. Comput. **15**(4), 577–590 (2018)
9. Lin, Y., Wang, X., Ma, H., et al.: An efficient approach to sharing edge knowledge in 5G-enabled industrial Internet of Things. IEEE Trans. Industr. Inf. (2022). https://doi.org/10.1109/TII.2022.3170470
10. Liu, W., et al.: Global dynamics of knowledge global dynamics of knowledge transmission model on scale-free networks. In: 2019 Chinese Control Conference. IEEE, Guangzhou, China (2019)
11. Wang, H., Wang, J., Small, M.: Knowledge transmission model with differing initial transmission and retransmission process. Phys. A **507**, 478–488 (2018)
12. Liao, S., Yi, S.: Modeling and analysis knowledge transmission process in complex networks by considering internalization mechanism. Chaos Soliton Fract. **143**, 110593 (2021)
13. Wang, Y., Cao, J.: Global dynamics of a network epidemic model for waterborne diseases spread. Appl. Math. Comput. **237**, 474–488 (2014)
14. Li, M., Shuai, Z.: Global-stability problem for coupled systems of differential equations on networks. J. Diff. Equ. **248**(1), 1–20 (2010)
15. Wang, H., Wang, J., Ding, L., et al.: Knowledge transmission model with consideration of self-learning mechanism in complex networks. Appl. Math. Comput. **304**, 83–92 (2017)

The Impact of Time Delay and User's Behavior on the Dissemination Process of Rumor in Mobile Social Networks

Chengxin Zhang, Xiaoming Wang$^{(\boxtimes)}$, Yaguang Lin, and Yumeng Hao

Shaanxi Normal University, Xi'an 710119, Shaanxi, China
wangxm@snnu.edu.cn

Abstract. Mobile social networks facilitate people's communication and exchange. However, the dissemination of rumor in mobile social networks is not conducive to building a harmonious network environment. Studying the dissemination mechanism of rumor in mobile social networks can reduce the harm caused by rumor to the network environment. Hence, we propose a new model of rumor dissemination in mobile social networks considering the difference of user's reaction when receiving information and the difference of user's behavior when processing information. Then, we make a stability analysis of the model. Finally, we conduct simulation experiments on the dissemination process of rumor in mobile social networks. The simulation results show that our proposed rumor dissemination model can effectively predict the dissemination trend of rumor in mobile social networks. Therefore, our work will contribute to the study of the dissemination mechanism of rumor in mobile social networks.

Keywords: Mobile social networks · Dissemination of rumor · User's behavior · Time delay · Stability analysis

1 Introduction

With the progress of science and technology, mobile social networks [1,2] have developed vigorously. Mobile social networks make communication between people more convenient. Users can perform actions such as forwarding and commenting on the opinions expressed by other users in mobile social networks.

However, the spread of rumors in mobile social networks present a massive social threat [3]. Internet rumors have become new challenges for Internet governance [4]. Therefore, in order to suppress the dissemination of rumor in mobile social networks, we need to explore the dissemination mechanism of rumor.

In recent years, the dissemination of information in social networks has become a hot topic for scholars [5–9]. Since the process of information dissemination in mobile social networks is similar to the process of infectious diseases

This work was supported by the National Natural Science Foundation of China (Grant Nos. 61872228, 62102240), the China Postdoctoral Science Foundation (Grant No. 2020M683421).

spreading among people, many scholars use epidemic models [10–13] to simulate the dissemination of information in mobile social networks. He et al. proposed a heterogeneous-network-based epidemic model to describe rumor spreading in mobile social networks [3]. Their work helped to explore the mechanism by which rumor disseminate. Liu et al. developed a dynamic system to model rumor spreading dynamics by the compartment method [14]. Their work considered user's ability to distinguish rumor.

However, there are still some factors that need to be taken into account when rumor disseminate in mobile social networks. Firstly, information delay is a common phenomenon in natural system [15]. Secondly, rumor propagation and behavior spreading are usually closely coupled with each other and the interaction will have great influence on the spreading dynamics [16].

Therefore, we consider the above factors and propose a new TD-SAOMR (Time Delay-Susceptible-Acceptable-Only-Multiple-Recovery) rumor dissemination model to describe the dissemination mechanism of rumor in mobile social networks. Our main contributions are as follows:

1) We propose a new rumor dissemination model, called TD-SAOMR model, which takes into account the time delay and the difference of user's behavior to make it more realistic.

2) We theoretically analyse the stability of the TD-SAOMR model and calculate the equilibrium points.

3) Through simulation experiments, we discuss the impact of the time delay and the difference of user's behavior on the dissemination of rumor in mobile social networks.

The rest of this paper is organized as follows. In the second section, we introduce the construction of the system model. In the third section, we theoretically analyse the stability of the equilibrium points. In the fourth section, we conduct simulation experiments. In the fifth section, we conclude the paper.

2   System Model

In this section, we explain the TD-SAOMR model and define the dissemination mechanism.

We divide user nodes in mobile social networks into the following five states: 1) The susceptible state (S) indicates that the current user node has not received the rumor; 2) The information accepting state (A) indicates that the current user node has received the rumor and is considering whether to deal with the rumor; 3) The state of only one behavior (O) indicates that the current user node only performs a single behavior on the rumor, such as only commenting on the rumor or only forwarding the rumor; 4) The multiple behavior state (M) indicates that the current user node performs a variety of behaviors for the rumor. For example, the user not only comment on the rumor, but also forward it; 5) The information recovery state (R) indicates that the current user node does not believe and not process the rumor for a period of time. We use S(t), A(t), O(t), M(t), and R(t) to represent the proportion of user nodes in the current mobile social network in

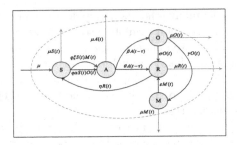

Fig. 1. The state transition diagram of the TD-SAOMR model.

Table 1. The main parameters in TD-SAOMR model and their definitions.

Parameter	Definition
μ	The rate at which user nodes enter and leave the current network
q	The contact probability between user nodes in each state
α	The probability of S transferred to A after contacting O
ξ	The probability of S transferred to A after contacting M
θ	The probability of A transferred to R due to distrust of the rumor
β	The probability of A transferred to O due to belief in the rumor
σ	The probability of O transferred to R due to distrust of the rumor
γ	The probability of O transferred to M due to belief in the rumor
ε	The probability of M transferred to R due to distrust of the rumor
η	The probability of R transferred to S due to forget the rumor

the above five states at time t, respectively. Table 1 shows the key parameters and their definitions in the TD-SAOMR model.

Combined with the actual situation that users have a period of reaction time, we add the information response delay τ. The state transition mechanism between user nodes in the TD-SAOMR model is shown in Fig. 1. According to the state transition mechanism defined above, we can obtain the dynamic differential equations of the TD-SAOMR model:

$$\begin{cases} \frac{dS(t)}{dt} = \mu - q\alpha S(t)O(t) - q\xi S(t)M(t) + \eta R(t) - \mu S(t) \\ \frac{dA(t)}{dt} = q\alpha S(t)O(t) + q\xi S(t)M(t) - (\theta + \beta)A(t - \tau) - \mu A(t) \\ \frac{dO(t)}{dt} = \beta A(t - \tau) - (\sigma + \gamma + \mu)O(t) \\ \frac{dM(t)}{dt} = \gamma O(t) - (\varepsilon + \mu)M(t) \\ \frac{dR(t)}{dt} = \varepsilon M(t) + \sigma O(t) + \theta A(t - \tau) - (\eta + \mu)R(t) \end{cases} \tag{1}$$

3   Stability Analysis

In this chapter, we calculate equilibrium points and perform stability analysis. When $\tau = 0$, we set the value of each differential equation in Eq. (1) to 0, and substitute $R(t) = 1 - S(t) - A(t) - O(t) - M(t)$ into it. Through calculation, we can get $E_0 = (1,0,0,0,0)$ which is called the rumor-free equilibrium point and $E_1 = (St_2, At_2, Ot_2, Mt_2, Rt_2)$ which is called the rumor equilibrium point. in which

$$St_2 = \frac{\beta\mu^2+\varepsilon\mu^2+\gamma\mu^2+\sigma\mu^2+\theta\mu^2+\mu^3+\beta\varepsilon\gamma+\beta\varepsilon\mu+\beta\gamma\mu+\varepsilon\gamma\mu+\beta\varepsilon\sigma+\varepsilon\gamma\theta+\beta\mu\sigma+\varepsilon\mu\sigma+\varepsilon\mu\theta+\gamma\mu\theta}{\beta(\alpha\varepsilon q+\alpha\mu q+\gamma\xi q)}$$
$$+\frac{\varepsilon\sigma\theta+\mu\sigma\theta}{\beta(\alpha\varepsilon q+\alpha\mu q+\gamma\xi q)}, At_2 = \frac{(\sigma+\gamma+\mu)(\varepsilon+\mu)}{\beta\gamma}Mt_2, Ot_2 = \frac{\varepsilon+\mu}{\gamma}Mt_2.$$

Then, we analyse the stability of the rumor equilibrium point E_1, we can get the following Theorem 1.

Theorem 1. *When* $\tau \in (0, \tau_0)$ *, the rumor equilibrium point tends to be locally stable. When* $\tau \geq \tau_0$ *, the rumor equilibrium point starts to lose stability, and Hopf bifurcation occurs.*

Proof. When $\tau \neq 0$, the corresponding eigenmatrix M can be obtained by calculating Eq. (1). Let M = 0, we can get the characteristic equation (2). The expressions of M and Eq. (2) are as follows.

$$M = \begin{bmatrix} \lambda + m_{11} & 0 & m_{13} & m_{14} & m_{15} \\ m_{21} & \lambda + m_2 & m_{23} & m_{24} & 0 \\ 0 & m_{32}e^{-\lambda\tau} & \lambda + m_{33} & 0 & 0 \\ 0 & 0 & m_{43} & \lambda + m_{44} & 0 \\ 0 & m_{52}e^{-\lambda\tau} & m_{53} & m_{54} & \lambda + m_{55} \end{bmatrix},$$

$$\lambda^5 + a_4\lambda^4 + a_3\lambda^3 + a_2\lambda^2 + a_1\lambda + a_0 + (b_4\lambda^4 + b_3\lambda^3 + b_2\lambda^2 + b_1\lambda + b_0)e^{-\lambda\tau} = 0 \tag{2}$$

in which

$m_{00} = \mu, m_{11} = q\alpha Ot_2 + q\xi Mt_2 + \mu, m_{13} = q\alpha St_2, m_{14} = q\xi St_2, m_{15} = -\eta,$
$m_{24} = -q\xi St_2, m_{21} = -q\alpha Ot_2 - q\xi Mt_2, m_{22} = \theta + \beta, m_{23} = -q\alpha St_2,$
$m_{32} = -\beta, m_{33} = \sigma + \gamma + \mu, m_{43} = -\gamma, m_{44} = \varepsilon + \mu, m_{52} = -\theta, m_{53} = -\sigma,$
$m_{54} = -\varepsilon, m_{55} = \eta + \mu, m_2 = m_{22}e^{-\lambda\tau} + m_{00}, a_4 = m_{00} + m_{11} + m_{33} + m_{44}$
$+m_{55}, a_3 = m_{00}m_{11} + m_{00}m_{33} + m_{00}m_{44} + m_{11}m_{33} + m_{00}m_{55} + m_{11}m_{44}$
$+m_{11}m_{55} + m_{33}m_{44} + m_{33}m_{55} + m_{44}m_{55}, a_2 = m_{00}m_{11}m_{33} + m_{00}m_{11}m_{44}$
$+m_{00}m_{11}m_{55} + m_{00}m_{33}m_{44} + m_{00}m_{33}m_{55} + m_{11}m_{33}m_{44} + m_{00}m_{44}m_{55}$
$+m_{11}m_{33}m_{55} + m_{11}m_{44}m_{55} + m_{33}m_{44}m_{55}, a_1 = m_{00}m_{11}m_{33}m_{44}$
$+m_{00}m_{11}m_{33}m_{55} + m_{00}m_{11}m_{44}m_{55} + m_{00}m_{33}m_{44}m_{55} + m_{11}m_{33}m_{44}m_{55},$
$a_0 = m_{00}m_{11}m_{33}m_{44}m_{55}, b_4 = m_{22}, b_3 = m_{11}m_{22} + m_{22}m_{33} - m_{23}m_{32}$
$+m_{22}m_{44} + m_{22}m_{55}, b_2 = m_{11}m_{22}m_{33} - m_{11}m_{23}m_{32} + m_{13}m_{21}m_{32}$
$+m_{11}m_{22}m_{44} + m_{11}m_{22}m_{55} + m_{15}m_{21}m_{52} + m_{22}m_{33}m_{44} - m_{23}m_{32}m_{44}$
$+m_{24}m_{32}m_{43} + m_{22}m_{33}m_{55} - m_{23}m_{32}m_{55} + m_{22}m_{44}m_{55},$
$b_1 = m_{11}m_{22}m_{33}m_{44} - m_{11}m_{23}m_{32}m_{44} + m_{11}m_{24}m_{32}m_{43} + m_{13}m_{21}m_{32}m_{44}$
$-m_{14}m_{21}m_{32}m_{43} + m_{11}m_{22}m_{33}m_{55} - m_{11}m_{23}m_{32}m_{55} + m_{13}m_{21}m_{32}m_{55}$
$-m_{15}m_{21}m_{32}m_{53} + m_{15}m_{21}m_{33}m_{52} + m_{11}m_{22}m_{44}m_{55} + m_{15}m_{21}m_{44}m_{52}$
$+m_{22}m_{33}m_{44}m_{55} - m_{23}m_{32}m_{44}m_{55} + m_{24}m_{32}m_{43}m_{55},$
$b_0 = m_{11}m_{22}m_{33}m_{44}m_{55} - m_{11}m_{23}m_{32}m_{44}m_{55} + m_{11}m_{24}m_{32}m_{43}m_{55}$
$+m_{13}m_{21}m_{32}m_{44}m_{55} - m_{14}m_{21}m_{32}m_{43}m_{55} + m_{15}m_{21}m_{32}m_{43}m_{54}$
$-m_{15}m_{21}m_{32}m_{44}m_{53} + m_{15}m_{21}m_{33}m_{44}m_{52}.$

Proposition 1. *The following conditions exist:*

$$P_1 : a_1 > 0, \begin{vmatrix} a_4 & 1 \\ a_2 & a_3 \end{vmatrix} > 0, \begin{vmatrix} a_4 & 1 & 0 \\ a_2 & a_3 & a_4 \\ a_0 & a_1 & a_2 \end{vmatrix} > 0, \begin{vmatrix} a_4 & 1 & 0 & 0 \\ a_2 & a_3 & a_4 & 1 \\ a_0 & a_1 & a_2 & a_3 \\ 0 & 0 & a_0 & a_1 \end{vmatrix} > 0, \begin{vmatrix} a_4 & 1 & 0 & 0 & 0 \\ a_2 & a_3 & a_4 & 1 & 0 \\ a_0 & a_1 & a_2 & a_3 & a_4 \\ 0 & 0 & a_0 & a_1 & a_2 \\ 0 & 0 & 0 & 0 & a_0 \end{vmatrix} > 0.$$

When P_1 is established, the Routh-Hurwitz criterion [17] can prove that the rumor equilibrium point is locally asymptotically stable.

When $\tau > 0$, let $\lambda = i\omega(\omega > 0)$ be the root of equations (1), and separate the real part and imaginary part of the equation to obtain the following Eq. (3).

$$\begin{cases} (-b_3\omega^3 + b_1\omega)\sin(t\omega) + (b_4\omega^4 - b_2\omega^2 + b_0)\cos(t\omega) = a_2\omega^2 - a_4\omega^4 - a_0 \\ (-b_3\omega^3 + b_1\omega)\cos(t\omega) - (b_4\omega^4 - b_2\omega^2 + b_0)\sin(t\omega) = a_3\omega^3 - \omega^5 - a_1\omega \end{cases} \quad (3)$$

Add the squares on both sides of the equal sign of the two equations of Eq. (3), we can get Eq. (4), as follows:

$$\omega^{10} + A_4\omega^8 + A_3\omega^6 + A_2\omega^4 + A_1\omega^2 + A_0 = 0 \quad (4)$$

in which

$A_4 = -2a_3 + a_4^2 - b_4^2, A_3 = 2a_1 - 2a_2a_4 + a_3^2 + 2b_2b_4 - b_3^2, A_0 = a_0^2 - b_0^2,$
$A_2 = 2a_0a_4 - 2a_1a_3 + a_2^2 - 2b_0b_4 + 2b_1b_3 - b_2^2, A_1 = -2a_0a_2 + a_1^2 + 2b_0b_2 - b_1^2.$

Proposition 2. P_2 :*Eq. (4) has at least one positive real root.*

Equation (5) can be obtained through calculation, as follows:

$$\tau_0 = \frac{1}{\omega_0}\arccos\frac{(b_4\omega_0{}^4 - b_2\omega_0{}^2 + b_0)B_1 + (-b_3\omega^3 + b_1\omega)B_2}{(b_4\omega^4 - b_2\omega^2 + b_0)^2 + (-b_3\omega^3 + b_1\omega)^2} \quad (5)$$

in which

$$B_1 = a_2\omega^2 - a_4\omega^4 - a_0, B_2 = a_3\omega^3 - \omega^5 - a_1\omega.$$

Take the derivative of Eq. (2) of λ with respect to τ, and substitute $\lambda = i\omega(\omega > 0)$ into it, we can get the Eq. (6), as follows:

$$\mathrm{Re}\left(\frac{d\lambda}{d\tau}\right)^{-1}\bigg|_{\tau=\tau_0} = \frac{G_1H_1 + G_2H_2}{H_1{}^2 + H_2{}^2} \quad (6)$$

in which

$G_1 = (5\omega_0^4 - 3a_3\omega_0^2 + a_1)\cos(\omega_0\tau_0) - (-4a_4\omega_0^3 + 2a_2\omega_0)\sin(\omega_0\tau_0) - 3b_3\omega_0^2 + b_1,$
$G_2 = (5\omega_0^4 - 3a_3\omega_0^2 + a_1)\sin(\omega_0\tau_0) + (-4a_4\omega_0^3 + 2a_2\omega_0)\cos(\omega_0\tau_0) - 4a_4\omega_0^3$
$\quad +2b_2\omega_0, H_1 = b_3\omega_0^3 - b_1\omega_0, H_2 = b_4\omega_0^4 - b_2\omega_0{}^2 + b_0.$

Proposition 3. $P_3 : \frac{G_1H_1 + G_2H_2}{H_1{}^2 + H_2{}^2} \neq 0$

According to Hopf bifurcation theory [18] and TD-SAOMR model, we can get that if $P_1 - P_3$ are established at the same time, the rumor equilibrium point tends to be locally stable when $\tau \in (0, \tau_0)$, meanwhile, the rumor equilibrium point starts to lose stability and produce local Hopf bifurcation when $\tau \geq \tau_0$. $\square$

4   Simulation Experiment

In this section, we explore the impact of time delay and user's behavior on the dissemination of rumor in mobile social networks through simulation experiments.

We set the parameters for different scenarios. Scenario 1: $\alpha = 0.1$, $\xi = 0.85$, $\eta = 0.1$, $\theta = 0.1$, $\beta = 0.85$, $\sigma = 0.1$, $\gamma = 0.8$, $\varepsilon = 0.1$, $q = 0.1$, $\mu = 0.05$, $\tau = 0$. At the same time, we set the initial value of the proportion of each state in Scenario 1 as: $S(0) = 0.09$, $A(0) = 0.78$, $O(0) = 0.1$, $M(0) = 0.025$, $R(0) = 0.005$. Scenario 2: $\alpha = 0.65$, $\xi = 0.3$, $\eta = 0.01$, $\theta = 0.001$, $\beta = 0.6$, $\sigma = 0.38$, $\gamma = 0.6$, $\varepsilon = 0.001$, $q = 0.6$, $\mu = 0.1$. According to the calculation, $E_1 = (0.8647, 0.0208, 0.0116, 0.0687, 0.0342)$, the $\tau_0 = 3.4597$. In scenario 2, when τ is 0.6 and 5, respectively, the change trend of the proportion of user nodes in each state is shown in Fig. 2.

The Hopf bifurcation appears in Fig. 2(b). Compared with Fig. 2 (a), the final change trend of the proportion of user nodes in each state in Fig. 2(b) has fluctuated. It shows that in the case of $\tau > \tau_0$, the dissemination of rumor in mobile social networks is unstable.

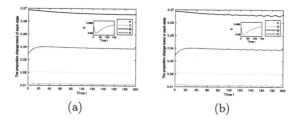

(a)   (b)

Fig. 2. The proportion change trend of user nodes in each state after being fitted by TD-SAOMR model. (a) $\tau = 0.6$. (b) $\tau = 5$.

In scenario 1, we change the size of parameters σ and ε respectively to observe its impact on the proportion of user nodes in R state, as shown in Fig. 3. When $\varepsilon = 0.1$ remains unchanged and σ increases from 0.001 to 0.3, it shows that the proportion of user nodes in R state in Fig. 3(b) has increased obviously compared with Fig. 3(a).

In scenario 2, when $\tau = 0.6$ and $\tau = 5$ respectively, we draw the three-dimensional graphs which are shown in Fig. 4. Comparing (a) and (b) in Fig. 4, it can be seen that when the $\tau < \tau_0$, the proportion of user nodes in state S in (b) decreases greatly. Similarly, Comparing (c) and (d) in Fig. 4, it can be seen that when the $\tau > \tau_0$, the proportion of user nodes in state S in (d) decreases greatly.

In conclusion, in above cases, the proportion of user nodes in the M state has a greater impact on the proportion of user nodes in the S and R states. This shows that the model we proposed is reasonable.

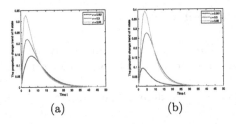

(a)   (b)

Fig. 3. When the value of σ and ε are different, the proportion change trend of user nodes in R state. (a) $\varepsilon = 0.1$, $\sigma = 0.001, 0.3, 0.95$. (b) $\sigma = 0.1$, $\varepsilon = 0.001, 0.3, 0.95$.

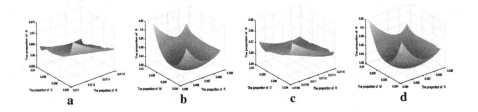

     a   **b**   **c**   **d**

Fig. 4. The impact of user's behavior on user nodes in the R and S states. (a) The interaction between O, R and S states, $\tau = 0.6$. (b) The interaction between M, R and S states, $\tau = 0.6$. (c) The interaction between O, R and S states, $\tau = 5$. (d) The interaction between M, R and S states, $\tau = 5$.

5   Conclusion

This paper proposes a new rumor dissemination model considering the difference of user's behavior and time delay. The experiment shows that the TD-SAOMR model can effectively explore the dissemination mechanism of rumor in mobile social networks. Our work proves that the user's behavior influence the disseminate of rumor in mobile social networks, and the relationship between the real time delay of rumor dissemination and the delay threshold influence the stability of rumor dissemination. In the future, we will consider the impact of different control measures on the dissemination of rumor.

References

1. Safi, S.M., Movaghar, A., Ghorbani, M.: Privacy protection scheme for mobile social network. J. King Saud Univ. Comput. Inf. Sci. **34**(7), 4062–4074 (2022)
2. Tulu, M.M., Mkiramweni, M.E., Hou, R., Feisso, S., Younas, T.: Influential nodes selection to enhance data dissemination in mobile social networks: A survey. J. Netw. Comput. Appl. **169**, 102768 (2020)
3. He, Z., Cai, Z., Yu, J., Wang, X., Sun, Y., li, Y.: Cost-efficient strategies for restraining rumor spreading in mobile social networks. IEEE Trans. Veh. Technol. **66**(3), 2789–2800 (2017)

4. Han, H., Guo, X.: Construction on framework of rumor detection and warning system based on web mining technology. In: 2018 IEEE/ACIS 17th International Conference on Computer and Information Science, pp. 767–771. IEEE, Singapore (2018)
5. Cai, Z., He, Z., Guan, X., li, Y.: Collective data-sanitization for preventing sensitive information inference attacks in social networks. IEEE Trans. Depend. Sec. Comput. 15(4), 577–590 (2018)
6. He, Z., Cai, Z., Yu, J.: Latent-data privacy preserving with customized data utility for social network data. IEEE Trans. Veh. Technol. **67**(1), 665–673 (2018)
7. Zheng, X., Cai, Z., Yu, J., Wang, C., Li, Y.: Follow but no track: privacy preserved profile publishing in cyber-physical social systems. IEEE Internet Things J. **4**(6), 1868–1878 (2017)
8. Wang, Y., Cai, Z., Zhan, Z., Gong, Y., Tong, X.: An optimization and auction-based incentive mechanism to maximize social welfare for mobile crowdsourcing. IEEE Trans. Comput. Soc. Syst. **6**(3), 414–429 (2019)
9. Wang, X., Wang, X., Min, G., Hao, F., Chen, C.L.P.: An efficient feedback control mechanism for positive/negative information spread in online social networks. IEEE Trans. Cybern. **52**(1), 87–100 (2022)
10. Lin, Y., Wang, X., Ma, H., Wang, L., Hao, F., Cai, Z.: An efficient approach to sharing edge knowledge in 5g-enabled industrial Internet of Things. IEEE Trans. Industr. Inf. (2022). https://doi.org/10.1109/TII.2022.3170470
11. Hussein, B.A., Hasson, S.T.: A modeling and simulation approach to analyze and control transition states in epidemic models. In: 2019 2nd International Conference on Engineering Technology and its Applications, pp. 94–98. IEEE, Iraq (2019)
12. Muhamediyeva, D., Baxromova, Y.: Problems of building a mathematical model of epidemic taking into account vaccination. In: 2021 International Conference on Information Science and Communications Technologies, pp. 1–4. IEEE, Uzbekistan (2021)
13. Kapetanović, A.L., Poljak, D.: Modeling the epidemic outbreak and dynamics of COVID-19 in Croatia. In: 2020 5th International Conference on Smart and Sustainable Technologie,, pp. 1–5. IEEE, Croatia (2020)
14. Liu, W., Wu, X., Yang, W., Zhu, X., Zhong, S.: Modeling cyber rumor spreading over mobile social networks: a compartment approach. Appl. Math. Comput. **343**, 214–229 (2019)
15. Zhou, W., Zhong, G., Li, J.: Stability of financial market driven by information delay and liquidity in delay agent-based model. Phys. A **600**, 127526 (2022)
16. Zhang, Y., Su, Y., Li, W., Liu, H.: Interacting model of rumor propagation and behavior spreading in multiplex networks. Chaos, Solit. Fract. **121**, 168–177 (2019)
17. Lin, Y., Wang, X., Hao, F., et al.: Dynamic control of fraud information spreading in mobile social networks. IEEE Trans. Syst. Man Cybern. Syst. **51**(6), 3725–3738 (2021)
18. Wang, S., Cui, Y., Sun, G.: Hopf bifurcation analysis for a generalized Lorenz system with single delay. In: 2020 11th International Conference on Prognostics and System Health Management, pp. 486–489. IEEE, China (2020)

Minimizing the Embedding Cost of Service Function Chains with Adjustable Order

Pengxin Zheng[1], Quan Chen[1(✉)], Feng Wang[2(✉)], Longqu Li[1], and Lianglun Cheng[1]

[1] School of Computers, Guangdong University of Technology, Guangzhou 510006, China
{2112005220,2112005021}@mail2.gdut.edu.cn, {quan.c,llcheng}@gdut.edu.cn
[2] School of Information Engineering, Guangdong University of Technology, Guangzhou 510006, China
fengwang13@gdut.edu.cn

Abstract. Network Function Virtualization (NFV) has becoming an emerging technology for ensuring the reliability and security of data flows. The virtual network function (VNF) embedding problem, which tries to minimize the embedding cost has attracted extensive interests recently. However, the existing works always assume the fixed execution order of VNFs, which limits their application. Thus, we investigate the VNF embedding problem without such limitations in this paper. Firstly, a general transformation framework is proposed for the NFV-enabled unicast routing with adjustable order. Then, an optimal algorithm is proposed for the unicast VNF embedding without delay constraints. Additionally, an efficient algorithm is also proposed for such problem with delay constraints. Finally, we evaluate the proposed algorithms via numerical results, which show that our algorithms significantly outperform the existing benchmarks.

Keywords: Software-defined network · Network function virtualization · Delay-aware unicast routing · Service function chain

1 Introduction

Recently, the Network Function Virtualization (NFV) technology, which can execute network functions on virtual machines, has emerged as a promising technique for ensuring the reliability and security of data flows while reducing the maintenance and deployment cost [1]. For example, the Virtual Network Functions(VNFs), such as network address translation, proxies, firewalls, intrusion detection systems, deep packet inspection, has been embedded on different server nodes to ensure the reliability and security of data flows. On the other hand,

H. Ma et al. (Eds.): CWSN 2022, CCIS 1715, pp. 162–181, 2022.
https://doi.org/10.1007/978-981-19-8350-4_14

unicast and multicast have been an important way of disseminating data in the network [2,3]. As for unicast routing in network traffic engineering, it usually needs to go through a series of designated VNFs, referred as Service Function Chain (SFC), before reaching the destination, which is known as NFV-enabled unicast.

To enabling NFV-enabled unicast services in SDN networks, the following two issues need to be addressed, i.e., the deployment location of VNFs, which is related to the VNF deployment cost, and the routing path of the data traffic, which is related to the link connection cost. Additionally, some NFV-enabled unicast requests often include a predetermined end-to-end delay constraint. To handle above challenges, there have been several works investigated the NFV-enabled unicast orchestration designs to achieve different goals, including lowering the total traffic delivery cost [4], achieving end-to-end delay specifications [5], and maximizing throughput [6], etc. To minimize the total traffic delivery cost, the authors in [4,7–13], have proposed many efficient methods by considering the VNF placement and link bandwidth consumption balance, such as a general transformation framework, a service function chain into a service function tree, a virtual network customization framework that can replicate functions in advance, and other innovations. However, all these existing works assume the SFCs follow a fixed order, which limits their application, especially when some NFV nodes can only instantiate specific VNFs. For example, assuming the SFC required for a unicast request are (f_1, f_2, f_3, f_4), after f_1, the next more adjacent node attached with server can only instantiate f_3 but not f_2, which may increase the link connection cost. Conversely, changing the execution order of f_2 and f_3 may yield a decreased link connection cost.

Figure 1 provides an example for different SFCs embedding with the same VNFs requirement in a target network. As shown in Fig. 1(a), 1) the target network consists of 11 nodes and 19 links, in which the source node is S, the destination node is d_1, and the nodes attached with servers are $\{A, B, C, D, E, F, G, H, I\}$, where the capacity of each node is set to be 1; 2) Adjacent to the server node is the VNF and its deployment cost. Among them, all of the four server nodes $\{E, F, G, I\}$ can instantiate both f_3 and f_4, but different server nodes have different deployment costs; 3) The weight attached to the link is the connection cost. 4) The unicast task is to flow from the source node S to the target node d_1 through the required VNF. Assuming that the unicast SFC demand consists of $\{f_1, f_2, f_3, f_4, f_5\}$, and the traditional SFC is embedded in a fixed order $(f_1 \rightarrow f_2 \rightarrow f_3 \rightarrow f_4 \rightarrow f_5)$, then Fig. 1(b) and Fig. 1(c) give their respective SFC embedding scheme, where the total traffic delivery costs are 62 and 46, respectively. It observed that different VNF execution strategies lead to different total traffic delivery costs. This example will be further explained in detail in Sect. 3.

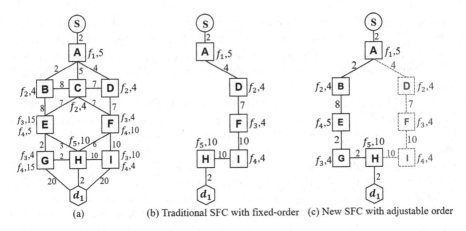

Fig. 1. Different SFC embedding strategies for the same VNF requirements in the target network, where the SFC contains five function demands: $\{f_1, f_2, f_3, f_4, f_5\}$.

In this paper, we investigate the first work for the SFC embedding problem with adjustable order for unicast in SDN. To minimize the total traffic delivery cost, a general transformation framework and several efficient algorithms are proposed. Our contributions are summarized as follows:

i) The SFC embedding problem with adjustable order is formulated, and it is proved to be NP-hard under the delay constraint. A transformation framework is proposed for SFCs embedding with adjustable order.

ii) To minimize the total traffic delivery cost, an optimal algorithm is proposed for unicast routing. When given a delay constraint, an efficient algorithm is also proposed, which has the benefit of deriving a lower bound on the theoretical optimal solution.

iii) We evaluate the proposed algorithms through experimental simulations in both synthetic network and real network. Experimental results show that the proposed algorithms outperform the existing benchmarks.

The rest of the paper is organized as follows. Section 2 reviews the related work. In Sect. 3, we formally define our problem. In Sect. 4, we introduce the construction of a general transformation framework and design efficient algorithms for a single NFV-enabled request with and without the end-to-end delay constraints, respectively. Section 5 presents the performance evaluation of the proposed algorithms. Finally, we draw the conclusion in Sect. 6.

2   Related Work

In recent years, there have been extensive studies on unicast and multicast routing combined with new technologies such as SDN and NFV. Most of the existing works studied the NFV-enabled unicast deployments based on various specific goals, such as minimum total traffic delivery cost [4], delay constraint [5], maximum network throughput [6], or comprehensive of the aforementioned all aspects [14].

To minimize the traffic delivery cost, the NFV-enabled unicast problem is studied by [4,7–10]. Chen and Wu [7] proposed VNFs placement algorithms to minimize the total traffic delivery cost of NFV-enabled unicast request by balancing the costs of VNF placement and link bandwidth consumption. Yu et al. [8] studied the profit maximization associated with placing VNFs into a set of locations, taking into account the delay constraint for each unicast request. Mirjalily et al. [9] study the problem of optimal network function virtualization for providing multicast services with minimum total cost in wireless mesh networks and propose a two-stage heuristic method. Kuo et al. [15] designed a heuristic algorithm for NFV-enabled request routing in SDN networks by considering bandwidth requirements and utilizing dynamic programming strategies. Some studies had considered delay constraint. Jin et al. [16] design a novel two-stage delay-aware VNF deployment scheme and propose three heuristics for effectively solving the problem of deploying VNF chains with latency guarantees and resource efficiency in the network edge. Li et al. [17] considered requests from a single tenant with end-to-end delay constraints and provided a solution with a dynamic strategy. Some comprehensive studies. To minimize the total traffic delivery cost and maximize the throughput of NFV-enabled unicast in SDN networks, Mike et al. [10] proposed a general framework for the delay-bounded unicast. In mobile edge networks, Ren et al. [18] propose an approximation algorithm with a provable approximation ratio for single request admission, and then design an efficient heuristic algorithm for a given set of latency-aware NFV-enabled request admission. Xu et al. [19] considered the delay-aware task offloading designs with network functional requirements in MEC networks, in which they proposed efficient online algorithms with provable competition ratios guarantee. Yue et al. [20] aimed to optimize the throughput of SFC requests (SFCR) and then devised a adjustment algorithm to optimize the mapped SFCRs in MEC-NFV-enabled networks.

Asgarian et al. [21] propose a source-destination-vnf (SDV) graph-based two-stage SDV-based (TSDV) approach to address the problem of embedding multicast service chains onto NFV-enabled underlying networks. With the advent of the 5G era, some people have combined 5G networks and NFV to conduct research. For example, Gharbaoui et al. [22] proposed a service chain orchestration system, which reproduces a typical 5G network deployment with virtualization functions in geographically distributed edge clouds. Kumazaki et al. [23] proposed a dynamic service chain construction based on Model Predictive Control (MPC) to utilize network resources. Pei et al. [24] study the differential routing problem considering SFC (DRP-SFC) in SDN and NFV-enabled networks, and propose a resource-aware routing algorithm (RA-RA) to solve DRP-SFC.

Note that the aforementioned works have not yet consider the adjustable order of VNFs, which may result in the SFCs embedded in a non-optimal order.

Motivated by this, in this paper, we investigate the NFV-enabled unicast problem by considering the SFC with adjustable order.

3   Network Model and Problem Definition

3.1   Network Model

Model of Target Network System: A SDN graph $G = (V, E)$, where V and E are the sets of nodes and links, respectively. The nodes are composed of switch nodes (represented by V_S) and server nodes (represented by set V_M), i.e., $V = V_S \cup V_M$. Switches nodes are capable of forwarding and replicating traffic, and server nodes not only can play the role of switch nodes, but also are capable of hosting and operating VNFs to process traffic. Each node $v \in V_M$ is treated as a switch node without an attached server if its server is not used for implementing VNF functions deployed on VMs. Otherwise, the VNFs implementation cost of node v must be taken into account. Let $cap(v)$ denote the computing capacity of the server node $v \in V_M$, B_e represent the bandwidth capacity of each link $e \in E$, and c_e denote the usage costs of one unit of bandwidth at each edge $e \in E$. When data is transmitted, the traffic delivery cost and transmission delay will be incurred on the link $e \in E$. In G, there is an SDN controller in charge of managing the allocation of resources for each admitted unicast request, and the above propoerties of each switch can be obtained by the controller by the methods as in [25,26]. Figure 2 is an example of a SDN network with VNFs.

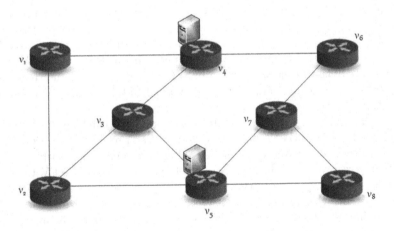

Fig. 2. System Model. An SDN Network G with VNFs, a node set $V_S = \{v_1, v_2, v_3, v_4, v_5, v_6, v_7, v_8\}$ which can transfer the traffic, meanwhile a subset $V_M = \{v_4, v_5\}$ of V that are attached with servers.

Model of VNF Deployment: Consider the VNF providers supplying $m \geq 1$ categories of VNFs in the network G. We define the VNF set $\mathcal{F} = \{f_1', f_2', f_3', ..., f_m'\}$. Furthermore, we let f_0 denote the dummy VNF instantiated on the source node s_k. Any VNF will incur a deployment cost when deployed on a server node. For simplicity, we assume that each VNF instance can serve traffic flows of any size.

Model of Unicast Task: In a given SDN network G, the NFV-enabled unicast request r_k is represented by a five-element tuple $r_k = (s_k, t_k, b_k, SC_k, P_{loc})$, which implies transferring the data traffic from a source node s_k to a destination node t_k through the SFC with adjustable order $SC_k = (f_1, f_2, f_3, ..., f_l)$, where $SC_k \in \mathcal{F}$ and $l \leq m$. In addition, b_k represents the given bandwidth resource required, which can be derived from historical information, and P_{loc} indicates the starting position of each adjustable order part in the SC_k.

3.2   NFV-Enabled Unicasting Problem

In an SDN network, network service providers need to flow traffic through a series of VNFs to ensure services are provided to users. Accordingly, the total traffic delivery cost includes the computing resource consumption cost of the server nodes and the link bandwidth resource usage cost.

Definition 1 (The Resource-constraint NFV-enabled Unicasting Problem). *For a unicast task $r_k = (s_k, t_k, b_k, SC_k, p_{loc})$, under the condition that the computational resources of each sever node $v \in V_M$ and the bandwidth resources of each link $e \in E$ in G are constrained, the resource-constraint NFV-enabled unicasting problem is to find the routing path such that i) the unicast request is satisfied and ii) the total traffic delivery cost, in terms of computing and bandwidth resource consumption, is minimized.*

Definition 2 (The Delay-aware NFV-enabled Unicasting Problem). *Based on Definition 1, the delay-aware NFV-enabled unicasting problem in an SDN $G = (V, E)$ for an NFV-enabled request $r_k = (s_k, t_k, b_k, SC_k, p_{loc})$ is to find a routing path for r_k, such that its total traffic delivery cost is minimized while the end-to-end delay of the path is no greater than a given end-to-end delay constraint D_k.*

As shown in Sect. 1, Fig. 1(a) depicts a network model. For simplicity, the switch nodes between NFV nodes are removed. In Fig. 1, the source node is S, the destination node is d_1, and the SFC required by the unicast task is $(f_1, f_2, f_3, f_4, f_5)$ with adjustable order between f_3 and f_4, where we refer to $\{f_3, f_4\}$ as the **adjustable order part** (AOP) and the rest of the SFC as the **fixed-order part** (FOP). For this particular unicast request, Fig. 3 provides 4 different solutions. In Fig. 3(a), we have deployed f_1, f_2, f_3, f_4 and f_5 on A, B, E, G, H, respectively, and the total traffic delivery cost is 67. Another solution for the SFC deployment order of $(f_1 \rightarrow f_2 \rightarrow f_3 \rightarrow f_4 \rightarrow f_5)$ is shown in Fig. 3(b) with the cost 62. In the same way, there are also two routing schemes for the sequence SFC such as $(f_1 \rightarrow f_2 \rightarrow f_4 \rightarrow f_3 \rightarrow f_5)$. The routing paths respectively are $(S \rightarrow A_{f_1} \rightarrow B_{f_2} \rightarrow E_{f_4} \rightarrow G_{f_3} \rightarrow H_{f_5} \rightarrow d_1)$ with the total traffic delivery cost 46 and $(S \rightarrow A_{f_1} \rightarrow D_{f_2} \rightarrow F_{f_4} \rightarrow I_{f_3} \rightarrow H_{f_5} \rightarrow d_1)$ with the total traffic delivery cost 74. For the SFC composed of $\{f_1, f_2, f_3, f_4, f_5\}$, the total traffic delivery cost of the request can be greatly reduced by exchanging the execution order of the VNFs with adjustable order. For example, the best scheme with execution order

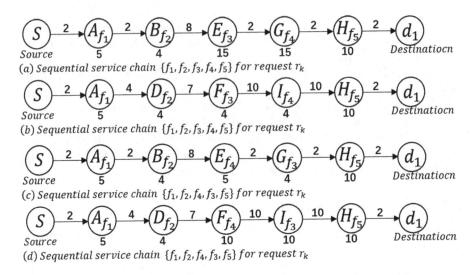

(a) Sequential service chain $\{f_1, f_2, f_3, f_4, f_5\}$ for request r_k

(b) Sequential service chain $\{f_1, f_2, f_3, f_4, f_5\}$ for request r_k

(c) Sequential service chain $\{f_1, f_2, f_4, f_3, f_5\}$ for request r_k

(d) Sequential service chain $\{f_1, f_2, f_4, f_3, f_5\}$ for request r_k

Fig. 3. The problem illustration of Fig. 1

$(f_1 \to f_2 \to f_4 \to f_3 \to f_5)$ can reduce the cost of admitting r_k by 25.8% compared to the other best with $(f_1 \to f_2 \to f_3 \to f_4 \to f_5)$.

Note that the number and categories of VNFs in SFC for each request are determined. But, the execution order between VNFs can be adjustable, that is, multiple versions of SFCs with adjustable order can complete the task (as shown in Fig. 3). In this case, considering the VNF deployment cost, link connection cost and node capacity, it is desirable to find the optimal execution order SFC embedding solution.

3.3 Delay Constraints of Unicast Requests

In implementing unicast requests, it is important to meet the end-to-end delay constraints of user services. For a delay-aware NFV-enabled unicast request, we consider both the processing delay in the selected server nodes and the data transmission delay on the links in network G, which are defined in the following.

Processing Delay. The processing delay of unicast request r_k consists of the data traffic that needs to be processed and the computing resources allocated to process the traffic. We consider that the processing delay $d^j_{p,k}$ of VNF f_j in SC_k with $1 \leq j \leq l$ for each unicast request r_k is proportional to the amount of traffic, i.e.,

$$d^j_{p,k} = \beta_j \cdot b_k \tag{1}$$

where β_j denotes a given proportional factor of VNF f_j. Therefore, the accumulative processing delay in SC_k of r_k is:

$$d_{p,k} = \sum_{f_j \in SC_k} d^j_{p,k} \tag{2}$$

Transmission Delay. Let P_k be a candidate of routing path from source s_k to destination t_k, and $d_{t,k}(e')$ be the transmission delay on link $e' \in P_k$. The transmission delay $d_{t,k}$ on path P_k is

$$d_{t,k} = \sum_{e' \in P_k} d_{t,k}(e') \tag{3}$$

As a result, the total delay experienced by r_k is

$$d_k = d_{p,k} + d_{t,k} \tag{4}$$

For a service satisfying the delay demand, the request processing delay time cannot be greater than the specified delay demand D_k, i.e.,

$$d_k \leq D_k \tag{5}$$

Theorem 1. *the delay-aware NFV-enabled unicasting problem is NP-hard.*

Proof. As in [27], the traditional delay-constrained shortest path problem is NP-hard. More difficult than the tradition delay-constrained shortest path problem, the problem we formulated also include the influence of server nodes. According to [28], even if G is a directed acyclic graph, this problem is still NP-hard.

4 Algorithms for a Single NFV-Enabled Unicast Request

In this section, we devise efficient algorithms for the NFV-enabled unicasting problem with and without end-to-end delay constraint. As the preparation of the algorithms, we first construct a parallel multilayer compression auxiliary diagram (PMCD) which includes all information of the original network.

4.1 Construction of PMCD

Note that different NFV nodes can instantiate the same VNF. Let V_{f_j} be the set of NFV nodes that can instantiate VNF f_j. The node set V_k in PMCD can be composed of source node s_k, destination node t_k, and NFV node sets V_{f_j}, i.e., $V_k = \bigcup_{j=1}^{l} V_{f_j} \cup \{s_k, t_k\}$. To guarantee the network functions of SC_k are traversed in the specified order, the nodes in V_k are connected according to all possible SFC chains. The specific steps to construct PMCD as shown in Fig. 4 are as follows:

- First, according to the feature of SFC with adjustable order, we divide the SFC into multiple subsets. For example, we consider a SFC $= (f_1, f_2, f_3, f_4, f_5, f_6, f_7)$, where two AOPs $\{f_1, f_2, f_3\}$ and $\{f_5, f_6\}$. In this case, the SFC is modeled as $(\{f_1, f_2, f_3\} \rightarrow \{f_4\} \rightarrow \{f_5, f_6\} \rightarrow \{f_7\})$. We arrange the V_{f_j} corresponding to each element of each partitioned subset in SFC into a column from top to bottom, and then copy this column k times, where k represents the number of elements in each divided subset. Let $V_{i^{th}}$ denote the NFV node set of the i-th column, where $i = (1, 2, ..., l)$, and l is the length of SC_k.

- All the nodes in the left column are connected to all nodes in their non-identical functional right adjacency columns by directed edges. If different adjacent VNFs are implemented on the same server node, then the weight of this edge is 0.
- Connect the source node s_k to the node $v \in V_{1^{th}}$ in the first column with a directed edge, and set the edge weight to be the shortest path [29] between the source nodes s_k and $v \in V_{1^{th}}$ in graph G, if this edge exists. Similarly, connect the nodes $v \in V_{l^{th}}$ in the last column with destination t_k, and assign the edge weight as the shortest path between the node $v \in V_{l^{th}}$ and t_k in graph G, if this edge exists. Therefore, there is an edge set for PMCD $E_k = \bigcup_{j=1}^{l-1}\{\langle u, v\rangle | u \in V_{j^{th}} \& v \in V_{(j+1)^{th}} \& u_f \neq v_f\} \cup \{\langle s_k, v\rangle | v \in V_{1^{th}}\} \cup \{\langle v, t_k\rangle | v \in V_{l^{th}}\}$, where u_f denotes the VNF deployed on node u.

The above three steps can transform any NFV-enabled unicast task with certain SFC requirements into a specific PMCD graph. The process of building the PMCD auxiliary graph ensures that the original network is a subgraph of the PMCD, which guarantees the auxiliary does not lack any information. To facilitate the calculation of the shortest path, we incorporate the node weight into the incoming edge weight of this node in the algorithm.

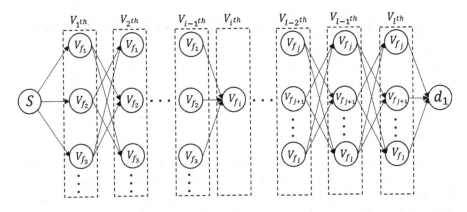

Fig. 4. A standard parallel multilayer compression auxiliary diagram PMCD, where $V_{f_1}, ..., V_{f_l}$ represent the sets of candidate nodes for each service in the service chain.

4.2 The Optimal Algorithm for Handling Unicast Request Without Delay Constraints

For a unicast request with more than two functions with adjustable order in the SFC, if the traditional shortest path algorithm is used, then the SFC in the solution obtained through this PMCD may be $(f_1, ..., f_i, f_{i+1}, f_i, f_{i+3}, ..., f_l)$. This shows that the PMCD may result in some undesirable solutions, where some functions is duplicated or missing. To address this issue, we propose an exclusive shortest path algorithm belonging to the PMCD auxiliary graph. The detailed steps to find a feasible solution are presented as follows:

- Step 1: Start a column-by-column forward search from the source node s_k.
- Step 2: Calculate the shortest path of each node v on each column from the source node s_k. Get the all shortest paths from the source node s_k to the nodes in the previous column of v, respectively, and we call such a fore node a predecessor node of v. Then, add these distances correspondingly to the shortest distances from the predecessor nodes to node v. Finally, preserve the predecessor nodes of v, the shortest path from s_k to v and the all VNFs deployed up to the predecessor node location.
- Step 3: Repeat the Step 2, and iteratively calculate the shortest path of each node in each column until the last column.
- Step 4: Finally, the nodes on the last column are connected to the destination node respectively, and the shortest path from the source node to the destination node can be obtained by comparison, and this path includes the SFC for realizing the unicast request.

Note that the source node s_k is the predecessor of all nodes in the first column. When processing the function deployment of each column, it is necessary to determine whether the function has been deployed. Also note that the total amount of resources of each node and link is limited. Hence, the routing path P_k obtained by Step 4 may not be suitable for practical scenarios. In this case, we need to check the obtained routing path, so as to satisfy the resource constraints.

Based on this idea, we further check whether there exists any overload problems. Specifically, an auxiliary diagram PMCD of G for r_k is constructed, where the remaining resource of link $e \in E_k$, denoted by R_e, is no less than $2 \cdot b_k$. If $R_e < 2 \cdot b_k$, we remove the corresponding link e in PMCD, and otherwise, we keep it unchanged. Furthermore, we check all VNFs in the SFC in turn. If the resources required to deploy $f_j \in SC_k$ on node $v \in V_M$ are greater than the remaining resources R_v on the node $v \in V_M$, we disconnect the link between the overloaded node and its connected nodes.

Theorem 2. *For the NFV-enabled unicasting problem with resource constraints, the optimal solution with the optimal VNFs execution order can be obtained through Algorithm 1, which takes $O(|V|^3)$ time.*

Proof. Since the proposed Algorithm 1 computes the function deployment path and the traffic delivery path separately, there may be an edge e that is traversed at least twice in data traffic routing of request r_k: one is when e in the path between the source s_k and a server node $v \in V_M$, the other is that e is in the path between the server node $v \in V_M$ and the destination t_k at the same time. When PMCD is constructed, each edge maintains at least $2 \cdot b_k$ of bandwidth resources, which ensures that the traffic of request r_k can be routed from the source s_k to the destination t_k. Via the construction process of PMCD, it is guaranteed that the SFC required by the request r_k can be completely embedded.

We first demonstrate that a feasible solution can be obtained by Algorithm 1. Next, we prove by mathematical induction that the shortest path from the source node to any node in any substructure $V_{f_j}, \forall f_j \in SC_k$ can be obtained by column-wise forward search (i.e., Step 2). For the nodes on the 1-th column, the shortest edge weight from the source s_k to any node in the first column $V_{1^{th}}$ is obtained by the shortest path algorithm. Then, for the nodes on the $(l-1)$-th column, assuming that the shortest path from the source s_k to any node in the $(l-1)$-th column $V_{(l-1)^{th}}$ is obtainable, represented by $c(p_{s_k,v_{l-1}})$. For the nodes on the l-th column, the shortest path from s_k to any node in l-th column $V_{l^{th}}$ is expressed as: $c(p_{s_k,v_{l-1}}) + \min(c(e)|e \in \langle v_{l-1}, u_l \rangle, \forall v_{l-1} \in V_{(l-1)^{th}}, \forall u_l \in V_{l^{th}})$. Finally, since PMCD considers the adjustable order of VNFs, the solution obtained by Algorithm 1 is also an optimal path with the optimal VNF ordering.

We then analyze the time complexity of Algorithm 1. The construction of PMCD$=(V_k, E_k)$ takes $O(|V|^3)$ time, as $|V_k| = \sum_{i=1}^{l} |V_{i^{th}}| + 2 \le |V|^2$ and $|E_k| \le \sum_{i=1}^{l} (|V_{i^{th}}| \times |V_{i^{th}}|) \le |V|^3$. The weight distribution of the edges in the PMCD graph can be realized by calculating the shortest path between the corresponding two nodes in graph G, which takes $O(|V|^3)$ time. Since the PMCD is a directed acyclic graph, it takes a linear time to find the shortest path [26]. Therefore, finding the shortest path in PMCD from s_k to t_k takes $O(|V_k| + |E_k|) = O(|V|^3)$ time. After finding the shortest path, convert it to the corresponding path in the original network graph, which takes $O(|V| + |SC_k|)$. Thus, Algorithm 1 takes $O(|V|^3)$ time.

Algorithm 1. Handle unicast request without delay constraints

---

Input: A network $G = (V, E)$, request $r_k = (s_k, t_K, b_k, SC_k, P_{loc})$, server nodes V_M, the resources of server nodes $cap(v)$, link resources B_e
Output: A solution shortest path P_k, and its cost C_k.
1: Delete edges in PMCD that do not have sufficient resources.
2: Construct an auxiliary graph G' under the node resource constraints.
3: **if** insufficient in link or node resources **then**
4:    return 0.
5: **end if**
6: **for** v of each column in G' **do**
7:    Calculate the shortest distance from s_k to v, save the distance, the predecessor nodes of v, and the
        deployed functions.
8: **end for**
9: **for** each node v of the last column in G' **do**
10:    Connect node v to dedtination t_k in minimum total cost C_v, meanwhile, store the C_v in the cost set
        and the shortest path P_v in path set, respectively.
11: **end for**
12: Compare each C_v in cost set to get the smallest cost C_k and its corresponding path P_k.
13: return C_k and P_k.

4.3   Handle Unicast Request with Delay Constraints

In practical, the routing requests often include a predetermined end-to-end delay constraint [30, 31]. In this section, we propose the method for delay-aware NFV-enabled unicast problem with delay constraints, which is NP-hard [32].

The basic idea behind this algorithm is to find the shortest path P'_k with delay limitation D_k based on the PMCD $= (V_k, E_k, c_k(v), c_k(e), d_{p,k}(v), d_{t,k}(e))$, where $c_k(v)$ and $d_{p,k}(v)$ represent the processing cost and delay in the node v, respectively, similarly, in addition to link transmission cost $c_k(e)$, a transmission delay $d_{t,k}(e)$ is assigned too.

Note that the delay-aware NFV-enabled unicast problem is similar to the delay constrained least cost (DCLC) path problem [33]. The special feature is that each node in the PMCD graph has been attached server to implement the VNFs, which incurs node consumption in the total traffic delivery cost and processing delay $d_{p,k}(v)$ at the server node $v \in V_M$. Therefore, Definition 2 can be formulated in terms of the DCLC problem, i.e., $\min\{C_P | P \in \mathcal{P}_{s_k, t_k} \& d_{k,P} \leq D_k\}$, where $\mathcal{P}_{s_k, t_k}$ represents the path set from the s_k to the t_k for the request r_k, $V(P)$ denotes all used server nodes on path P, C_P denotes the total traffic delivery cost defined in (1), and $d_{k,P} = \sum_{v \in V(P)} d_{p,k}(v) + \sum_{e \in P} d_{t,k}(e)$ denotes the total delay of P. We next propose a modified edge cost function, i.e., $c(e_\lambda) = c_k(e) + c_k(v) + \lambda \cdot (d_{p,k}(v) + d_{t,k}(e))$, where $\lambda \geq 0$. With the adjusted edge weights, we can find a path P_λ with total cost $C_{P,\lambda}$ by Algorithm 1. When $d_{k,P_\lambda} > D_k$, we perform to find the suitable solution for r_k to meet the delay constraint by changing the value of λ.

In general, we adopt the ideas of Juttner et al. [27], which uses the concept of aggregated costs and exploits an efficient lagrange relaxation based algorithm to get the delay constrained routing path. Based on the PMCD graph, the detailed operations to find a feasible solution are stated as follow.

- Step 1: Set $\lambda = 0$, find the shortest path P_c from s_k to t_k with C_{P_c} by Algorithm 1. If the path P_c found meets the delay constraints D_k, stop the algorithm and return the optimal path P_c as P'_k.
- Step 2: Otherwise, store the path P_c and d_{k,P_c}. Then, using the link delay $d_{t,k}(e)$ and node delay $d_{p,k}(v)$ as the cost of the PMCD graph, calculate whether there is a path P_d that meets the delay constraint from s_k to t_k. If the obtained path P_d satisfies the delay constraint, the path P_d with total delay d_{k,P_d} is stored as the best path found so far, and go to Step 3. Otherwise, there is no suitable path in the network that can meet the delay constraint for this request r_k, and then the algorithm is stopped.
- Step 3: Calculate λ by $\lambda = \frac{C_{P_c} - C_{P_d}}{d_{k,P_d} - d_{k,P_c}}$. Adjust the edge weights in PMCD by λ. Then use the Algorithm 1 to find another path P_r. If $d_{k,P_r} \leq D_k$, $P_d = P_r$, otherwise, $P_c = P_r$.
- Step 4: Repeat Step 3 until $C_{P_r,\lambda} == C_{P_c,\lambda}$. Return the path P_d as P'_k.
- Step 5: Finally, we replace all of the edges in P'_k with its corresponding shortest path in network G to derive the delay-constrained shortest path.

Theorem 3. *Let* $LB(\lambda) = min\{C_{P,\lambda}|P \in \mathcal{P}_{s_k,t_k}\} - \lambda \cdot D_k$, *for any* $\lambda \geq 0$. *Then* $LB(\lambda)$ *is the lower bound to Definition 2.*

Proof. Let P_{opt} denote the optimal solution to Definition 2, and let the minimum cost of implementing an NFV-enabled unicast request with delay constraint be $C_{P_{opt}}$. Then, we have

$$
\begin{aligned}
LB(\lambda) &= min\{C_{P,\lambda}|P \in \mathcal{P}_{s_k,t_k}\} - \lambda \cdot D_k \\
&\leq C_{P_{opt},\lambda} - \lambda \cdot D_k \\
&= C_{P_{opt}} + \lambda \cdot \left(\sum_{v \in V(P_{opt})} d_{p,k}(v) + \sum_{e \in P_{opt}} d_{t,k}(e) - D_k \right) \\
&\leq C_{P_{opt}}
\end{aligned}
\tag{6}
$$

5   Experimental Evaluation

In this section, we introduce the evaluation environment, the relevant parameters, the benchmark algorithms, and then we demonstrate the performance of the proposed algorithms.

5.1   Experiment Setting

To evaluate our algorithm, we conduct experiments using the network generated by the ER random graph algorithm and the real network topology GÉANT [34], respectively. We give the settings of the required parameters.

- Network size: Following the previous work [11,34], we set the network size in the range of [50, 250], covering both small and large networks.
- Network connectivity: Each node has an average of 3 connecting edges.
- Edge weight and Link resource: The usage cost of one unit of bandwidth per edge c_e and link resource limit are randomly generated between [1, 50] and [500, 1000] Mbps, respectively.
- Server node ratio: The number of server nodes accounts for 10% of the total network nodes.
- Computing resources: The computing resources of the server nodes are randomly generated at [4000,12000] MHz.
- Unicast request task: For each simulated NFV unicast request, we also use a random generation method, such that the source node and the destination node are randomly selected from the target network.
- Bandwidth resource: The bandwidth resource b_k required by each request is between [1, 5].
- VNF deployment cost: The resource consumed by deploying function f_i on each node v is in the range of [1, 25].
- SFC size: According to [35], the original hardware-based network functions can be replaced with VNFs and incorporated into SFCs. Therefore, with the continuous exploration and market expansion of NFV, the SFC length will increase. We set the variation range of the SFC length to be between [5, 20], which is the actual deployment double [36].

With the above parameter settings, we run all the algorithms on a computer configured with an Intel CPU 11700 with a maximum frequency of 4.8 GHz and 16 GB of memory (RAM). Unless otherwise specified, these above parameter settings are taken as default parameters.

To the best of our knowledge, this is the first study of the SFC embedding problem with adjustable order in NFV-enabled unicast request problems. We compare Algorithm 1 (Min-path column-by-column iterative search algorithm, MCIS) with two other benchmark algorithms: i) In [37], Huang et al. proposed a method, which is referred to as ASR (Admitting a single request). ASR can map different resource usages in the SDN network G to the edge weights in the auxiliary graph G'. Then, the problem of handling NFV-enabled unicast requests r_k in graph G is transformed into the problem of finding the shortest path in graph G'. We consider this ASR approach as one of the benchmarks to evaluate the cost of transmitting NFV-enabled unicast without regard to delay. ii) Another benchmark algorithm (i.e., UNICAST) is proposed by Mike et al. [10]. The algorithm proposes a general framework for solving NFV-enabled unicast requests, builds an auxiliary graph of the request according to the framework, and then finds the shortest path from the source node to the target node in this auxiliary. The two benchmark algorithms for Algorithm 2 (Heu_Lag for short) are as follows: i) Based on the ASR, plus the delay limit, the requests that cannot meet the delay constraints are directly discarded, which is referred to as ASR_Delay; ii) The second contrast algorithm with delay constraints is proposed by Mike et al. [10]. The Lagrange relaxation algorithm is employed to balance the delay and resource constraints until the request result meets the delay constraint, which is referred to as UNICAST_Delay.

Since unicast requests that require VNFs with adjustable order can have choices of SFCs in different orders, our algorithm can calculate which permutation is better relative to the benchmark algorithms. For these benchmark algorithms, we randomly choose a function deployment order for them at each computation time. We conduct experiments using the generated random graphs of different sizes, taking the final consumption and running time of the algorithm as performance metrics. Furthermore, we perform experiments over the real network topology GÉANT.

5.2   Experiment on Synthetic Network

Performance Without Delay Constraints. To evaluate the impact of different network sizes, we set the network size to range from 50 to 300. In Fig. 5a, we observe that the solutions of these three methods possess different total traffic delivery costs. Algorithm 1 MCIS is lower than both ASR and UNICAST. The cost of MCIS is 143.06% lower than that of ASR, and 22.21% lower than that of UNICAST. This is because ASR only considers deploying all VNFs on one server node. Algorithms MCIS and UNICAST considering the deployment of VNFs on multiple server nodes can well avoid these server nodes with high deployment consumption, while ASR can only deploy all VNFs on one server, which increases the cost.

For the running time of those algorithms, as shown in Fig. 5b, the average running time of MCIS is similar to that of UNICAST. The average running time of MCIS is slightly lower than that of UNICAST. The average running time of ASR is low for the other two algorithms. This is because ASR simply considers the deployment of all functions on one server node, so ASR does not need to construct a complex auxiliary graph to calculate the deployment of VNFs. Therefore, the required average runtime of ASR is smaller than the other algorithms.

Performance with Delay Constraints. To evaluate the impact of different network sizes, we set the network size to range from 50 to 300. As shown in Fig. 6a, in different network scales, the cost of Algorithm 2 Heu_Lag is lower than that of ASR_Delay and UNICAST_Delay to accept a unicast request. The cost of algorithm 2 Heu_Lag is about 117.06% lower than that of ASR_Delay, and 18.27% lower than that of UNICAST_Delay. As shown in Fig. 6b, the average running time of Heu_Lag is about 15.04% less than that of UNICAST_Delay, while the average running time of Algorithm ASR_Delay is smaller. This is because ASR_Delay not only deploys all VNFs on a single server, but also directly rejects requests that do not meet the delay constraints and does nothing else.

5.3   Experiments on GÉANT

In the experiment of this subsection, we apply the real network topology of GÉANT, and evaluate our method by changing the SFC length.

Performance Without Delay Constraints. To evaluate the impact of SFC length, we set the SFC length to vary from 5 to 20, in which the number of functions with adjustable order is fixed at 3 and the number of server nodes is 5. As shown in Fig. 7a, as the SFC length increases, the total resource consumption amount increases. The consumption of Algorithm 1 MCIS and Algorithm UNICAST are basically remain unchanged. The consumption of MCIS is slightly lower than that of UNICAST about 2.31%, while the gap between MCIS and ASR is significantly large. In the network scale of GÉANT, the average consumption of MCIS is lower than that of ASR by about 46.98%. For the comparison of algorithm running time in Fig. 7b, the average running time of MCIS is about 36.26% lower than that of UNICAST, while ASR is lower than both MCIS and UNICAST. This is because ASR simply deploys all functions on one server node.

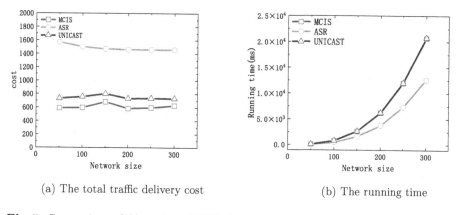

(a) The total traffic delivery cost   (b) The running time

Fig. 5. Comparison of Algorithms MCIS, ASR, UNICAST with respect to cost/ running time.

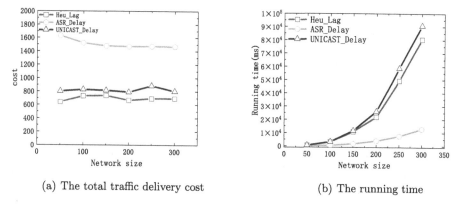

(a) The total traffic delivery cost   (b) The running time

Fig. 6. Comparison of Algorithms Heu_Lag, ASR_Delay, UNICAST_Delay with respect to cost/ running time.

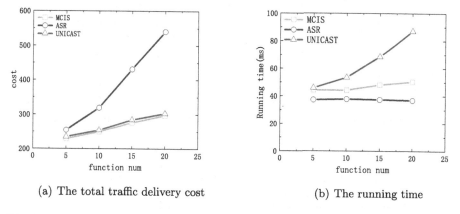

(a) The total traffic delivery cost   (b) The running time

Fig. 7. Comparison of Algorithms MCIS, ASR, UNICAST with respect to cost/ running time in GÉANT.

Performance with Delay Constraints. To evaluate the impact of SFC length, we set the SFC length to vary from 5 to 20, in which the number of functions with adjustable order is fixed at 3 and the number of server nodes is 5. As shown in Fig. 8a, the cost of Heu_Lag is lower than that of ASR_Delay and UNICAST_Delay to accept a unicast request. The cost of Heu_Lag is about 38.73% lower than that of ASR_Delay. The average running time of Heu_Lag is about 50.89% less than that of UNICAST_Delay, while the average running time of ASR_Delay is lower than that of the other two algorithms. This is because ASR_Delay not only deploys all VNFs on one server node, but also just makes a simple judgment on whether the delay constraint is met.

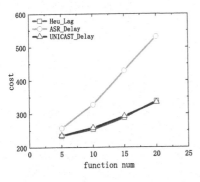
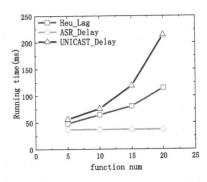

(a) The total traffic delivery cost   (b) The running time

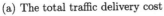

Fig. 8. Comparison of Algorithms Heu_Lag, ASR_Delay, UNICAST_Delay with respect to cost/ running time in GÉANT.

6   Conclusions

In this paper, we investigated the NFV-enabled unicast, by considering the case where SFCs have functions with adjustable order. First, we proposed a general PMCD transformation framework to simplify and normalize the handling of the SFC embedding problem with adjustable order. Then, we proposed the NFV-enabled unicast algorithms in SDN with and without end-to-end delay constraints, respectively, so as to minimize the total traffic delivery cost. Finally, we evaluate the performance of the proposed algorithms through experimental simulations. The results show that the proposed algorithms outperform the existing benchmark algorithms, when dealing with the NFV-enabled unicasting problem.

Acknowledgement. This work was partly supported by the R&D projects in key areas of Guangdong Province (2020B010164001), the Key Program of NSFC- Guangdong Joints Funds (U1801263, .U2001201), the Projects of Science and Technology Plan of Guangdong province under Grant NOs. 2022A1515011032, 2020A1515011132, GDNRC[2020]024, the industry university research innovation fund of Chinese Universities (2021FNA02010), and the Guangdong Provincial Key Laboratory of Cyber-Physical System under Grant NOs. 2020B1212060069.

References

1. Afolabi, I., Taleb, T., Samdanis, K., Ksentini, A., Flinck, H.: Network slicing and softwarization: a survey on principles, enabling technologies, and solutions. IEEE Commun. Surv. Tutor. **20**(3), 2429–2453 (2018)
2. Yao, B., Gao, H., Chen, Q., Li, J.: Energy-adaptive and bottleneck-aware many-to-many communication scheduling for battery-free wsns. IEEE Internet Things J. **8**(10), 8514–8529 (2021)
3. Chen, Q., Cai, Z., Cheng, L., Gao, H., Li, J.: Structure-free broadcast scheduling for duty-cycled multihop wireless sensor networks. IEEE Trans. Mob. Comput. **21**, 4624–4641 (2021)
4. Feng, H., Llorca, J., Tulino, A.M., Raz, D., Molisch, A.F.: Approximation algorithms for the NFV service distribution problem. In: IEEE INFOCOM 2017-IEEE Conference on Computer Communications, pp. 1–9. IEEE (2017)
5. Bremler-Barr, A., Harchol, Y., Hay., D.: Openbox: a software-defined framework for developing, deploying, and managing network functions. In: Proceedings of the 2016 ACM SIGCOMM Conference, pp. 511–524 (2016)
6. Kuo, J.-J., Shen, S.-H., Kang, H.-Y., Yang, D.-N., Tsai, M.-J., Chen, W.-T.: Service chain embedding with maximum flow in software defined network and application to the next-generation cellular network architecture. In: IEEE INFOCOM 2017-IEEE Conference on Computer Communications, pp. 1–9. IEEE (2017)
7. Chen, Y., Wu, J.: NFV middlebox placement with balanced set-up cost and bandwidth consumption. In: Proceedings of the 47th International Conference on Parallel Processing, pp. 1–10 (2018)
8. Ma, Yu., Liang, W., Zichuan, X., Guo, S.: Profit maximization for admitting requests with network function services in distributed clouds. IEEE Trans. Parallel Distrib. Syst. **30**(5), 1143–1157 (2018)
9. Mirjalily, G., Asgarian, M., Luo, Z.-Q.: Interference-aware NFV-enabled multicast service in resource-constrained wireless mesh networks. IEEE Trans. Netw. Serv. Manage. **19**(1), 424–436 (2021)
10. Jia, M., Liang, W., Huang, M., Zichuan, X., Ma, Yu.: Routing cost minimization and throughput maximization of NFV-enabled unicasting in software-defined networks. IEEE Trans. Netw. Serv. Manage. **15**(2), 732–745 (2018)
11. Ren, B., Guo, D., Tang, G., Lin, X., Qin, Y.: Optimal service function tree embedding for nfv enabled multicast. In: 2018 IEEE 38th International Conference on Distributed Computing Systems (ICDCS), pp. 132–142. IEEE (2018)
12. Ren, B., Guo, D., Shen, Y., Tang, G., Lin, X.: Embedding service function tree with minimum cost for NFV-enabled multicast. IEEE J. Sel. Areas Commun. **37**(5), 1085–1097 (2019)
13. Alhussein, O., et al.: A virtual network customization framework for multicast services in NFV-enabled core networks. IEEE J. Sel. Areas Commun. **38**(6), 1025–1039 (2020)
14. Zhang, Q., Xiao, Y., Liu, F., Lui, J.C.S., Guo, J., Wang, T.: Joint optimization of chain placement and request scheduling for network function virtualization. In: 2017 IEEE 37th International Conference on Distributed Computing Systems (ICDCS), pp. 731–741. IEEE (2017)
15. Kuo, T.-W., Liou, B.-H., Lin, K.C.-J., Tsai, M.-J.: Deploying chains of virtual network functions: On the relation between link and server usage. IEEE/ACM Trans. Network. **26**(4), 1562–1576 (2018)

16. Jin, P., Fei, X., Zhang, Q., Liu, F., Li, B.: Latency-aware VNF chain deployment with efficient resource reuse at network edge. In: IEEE INFOCOM 2020-IEEE Conference on Computer Communications, pp. 267–276. IEEE (2020)

17. Li, Y., Phan, L.T.X., Loo, B.T.: Network functions virtualization with soft real-time guarantees. In: IEEE INFOCOM 2016-The 35th Annual IEEE International Conference on Computer Communications, pp. 1–9. IEEE (2016)

18. Ren, H., et al.: Efficient algorithms for delay-aware NFV-enabled multicasting in mobile edge clouds with resource sharing. IEEE Trans. Parallel Distribut. Syst. **31**(9), 2050–2066 (2020)

19. Zichuan, X., Liang, W., Jia, M., Huang, M., Mao, G.: Task offloading with network function requirements in a mobile edge-cloud network. IEEE Trans. Mob. Comput. **18**(11), 2672–2685 (2018)

20. Yue, Y., Cheng, B., Li, B., Wang, M., Liu, X.: Throughput optimization VNF placement for mapping SFC requests in mec-nfv enabled networks. In: Proceedings of the 26th Annual International Conference on Mobile Computing and Networking, pp. 1–3 (2020)

21. Asgarian, M., Mirjalily, G., Luo, Z.-Q.: Trade-off between efficiency and complexity in multi-stage embedding of multicast VNF service chains. IEEE Commun. Lett. **26**(2), 429–433 (2021)

22. Gharbaoui, M., Contoli, C., Davoli, G., Borsatti, D., Cuffaro, G., Paganelli, F., Cerroni, W., Cappanera, P., Martini, B.: An experimental study on latency-aware and self-adaptive service chaining orchestration in distributed NFV and SDN infrastructures. Comput. Netw. **208**, 108880 (2022)

23. Kumazaki, M., Ogura, M., Tachibana, T.: Dynamic service chain construction based on model predictive control in NFV environments. IEICE Trans. Commun. **105**(4), 399–410 (2022)

24. Pei, J., Hong, P., Xue, K., Li, D.: Resource aware routing for service function chains in SDN and NFV-enabled network. IEEE Trans. Serv. Comput. **14**(4), 985–997 (2018)

25. Chen, Q., Gao, H., Li, Y., Cheng, S., Li, J.: Edge-based beaconing schedule in duty-cycled multihop wireless networks. In IEEE INFOCOM 2017-IEEE Conference on Computer Communications, pp. 1–9. IEEE (2017)

26. Chen, Q., Gao, H., Cheng, L., Li, Y.: Label coloring based beaconing schedule in duty-cycled multihop wireless networks. IEEE Trans. Mob. Comput. **19**(5), 1123–1137 (2019)

27. Juttner, A., Szviatovski, B., Mécs, I., Rajkó, Z.: Lagrange relaxation based method for the QoS routing problem. In: Proceedings IEEE INFOCOM 2001. Conference on Computer Communications. Twentieth Annual Joint Conference of the IEEE Computer and Communications Society (Cat. No. 01CH37213), vol. 2, pp. 859–868. IEEE (2001)

28. Wang, Z., Crowcroft, J.: Quality-of-service routing for supporting multimedia applications. IEEE J. Sel. Areas Commun. **14**(7), 1228–1234 (1996)

29. Floyd, R.W.: Algorithm 97: shortest path. Commun. ACM **5**(6), 345 (1962)

30. Chen, Q., Cai, Z., Cheng, L., Gao, H., Li, J.: Low-latency concurrent broadcast scheduling in duty-cycled multihop wireless networks. In: 2019 IEEE 39th International Conference on Distributed Computing Systems (ICDCS), pp. 851–860. IEEE (2019)

31. Chen, Q., Gao, H., Cheng, S., Fang, X., Cai, Z., Li, J.: Centralized and distributed delay-bounded scheduling algorithms for multicast in duty-cycled wireless sensor networks. IEEE/ACM Trans. Networking **25**(6), 3573–3586 (2017)

32. Book, R.V., Garey, M.R., Johnson, D.S.: Computers and intractability: a guide to the theory of np-completeness. Bulletin (New Series) Am. Math. Soc. **3**(2), 898–904 (1980)
33. Salama, H.F., Reeves, D.S., Viniotis, Y.: A distributed algorithm for delay-constrained unicast routing. In: Proceedings of INFOCOM 1997, vol. 1, pp. 84–91. IEEE (1997)
34. Xu, Z., Liang, W., Huang, M., Jia, M., Guo, S., Galis, A.: Approximation and online algorithms for NFV-enabled multicasting in SDNs. In: 2017 IEEE 37th International Conference on Distributed Computing Systems (ICDCS), pp. 625–634. IEEE (2017)
35. Brown, G., Analyst, S., Reading, H.: Service chaining in carrier networks, White paper (2015)
36. Luizelli, M.C., Raz, D., Sa'ar, Y.: Optimizing NFV chain deployment through minimizing the cost of virtual switching. In: IEEE INFOCOM 2018-IEEE Conference on Computer Communications, pp. 2150–2158. IEEE (2018)
37. Huang, M., Liang, W., Xu, Z., Jia, M., Guo, S.: Throughput maximization in software-defined networks with consolidated middleboxes. In: 2016 IEEE 41st Conference on Local Computer Networks (LCN), pp. 298–306. IEEE (2016)

MDLpark: Available Parking Prediction for Smart Parking Through Mobile Deep Learning

Md Tanvir Rahman[1], Yu Zhang[1(✉)], Samen Anjum Arani[1], and Wei Shao[2]

[1] School of Computer Science, Northwestern Polytechnical University, Xi'an, China
zhangyu@nwpu.edu.cn
[2] Electrical and Computer Engineering, University of California, Davis, USA
weishao@ucdavis.edu

Abstract. Problems with parking have resulted in traffic congestion, social phobia, and smog, as well as an inefficient allocation of resources as a result of the city's growing population. The importance of computer-aided methods and existing methods for parking prediction are analyzed. On this basis, the existing deep learning and mobile deep learning methods were investigated in depth and found that the existing methods are dependent on the cloud server and also have issues related to accuracy and response time. MDLpark, a novel mobile deep learning architecture-based approach for parking occupancy prediction is proposed. The method is based on Temporal Convolutional Network (TCN), which uses a one-dimensional fully convolutional network architecture through TCN, which utilizes its convolution and dilation to make it dynamically adaptive to the prediction window and prediction response. We restructured the residual block of TCN by replacing the weight normalization with batch normalization, which is more stable than weight normalization. The proposed MDLpark prediction method is implemented based on Keras and TensorFlow, and a mobile deep learning parking application is designed. Experimental results show that compared with other models (TCN, LSTM, GRU and MLP), MDLpark achieves higher prediction accuracy with 97.6% accuracy (97.3%, 84.3%, 95.6%, and 95.7% for TCN, LSTM, GRU, and MLP, respectively). At the same time, through the developed model, the traveler's time to find a parking space is reduced, and the function of direction to these parking lots is provided.

Keywords: MDLpark · Smart parking · TensorFlow · Time series analysis · TCN

1 Introduction

Every day, people all around the globe rely on cars for mobility. The time, energy, and expense of drivers who require a parking lot to look for parking

H. Ma et al. (Eds.): CWSN 2022, CCIS 1715, pp. 182–199, 2022.
https://doi.org/10.1007/978-981-19-8350-4_15

spots are growing day by day due to the enormous number of cars and the insufficient number of car parks in big metropolitan regions. As a result, there is a steady need for parking. In public locations, there are frequently allocated parking spaces that are used by a large number of individuals. Parking spaces in shared lots that are in the greatest location for the lowest price have grown more popular. Driving in busy metropolitan areas takes an average of 3.5 to 14 min [1], which results in people spending money and producing pollution, thereby raising the total cost of life for everyone in that region. Drivers motoring about seeking parking waste a lot of time and money, while also generating lots of unneeded carbon dioxide. As drivers get more angry, they are more likely to break the law. For example, it has been shown that the relationship between taking up a good parking spot and illegal parking, such as double parking and blocking crosswalks, bus stops, and so on, is exponential [2].

Cars may be detected entering and exiting parking spaces using a variety of external sensors and cameras. Sensor-based parking systems rely on sensors attached to parking spots or placed on the sides of automobiles, whereas camera-based parking systems use complex camera setups. As a consequence, conventional parking systems are too costly to construct and maintain as a consequence of these drawbacks. As a result, the system is not suitable for large-scale deployments since it requires more hardware and network capacity. Smartphone-based solutions, including OpenSpot, Roadify, Primsopt, and SpotScout have been introduced in the last several years, but these systems still require drivers to manually enter information into the system when they leave their parking spots [3]. Drivers are inconvenienced by this manual input. Drivers and people in charge of parking would both benefit from a low-cost system that can automatically tell when a car pulls into or out of a space.

It serves as inspiration for the development of an automated smart phone application based on deep learning algorithms. This is due to the fact that there is a significant need for real-time data all of the time in this situation. In addition, the response time, cost, and accuracy of the search are all factors that need to be taken into consideration. The most significant contribution made by this research is,

1. Study the impact of available parking predictions on metropolitan cities. It takes longer to locate a parking space in cities since the number of automobiles increases each year. Methods that have been used in the past don't work anymore. We show that there is a huge importance to having a time-saving and economical real-time parking availability prediction application.
2. Investigate the deep learning algorithms TCN, LSTM, GRU, and MLP for the prediction of empty parking spaces. We used TCN as the basis for our deep learning model. The LSTM model was selected for this purpose because it is a great variation of the RNN model, inheriting most of the properties of RNN models while also solving the vanishing gradient issue produced by the continuous decline of the gradient backpropagation process. Because it has a long-time memory function, it is particularly well suited for dealing with timing problems. To demonstrate the benefits of TCN, we use the LSTM

model, which has been shown to be a very excellent model, as a benchmark for TCN. Because they are created in a comparable manner and, in certain situations, achieve equally great outcomes, GRU can also be regarded as a variant of the LSTM. The TCN model's ability to predict outcomes is the primary topic of this thesis. We show that TCN networks are better at making predictions than previous deep neural network models, such as MLP, and deep learning models, such as LSTM and GRU.

3. To interrogate the mobile deep learning technology in the sector of predicting parking availability, we study and use the TensorFlow and TensorFlow-Lite libraries to compress the models that make the prediction models capable of being implemented in a mobile application. We propose an application design that will show the available parking lots using real-time data. The application will be built based on mobile deep learning.

2 Literature Review

Smart parking is becoming more popular in smart cities, as reported in industry papers [4,5]. As the authors point out, smart parking reduces congestion while generating revenue, uses a pricing system that adjusts according to demand for space during peak hours, and enforces traffic laws by utilizing cameras to identify violators, among other things. In a city [6], obtaining parking spots is one of the most important responsibilities, accounting for up to 31% of total ground use in big metropolitan regions. [7] states that, on average, a vehicle is in motion just 10% of the time, with the rest of the time spent still, either temporarily or permanently. When it comes to locating a parking spot, many people prefer the manual technique, according to the authors of [8]. Parking is difficult to come by for a large percentage of the vehicles on the road at any one time, with searches taking an average of 7–8 min. It is well documented that several research papers have been published in the previous few years that address various elements of intelligent parking systems, including occupancy detection [9,10], system development [11], and shared service design [12]. The parking assignment algorithms presented in several research publications [13–16] are reservation-based solutions built for regulated off-street parking facilities and are based on reservation-based solutions.

It was recommended in [17] that a new cloud-based intelligent vehicle parking system (SVPS) be implemented across ubiquitous VANETs in order to offer more reliable parking services. The suggested SVPS architecture incorporates a novel algorithm that provides easy parking space information, as well as reservation and recommendation choices, in order to assist cars in an efficient, real-time, and exact way, according to the requirements of the user. The results of the simulations show that the suggested design made the most optimal use of the parking resources available. A smart parking concept (SPARK) based on VANET technology was developed in [14] for big vehicle parks. They kept an eye on the vehicle park on all RSUs in a car park that was part of the SPARK program. They used the information they collected to give real-time parking guidance, intelligent theft prevention, and the dissemination of user-friendly parking information. It was discovered in [18] that a cloud-based architecture might be used to connect parking spot service providers and drivers. Through this method, park proprietors who provide services may market their offerings to visitors.

A study published in [19] investigated the energy and time consumption of algorithms employed in the search for parking places. When the hierarchy-based BST algorithm was applied, the efficiency of the method was shown to be greater than that of non-hierarchical aspects [3]. Looked at the subject from a different point of view than the previous two. Parking places were identified with the use of smart phones. When a motorist enters or exits a parking place, the location of the appropriate parking space may be determined. Although it is used in closed parking lots, it has a high accuracy rate.

The performance of the sensors that determine whether or not parking spots in car parks are occupied was investigated in [20], and the results were published. The performance of these sensors varies depending on the angle of the light and the distance between the sensors. In [21], there was talk about reducing the amount of traffic caused by staff at the car park's entry and departure. An automated barrier system with RFID readers at the entrances and exits was created and installed at various locations. They were able to cut labor expenses as well as the density of entrance and exit points [22]. Describes the development of a strategy that was based on reservations. They used Internet of Things sensors to monitor each region of the parking lot, and they developed a mobile application to serve as a reservation system.

The introduction of Internet of Things (IoT) devices in parking garages has also resulted in increased security concerns. These security issues were highlighted in [23], and an elliptical encryption scheme was presented as a solution. The efficiency of this approach was proved to be higher when compared to other encryption methods. [24] describes the results of a study done to determine the demands of drivers in terms of smart parking infrastructure services. Discussed were parking monitoring, parking reservations, and current developments that would be beneficial to both drivers and parking businesses. In order to predict parking spaces in a city as a whole, [25] propose a semi-supervised spatio-temporal learning framework called Semi-supervised Hierarchical Recurrent Graph Neural Network (SHARE), which takes into account both environmental context factors and sparse real-time parking availability data.

3   Methodology

3.1   Proposed Architecture

The end-to-end process of our real-time parking availability prediction program is depicted in Fig. 1. According to our concept, the driver launches the application and searches for the area where he or she wants to park their car. The driver can utilize the GPS system on his or her smartphone to enter their current position in real time. The MDLpark method, which is based on Mobile Deep Learning, is used in this system to find out how many parking spaces are available. The dataset we use is also connected to the real-time API. It is updated every two minutes with the most current information available in the database. As a consequence, the findings of our model analysis of the data are shown in real time. The whole procedure will be carried out on the interface of a smartphone application. Following the preparation of the predicted outcome, the applications display occupied or empty states. The driver will then be notified of the situation. Then he can choose from among the available parking spaces the one that is most convenient for him.

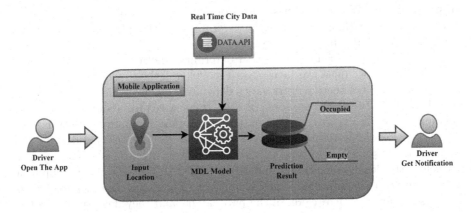

Fig. 1. MDLpark system architecture.

Our proposed architecture implementation can be broken down into three main components, which are as follows: data preprocessing, model training, and model evaluation/compression for mobile implementation. Data preprocessing begins with the collection of data from online resources and the preprocessing of the data so it would be more effective for chosen models. After that, prediction models are created and trained on the preprocessed data, and the process is repeated. Last but not least, compress the model and transform the pre-trained model into a tf.lite file that can be used to implement the model in a mobile application.

3.2   Data Preprocessing

Data preprocessing is the process of changing raw data into a format that can be read and used for training the model. It has become a vital part of deep learning algorithms perform best when they are presented in a way that emphasizes the relevant aspects are needed to solve a problem. The preprocessing portion of this research includes use of the Panda library, the Scikit-learn library, and the NumPy library, all of which are written in Python. For the purpose of predicting occupancy, we need to transform the data and add a new column that numerically represents the status, whether it is occupied or not. Because deep learning models are incapable of learning from plain text, "Unoccupied" status is defined as 1 and "present" as 0. Then MinMaxscaler has been used for feature scaling. This is a scaler type that sets the minimum and maximum values to 0 and 1. It is the change of the values of distinct numerical characteristics such that they fall within a comparable range to each other; this is known as feature scaling. As a result, it prevents supervised learning models from being biased towards a certain set of values. Figure 2 shows the portion of the status of being occupied or empty. We split the dataset into two portions: 70% for training and 30% for testing in MDLpark; 70% for training and 30% for testing in TCN; 70% for training and 30% for testing in LSTM; 80% for training and 20% for testing in GRU; and 70% for training and 30% for testing in MLP.

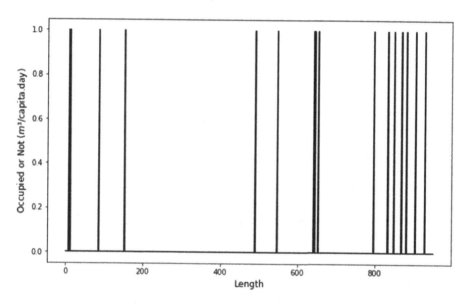

Fig. 2. Dataset status visualization.

3.3 Model Training

TCN is an acronym for Temporal Convolutional Network, which is composed of an enlarged, causal one-dimensional convolutional layer with the same input and output lengths as the input layer. First, a quick introduction to the convolutional network is necessary before moving on to temporal convolution. The convolution process is the fundamental operation of a convolutional neural network (CNN). Data and a set of fixed weight filter matrices are combined in the convolution process, which is the inner product of the two operations. While convolutional neural networks are commonly used in the image processing field, the need for parallel computing and improvement of RNN networks in the field of time series prediction has necessitated the transformation of the convolutional network into a time series convolutional network that is suitable for the needs of time series prediction [26].

Table 1. MDLpark model parameters

Parameter	Value
Train size	70%
Test size	16%
Scaling	MinMaxScaler
Epochs	100
Activation	Relu
Optimizer	Adam
Loss	Mean-squared-error
Batch size	32
Verbose	2

The TCN model serves as a foundation for our MDLpark model's design. It is possible to convolute a sequence of any length into one of the same length. There is no "leakage" of information from the future to the past since it is a causal convolution. A 1D FCN is used in the TCN design to achieve the first goal. It is a one-dimensional network. In other words, the length of each hidden layer will be increased by one in order to match the input layer's length. An output at a certain time t is convolved only with components from that time and previously in the preceding layer in order to get the second point. TCN is a mix of 1D FCN and causal convolutions in a single model. The core structure of TCN was used, however the residual block was restructured. Instead of weight normalization, batch normalization is utilized between convolutions since this method provides better accuracy than weight normalization on large networks Fig. 3. Training deep networks using Weight Normalization is less stable than training them with Batch Normalization, but it is faster than training them with batch normalization. The inclusion of batch normalization is a vital part of our model's design. It offers improved learning capabilities and raises the accuracy offered by the model as a result of the adaptability of mean and variance for each mini-batch. Adam optimizer is used for our model. Using a batch size of 16 and 100 epochs, we test the model's predictions. Model parameters are shown in Table 1.

We leveraged MDLpark for our deep learning model. TCN, LSTM, GRU, and MLP approaches were tested with our suggested model. TCN is our primary suggested based model, and it belongs to the CNN class. We run the model with a batch size of 16 and 100 epochs. The parameters of the model applied are given in Table 2.

Residual Block

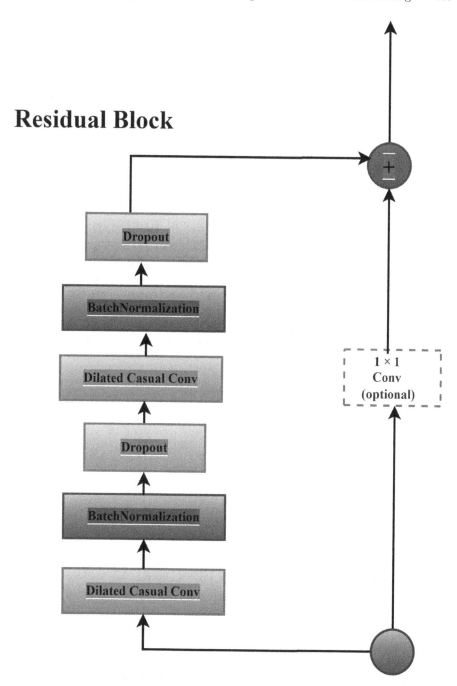

Fig. 3. Residual block of MDLpark.

Table 2. TCN model parameters

Parameter	Value
Train size	70%
Test size	16%
Scaling	MinMaxScaler
Epochs	100
Activation	Relu
Optimizer	Adam
Loss	Mean-squared-error
Batch size	16
Verbose	2

In addition to the three gates, [14] the LSTM cell has a cell update, which is represented by the tanh layer and is often included in the cell's state. Networks with feedback connections, such as LSTMs, differ from normal feed-forward networks. Time series of long-term relevance can be processed using the LSTM. By adding these gates, the network can choose to keep or forget old information, preventing gradient disappearance and explosion. We used a batch size of 64 and 100 epochs to run the model. The parameters of the models applied are given in Table 3.

Table 3. LSTM model parameters

Parameter	Value
Train size	70%
Test size	30%
Scaling	MinMaxScaler
Epochs	100
Activation	tanh
Optimizer	Adam
Loss	Mean-squared-error
Batch size	64
Verbose	1

The GRU can also be thought of as a variation on the LSTM because both are made in the same way. The update gate and the reset gate are used by GRU to tackle the vanishing gradient issue that occurs in a regular RNN. Two vectors decide what data should be output. These may be trained to retain old information without washing. Because the model is not washing away the new input information every time it is run, the vanishing gradient issue is eliminated. Instead, the model retains the important information and sends it down to the following time steps of the network. We run the model with a batch size of 64 and 100 epochs. The parameters of the models applied are given in Table 4.

Table 4. GRU model parameters

Parameter	Value
Train size	80%
Test size	20%
Scaling	MinMaxScaler
Epochs	100
Activation	sigmoid
Optimizer	sgd
Loss	Mean-squared-error
Batch size	64
Verbose	1

A multilayer perceptron (MLP) is a term used to describe a fully connected multi-layer neural network (MLP). It is composed of three layers, one of which is hidden. A feedforward artificial neural network, such as an MLP, is a common kind of artificial neural network. The backpropagation method is used for weight adjustment training. Propagate data from the input layer all the way to the output layer, starting with the input layer. The forward propagation stage is the next phase. Calculate the error, which is the difference between the predicted and actual result, based on the output of the program. It is necessary to keep the amount of error to a bare minimum. Retrace the steps that led to the error. Calculate the derivative of the function with respect to each weight in the network, and then update the network model. We run the model with a batch size of 64 and 100 epochs to see how it performs. The model loss and validation loss of the model are shown in the figure in proportion to the number of epochs. The parameters of the models applied are given in Table 5.

Table 5. MLP model parameters

Parameter	Value
Train size	85%
Test size	15%
Scaling	MinMaxScaler
Epochs	100
Activation	Relu
Optimizer	Adam
Loss	Mean-squared-error
Batch size	64
Verbose	1

3.4 TF-Lite Model Compression

After the trained models have been validated, they must be deployed to the edge device. In order to complete this level, the model's overall size must be decreased. Because of its smaller size, the model takes up less space on the user's device's hard drive or memory. It reduces the amount of RAM that is required as well as the amount of time that is spent inferencing results. Furthermore, the reduction in latency achieved by the reduction in inference time has an impact on the power consumption of the device in question. When TensorFlow Lite is utilized, it is possible to get the following benefits: An existing TensorFlow model may be converted to a TensorFlow Lite model using the TensorFlow Lite converter Fig. 4. The FlatBuffer format is an efficient format that may be recognised by the .tflite file extension being used. Developed by Google, FlatBuffer is a very efficient and portable method for storing data. TensorFlow's protocol buffer model format has a number of significant advantages over this format, including smaller size and faster inference. As a result, TensorFlow Lite is able to execute effectively on devices with limited computation and memory resources.

```
# Convert the model
converter = tf.lite.TFLiteConverter.from_saved_model(saved_model_dir) # path to the SavedModel directory
tflite_model = converter.convert()

# Save the model.
with open('model.tflite', 'wb') as f:
    f.write(tflite_model)
```

Fig. 4. Model conversion.

Following the saving of our model, we converted it into a TensorFlow lite file using the TensorFlow lite converter. The example below demonstrates how to convert a SavedModel to a TensorFlow Lite model.

3.5 Application Architecture

For drivers seeking parking, these applications not only provide a convenient alternative to driving around in circles looking for a place, but also make it possible to save the time and frustration of constantly searching. Figure 5 shows the software architecture of the application. Drivers who are first-time users of the program will be required to register their information with the system. Customers who have already registered themselves will be able to look for vacant parking spots available at their desired location. After that, the program will look for any nearby parking spaces. If there are any available, the user will choose the space that is most suitable for him. He will be able to specify the parking location on the application or obtain directions to the spot if it is accessible. Drivers also have the ability to share the location with other users. The real-time data API and Google Map will be connected with the application. The pre-trained model will be deployed in the application and it will take the real-time data and the user location as input.

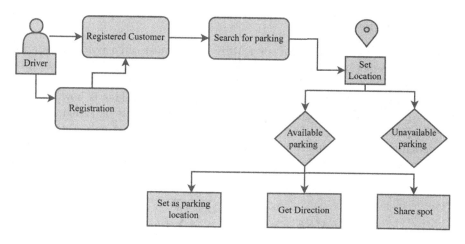

Fig. 5. Software architecture.

4   Evaluation

4.1   Dataset

The Melbourne open data platform [27] is used to gather the Historical Parking Records dataset. It is an open platform that provides several types of parking data for the city of Melbourne. With more than one million parking transactions reported every month in the City of Melbourne, there is a tremendous demand for parking spaces there. As a result, this platform is very well-known in the parking-related research area. It provides free access to a large number of data sets, which may be accessed in a variety of ways, including xml, xlsx, CSV, and API. All of the experiments were carried out using data from a dataset named "On-street parking bay sensors". The data was first collected in 2017, and it is still being updated every two minutes to this day. The dataset consists of 809 rows and 6 columns of information. Figure 6 shows the parameters of the dataset.

bay_id	st_marker_id	status	location	lat	lon
1471	1775S	Present	(-37.816754166072°, 14...	-37.8167541660727	144.96609310265694
1472	1777S	Present	(-37.816775252167844°, ...	-37.816775252167844	144.96602201405722
5875	C9202	Present	(-37.79848480646727°, 1...	-37.79848480646727	144.96551685131993
6056	13034N	Present	(-37.82117319038632°, 1...	-37.82117319038632	144.94391931390288
5345	8871W	Unoccupied	(-37.82543122206522°, 1...	-37.82543122206522	144.96054694628188
2635	10105W	Present	(-37.80341705438269°, 1...	-37.80341705438269	144.94793731799047
2653	10155W	Unoccupied	(-37.80476269838175°, 1...	-37.80476269838175	144.94922777133996
2660	10167W	Present	(-37.80440418442524°, 1...	-37.80440418442524	144.9492897972084
2667	10176E	Unoccupied	(-37.80415897928181°, 1...	-37.80415897928181	144.94952302106753

Fig. 6. On-street parking dataset.

4.2   Evaluation Metric

The Root Mean Squared Error, or RMSE, is the most often used statistic for measuring prediction accuracy [28]. The variance of the residuals is represented by the mean squared error (MSE), which is the average of the squared differences between the actual and predicted values in the data set. This is how the root mean squared error, or standard deviation of the residuals, is called the root mean squared error. The fact that the RMSE is measured as a ratio of the dependent variable's value helps to make it easier to understand. A lower RMSE number indicates a more accurate model, since it measures how distant the errors are from zero on average.

$$RMSE = \sqrt{MSE} = \sqrt{\frac{1}{N}\sum_{i=1}^{N}(y_i - \hat{y})^2} \qquad (1)$$

There is a greater penalty for large predictions when using the root mean squared error (RMSE). This means that for data sets with outliers, the mean absolute error (MAE), which quantifies the exact difference between real and predicted values, could be a more robust evaluation metric.

$$MAE = \sqrt{\frac{1}{N}\sum_{i=1}^{N}|y_i - \hat{y}|} \qquad (2)$$

For the purpose of predicting parking occupancy in parking garages, researchers most often use either (R)MSE or a combination of (R)MSE and MAE. This constraint may be overcome by using the Mean Absolute Scaled Error, which [29] however has the drawback of becoming infinite or undefinable as occupancy decreases towards zero (MASE). The test model's MAE is divided by the MAE of a random naive13 model to arrive at this result. According to [30], if all historical observations were similar, MASE would become infinite or undefined. Furthermore, MASE may demonstrate the value of each model in comparison to a benchmark model, providing stakeholders with fresh insights into the system's performance [28]. When compared to its less complicated siblings, MAE and (R)MSE, it is more time-consuming and computationally expensive to implement. Finally, it seems that MASE delivers a more helpful assessment during the inter-model comparison testing phase than it does during the training and validation of each model on its own.

$$MASE = \frac{MAE}{MAE_{naive}}, where\, MAE = \sqrt{\frac{1}{N}\sum_{i=1}^{N}|y_i - \hat{y}|} \qquad (3)$$

MAE and (R)MSE are used rather often in order to evaluate the performance of regression models; despite this, both of these metrics have a number of serious flaws, one of which is a propensity to become undefinable. On the other hand, these metrics are essential during the training and validation stages of each model since they provide stakeholders with a measurable indicator of the model's level of performance. This is why these phases are so crucial. In addition, the use of a loss function, which is often the MSE, is a prerequisite for the execution of some algorithms. As a consequence of this, we may deduce that there is a direct connection between the performance metric and the training of the model in this particular instance. Last but not least, when the models have been trained and confirmed, the MASE measure is a useful tool for comparing the models among themselves as well as analyzing how they perform in contrast to a baseline model, which enables a better understanding of the additional value that the model provides.

4.3   Experimental Result

The four-prediction model; LSTM, TCN, GRU and MLP was run for 100 epochs and the comparison in terms of accuracy. As we can see, from three different neural network models, the four algorithms have been able to achieve proper performances. All of the model run in the Historical parking records dataset is collected from the Melbourne open data platform. Figure 7 and Fig. 8 shows the comparative Loss/Epochs.

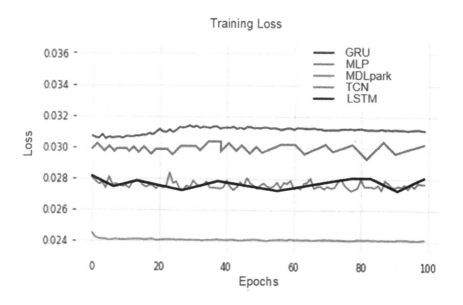

Fig. 7. Training loss.

Among the all models tested, the MDLpark model had the highest accuracy 97.6%, outperforming the others Fig. 9. The accuracy of TCN, LSTM, GRU, and MLP was 97.3%, 84.3%, 95.6%, 95.7% respectively.

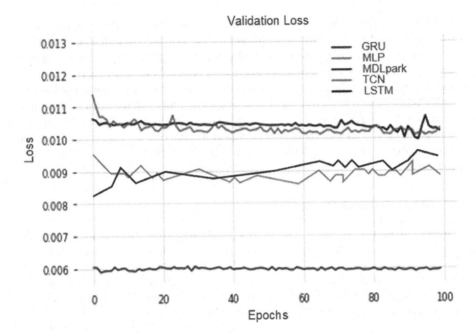

Fig. 8. Validation loss.

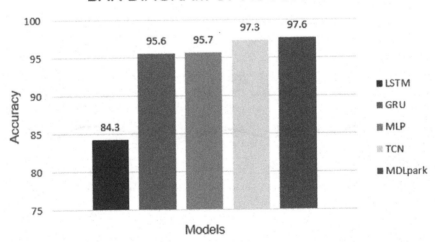

Fig. 9. Performance comparison.

Besides the accuracy calculation, we also evaluate the RMSE, MAE, and MSE. The lower the value of these error points, the more efficient any model is. From the Table 6, we can see that TCN gets the lowest value of RMSE, while GRU and MLP get similar values. On the other hand, LSTM gets the highest value of RMSE. It means TCN is the most efficient model among all of these models.

Table 6. Error assessment of models

Time series model	MAE	MSE	RMSE
LSTM	0.168	0.168	0.41
GRU	0.044	0.044	0.21
MLP	0.042	0.042	0.21
TCN	0.027	0.027	0.16
MDLpark	0.025	0.025	0.155

The GRU network is simpler than the LSTM network, it enables greater resampling rates, and it can be used to analyze both small and big datasets simultaneously. The experiments conducted revealed that the GRU neural network produces the best results since it is quicker and faster to train than other neural networks and produces consistently excellent outcomes. MLP performs in a manner similar to that of the GRU. Because LSTM is a great version of RNN and is particularly well suited for dealing with timing challenges, the LSTM model likewise exhibits outstanding performance. TCN is a new kind of algorithm that can be used to solve problems involving time series prediction and forecasting. TCN is a solution to the concurrency issue of the LSTM and GRU algorithms. TCN outperforms both the LSTM and the GRU models in our simulation by a rather slight margin. Deep learning's accuracy is dependent on the quantity of data available, and the amount of data available in this case is not very large. While MDLpark's speed has been considerably increased when compared to TCN, LSTM and GRU's, its overall performance has been enhanced even more when compared to LSTM, which is more appropriate for usage in a production environment. MDLpark model outperforms all other algorithms in terms of optimization.

5   Conclusion

It has been shown that many drivers spend a significant amount of time cruising about seeking available parking spaces. When there is no vacant parking space, frustration increases, which leads to a greater contempt for traffic regulations. It is anticipated that these issues will be reduced if drivers have access to real-time information regarding where parking spaces are available. According to the findings of this research, we have developed a deep neural network for searching parking spots that is based on a mobile device. For evaluating our proposed model, we demonstrate four different models: TCN, LSTM, GRU, and MLP using the same dataset. We utilized the open-source dataset named "On-street parking bay sensors" from the site City of Melbourne Open Data. Despite the fact that the data was initially gathered in 2017, it is still being updated every two minutes to this day. The dataset contains 809 rows of data and 6 columns of information. MDLpark was the most accurate on the used dataset, with an overall accuracy of 97.6%. The accuracy of TCN, LSTM, GRU, and MLP was 97.3%, 84.3%, 95.6%, and 95.7%, respectively. MDLpark also performed very well in the RMSE scale with a value of 0.154. On the other hand, TCN, LSTM, GRU, and MLP got 0.16, 0.41, 0.21, and 0.21. After that, MDLpark was converted into a .tflite file for deployment in the application by using the TensorFlow Lite converter. One of the most notable drawbacks of our method is the small size of the dataset. As we all know, huge datasets improve the performance of deep learning models.

Acknowledgment. This research was supported by the National Natural Science Foundation of China (Nos. 62172336 and 62032018).

References

1. Shoup, D.C.: Cruising for parking. Transp. Policy **13**(6), 479–486 (2006)
2. Alternatives, T.: No vacancy: park slope's parking problem and how to fix it. Transportation Alternatives, New York (2007). https://www.transalt.org/files/news/reports/novacancy.pdf
3. Lan, K.C., Shih, W.Y.: An intelligent driver location system for smart parking. Expert Syst. Appl. **41**(5), 2443–2456 (2014)
4. Emc, D.: Smart cities and communities gdt smart city solutions on IntelR-based Dell EMC infrastructure. Technical report (2017). Accessed Oct 2021
5. ITALTEL. SMART CITIES; Technical report (2017). https://www.italtel.com/content/uploads/2017/09/Italtel-Smart-Cities-White-Paper.pdf. Accessed Nov 2021
6. Lin, T., Rivano, H., Le Mouël, F.: A survey of smart parking solutions. IEEE Trans. Intell. Transp. Syst. **18**(12), 3229–3253 (2017)
7. Vancluysen, K., Boras, K.: Smart parking in the thinking city. Technical report (2016). Accessed Dec 2021
8. Geng, Y., Cassandras, C.G.: A new "smart parking" system infrastructure and implementation. Proc. Soc. Behav. Sci. **54**, 1278–1287 (2012)
9. Cherian, J., Luo, J., Guo, H., Ho, S.S., Wisbrun, R.: ParkGauge: gauging the occupancy of parking garages with crowdsensed parking characteristics. In 2016 17th IEEE International Conference on Mobile Data Management (MDM), vol. 1, pp. 92–101. IEEE (2016)
10. Grassi, G., Jamieson, K., Bahl, P., Pau, G.: ParkMaster: an in-vehicle, edge-based video analytics service for detecting open parking spaces in urban environments. In: Proceedings of the Second ACM/IEEE Symposium on Edge Computing, pp. 1–14 (2017)
11. Wang, H., He, W.: A reservation-based smart parking system. In: 2011 IEEE Conference on Computer Communications Workshops (INFOCOM WKSHPS), pp. 690–695. IEEE (2011)
12. Griggs, W., Yu, J.Y., Wirth, F., Häusler, F., Shorten, R.: On the design of campus parking systems with QoS guarantees. IEEE Trans. Intell. Transp. Syst. **17**(5), 1428–1437 (2015)

13. Tang, V.W., Zheng, Y., Cao, J.: An intelligent car park management system based on wireless sensor networks. In: 2006 First International Symposium on Pervasive Computing and Applications, pp. 65–70. IEEE (2006)

14. Lu, R., Lin, X., Zhu, H., Shen, X.: SPARK: a new VANET-based smart parking scheme for large parking lots. In: IEEE INFOCOM 2009, pp. 1413–1421. IEEE (2009)

15. Jin, C., Wang, L., Shu, L., Feng, Y., Xu, X.: A fairness-aware smart parking scheme aided by parking lots. In: 2012 IEEE International Conference on Communications (ICC), pp. 2119–2123. IEEE (2012)

16. Geng, Y., Cassandras, C.G.: New "smart parking" system based on resource allocation and reservations. IEEE Trans. Intell. Transp. Syst. **14**(3), 1129–1139 (2013)

17. Safi, Q.G.K., Luo, S., Pan, L., Liu, W., Hussain, R., Bouk, S.H.: SVPS: cloud-based smart vehicle parking system over ubiquitous VANETs. Comput. Netw. **138**, 18–30 (2018)

18. Atif, Y., Ding, J., Jeusfeld, M.A.: Internet of things approach to cloud-based smart car parking. Proc. Comput. Sci. **98**, 193–198 (2016)

19. Kizilkaya, B., Caglar, M., Al-Turjman, F., Ever, E.: Binary search tree based hierarchical placement algorithm for IoT based smart parking applications. Internet Things **5**, 71–83 (2019)

20. Bachani, M., Qureshi, U.M., Shaikh, F.K.: Performance analysis of proximity and light sensors for smart parking. Proc. Comput. Sci. **83**, 385–392 (2016)

21. Pala, Z., Inanc, N.: Smart parking applications using RFID technology. In: 2007 1st Annual RFID Eurasia, pp. 1–3. IEEE (2007)

22. CIEC: The essential chemical industry Online. In: Proceedings of International Conference on Internet Things Application, pp. 266–270 (2016)

23. Chatzigiannakis, I., Vitaletti, A., Pyrgelis, A.: A privacy-preserving smart parking system using an IoT elliptic curve based security platform. Comput. Commun. **89**, 165–177 (2016)

24. Polycarpou, E., Lambrinos, L., Protopapadakis, E.: Smart parking solutions for urban areas. In: 2013 IEEE 14th International Symposium on "A World of Wireless, Mobile and Multimedia Networks" (WoWMoM), pp. 1–6. IEEE (2013)

25. Zhang, W., Liu, H., Liu, Y., Zhou, J., Xiong, H.: Semi-supervised hierarchical recurrent graph neural network for city-wide parking availability prediction. In: Proceedings of the AAAI Conference on Artificial Intelligence, vol. 34, no. 01, pp. 1186–1193 (2020)

26. Gu, J., et al.: Recent advances in convolutional neural networks. Pattern Recogn. **77**, 354–377 (2018)

27. https://data.melbourne.vic.gov.au/Transport/On-street-Parking-Bay-Sensors/. Accessed January 2022

28. Kuhn, M., Johnson, K.: Applied Predictive Modeling, vol. 26, p. 13. Springer, New York (2013). https://doi.org/10.1007/978-1-4614-6849-3

29. Provoost, S., Ruwaard, J., Van Breda, W., Riper, H., Bosse, T.: Validating automated sentiment analysis of online cognitive behavioral therapy patient texts: an exploratory study. Front. Psychol. **10**, 1065 (2019)

30. Hyndman, R.J.: Another look at forecast-accuracy metrics for intermittent demand. Foresight Int. J. Appl. Forecast. **4**(4), 43–46 (2006)

Image Attribute Modification Based on Text Guidance

Liang Zhao$^{(\boxtimes)}$, Xiaoyuan Li, Chunjiang Fu, and Zhikui Chen

Dalian University of Technology, Dalian, China
liangzhao@dlut.edu.cn

Abstract. The goal of this paper is to manipulate image attributes using text description. Although many methods can synthesize images with new properties from text, they cannot fully preserve the text-independent content of the original image. There are two major limitations: (1) Some important details in image sub-region will be lost in the process of image modification; (2) Compared with the original image, the shape and edge of the object in the modified image will be more blurred. Therefore, we propose a novel framework edge aware generative adversarial network (EA-GAN) that uses edge information to guide image modification, which ensures the network's ability to identify local regions and realizes accurate modification of image sub-regions. At the same time, an edge reconstruction loss (ERLoss) is added to the generator to constrain the generation of edges, generate sharper edges, and improve the clarity of the image. The experimental data on the CUB and Oxford-102 datasets show that the algorithm used in this paper can well distinguish the corresponding image features in the conditional text, and modify the image attribute of specific regions in the image.

Keywords: Text to image generation · Generative adversarial network · Image modification

1 Introduction

With the popularity of mobile phones and the decline in the cost of photography, people's demand for personalized modification of pictures is gradually increasing. The great advances made in deep generative models, boost a remarkable evolution in automatic image manipulation, including image inpainting [25,26], image colourisation [27], style transfer [28,29], and domain or attribute translation [30,31].

Most of the above works is done on the single mode of image, and only a few works focus on text to image modification. Text description is the most natural and convenient medium for human being to manipulate images. This paper aims to manipulate image attributes using text description while preserve text-irrelevant contents.

Rather than image manipulating, approaches based on Generative adversarial networks(GANs) [1,19–21] have achieved promising results on this task.

H. Ma et al. (Eds.): CWSN 2022, CCIS 1715, pp. 200–211, 2022.
https://doi.org/10.1007/978-981-19-8350-4_16

A small brown bird with a brown crown has a white belly.

A light pink flower with pointed petals and a yellow circle.

Original   TAGAN   Ours

Fig. 1. Manipulating text-relevant contents using previous work (TAGAN [3]) and our work respectively. The image generated by TAGAN is blurred and the background of the image is not well preserved. Our method not only retains more text-irrelevant information, but also modifies the text-relevant information more accurately.

GANs are capable of generating realistic-looking images that adhere to characteristics described in text. Most networks are conditioned on an embedding of text description and generate a new image. However, these approaches only condition on an embedding of the complete textual description, without effectively distinguishing text-relevant regions from the original image and preserving text-irrelevant regions such as background. Some approaches tackle this by relying on similarity between encoded image and the sentence vector pretrained [2] or using word level discriminator [3] or affine combination module [32]. Though these models can be used to modify image attribute, they only fuse text description and original image while generating new image. Because of the lack of image sub regions and object shape information, there normally exists edge blur and object distortion in the modified images. As shown in 1, in the bird image modified by TAGAN [3], the round bird eyes and the human hands in the background can hardly be seen. Similarly, the image of flowers generated by TAGAN is very blurred, and the stamens and petals are mixed together.

In order to help the network better fuse text and image features and achieve more accurate modification of images, we add the edge information to the network. The recent study [4] discovered that edge played a key role when people recognize an object. To tackle these problems, we propose edge aware generator (EAG) that not only fuse text description and images, but also concatenate edge information extracted by canny operator. It enables the network to better distinguish different regions of the image (such as objects and backgrounds), modify specific areas related to the text while preserving content unrelated to the text. Meanwhile, a joint edge reconstruction loss (JERLoss) is added to the generator. It calculates the difference between the images before and after the modification. This not only prevents the loss of detailed information, but also ensures that the shape of the object is not changed.

2   Related Work

2.1   Text-to-Image Generation

With the success of deep generative models, T2I generation is becoming a hot topic both in CV field. Our work is particularly related to GANs. Reed et al. [5] used text to control the generation of images for the first time. To improve the resolution of the images, StackGAN [6] uses multiple stacked generator-discriminator pairs to gradually generate images from coarse to fine, increasing the image resolution. Li et al. [7] applied the attention mechanism to the stacking model, while proposing a semantic-visual model with training, which generated more refined images. To address the problem of multiple-stage GANs using too much computational resources, Ming et al. [23] proposed a one-stage structure that uses only a pair of generator and discriminator to generate images. In order to better fuse text and image features, SD-GAN [22] proposes to use Semantic-conditioned batch normalization (CBN) for image and text fusion. DF-GAN [23] uses stacked affine transformation to better fuse image features and text features. Hu et al. [33] proposed Semantic-Spatial Condition Batch Normalization (SSCBN) which use spatial mask maps to guide the learned text adaptive affine transformation. With the development of contrastive self-supervised pretraining, some recent works [36,37] use VQVAE [35] to represent images as discrete features, and generate images through transformer, which achieves better results than GANs. However, the above work is to generate a new image with text instead of manipulating the content of an existing image.

2.2   Conditional Image Synthesis

Our work is related to conditional image synthesis. Various methos based on Conditional Generative Adversarial Networks(CGANs) [8] have acheived paired image-to-image translation [9–11], or unpaired translation [12,13]. Except from same-domain image translation, image generation also make big progress in cross-domain. Esser et al. [34] proposed a new conditional generation model by combining vqvae and transformer, and generated high-resolution images. Compared to other conditional variables such as category or layout, text descriptions are the most convenient and direct way for people to control images. However, these methods mostly focus on the generation of the same image domain. This paper mainly studies the cross modal problem from text to image.

2.3   Text-Guided Image Manipulation

There are few works focusing on image manipulation using natural language descriptions. Dong et al. [2] use an encoder-decoder architecture and pre-trained text based on GAN to achieve image manipulation with text while maintaining the original image layout. In order to achieve only modifying image regions related to the descriptive text, Nam et al. [3] proposed a text adaptive discriminator to focus on word-level features in the text. Our framework follows its structure to get word-level feedback. However, both methods will have the problem that the modified image is not clear and the texture is blurred. To effectively manipulate text-relevant area, ManiGAN [32] uses affine transformation instead of concatenation to fuse text and image. However, the above methods only use the original image and text information to realize the manipulation of the image. These works not effectively utilize the edge information to generate a finer picture.

3 Generative Adversarial Networks for Image Modification

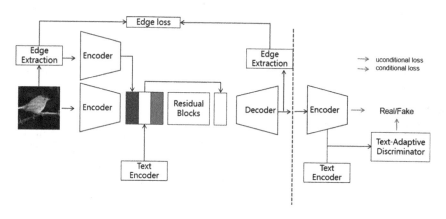

Fig. 2. The framework of the proposed algorithm.

Let x, t, $\hat{t}$, denote an image, a positive text where the description matches the image, and a negative text that does not correctly describe the image, respectively. Given an image x and a target negative text $\hat{t}$, our task is to semantically manipulate x according to $\hat{t}$ so that the visual attributes of the manipulated image $\hat{y}$ match the description of $\hat{t}$ while preserving other information. We use GAN as framework, in which the generator is trained to produce $\hat{y} = \text{G}(x, \text{E}(x), \hat{t})$. Similar to text-to-image GANs, we train our GAN to generate a realistic image that matches the conditional text semantically.

3.1 Edge Aware Generator

The existing work only fuses the original image and text, which makes the network unable to accurately manipulate the image sub regions, and thus unable to effectively generate fine-grained images. In order to help the network more accurately modify the text-relevant contents without changing the text-irrelevant contents, we use a generator that adds edge information to assist the network to identify the image sub areas. The generator is an encoder-decoder network as shown in Fig. 2. It first input an image to two modules. The fist is an encoder which will output image features. The second is an edge extraction module which is the key point of our network. It extract edge of the input image and encode it to edge features. To make image and text fusion better, edge information is added to fusion block, image features is transformed to a semantically manipulated representation according to the features of the given conditional text and the extracted edge. For the text representation, we use a bidirectional RNN to encode the whole text. we train the RNN from scratch, without pretraining. Additionally, we adopt the conditioning augmentation method for smooth text representation and the diversity of generated outputs. As shown in Fig. 2, manipulated contents are generated through several residual blocks with a skip connection. This process may generate a new background and other contents that are not described in the text. Therefore, we use the reconstruction loss [24] when a positive text is given, which enforces the generator to reconstruct the text-irrelevant contents from the input image instead of generating new contents:

$$\mathcal{L}_{rec} = \|x - G(x,t)\| \tag{1}$$

3.2 Edge Reconstruction Loss

Although reconstruction loss can help the network preserve text-irrelevant information, there has no constraint when a negative text is given. Therefore, we proposed an edge reconstruction loss when a negative text is given, which can ensure that the shape and other information irrelevant to the text will not change after the input image is modified. We input negative text to the generator and extract the edge information of the input image and the output image. Then we calculate the difference between these two images with MSE loss. Let E denote edge extractor, and the loss is defined as:

$$e = E(x), \quad \hat{e} = E(G(x))$$
$$\mathcal{L}_{rec_e} = \|E(x) - E(G(x,\hat{t}))\| \tag{2}$$

3.3 Discriminator

To get word-level feedback from discriminator, we adopt text adaptive discriminator structure proposed by TAGAN [3]. It can be seen from the Fig. 2 that the identification used in this paper has two outputs, one is to identify whether the image is true, and the other is to identify whether the image conforms to the textual description. The discriminator can be regarded as a classifier of the Encoder structure, which generates true and false labels to guide the generation of the generator.

3.4 Loss Function

The final GAN objective consists of both unconditional adversarial losses for $D(x)$, text-conditional losses for $D(x,\hat{t})$. In order to reduce the generation of irrelevant information, we use the reconstruction loss as shown in Eq. 1 for the real image and the edge reconstruction loss as shown in Eq. 2 for the generated image. The discriminator has two branches, which are used to identify the authenticity of the image and the correlation between the image and the text. Although there are two outputs, these two outputs share an encoder, which means their inputs are the same.Like other generative models, we train the discriminator, then the generator, and then alternate training until training stops.

The loss of discriminator consists of the loss of real data and the loss of generated data, so the loss function of the model is the sum of the loss of discriminator of real data and the loss of discriminator of generated data. When input real image, it will calculate the unconditional loss between output and 1. And it will calculate the conditional loss both between real image and matched text description and between real image and unmatched description. When input generated image, it will fist calculate the unconditional between output and 0. And then calculate the conditional loss between fake image and text description. It can be seen in equation

$$L_D = \mathbb{E}_{x,t,\hat{t} \sim P_{data}}[log D(x) + \lambda_1(log D(x,t)$$
$$+log(1 - D(x,\hat{t}))]$$
$$+\mathbb{E}_{x,t,\hat{t} \sim P_{data}} log(1 - G(x,\hat{t})) \qquad (3)$$

When it comes to generator, there are three parts of it. The fist is a adversarial loss. It calculate the distance between the output of discriminator and 1. The purpose of this loss is to make the results generated by the generator deceive the discriminator as much as possible. When input matched text to generator, the network will calculate reconstruction loss as shown in Eq. 1 which can ensure that the generated network will not produce content irrelevant to the text. When it comes to unmatched text, it will use edge reconstruction loss which means the distance between real image and generated image. It can ensure the generate work only generate content that is relevant to unmatched description and will not loss some important edge information.

$$L_G = \mathbb{E}_{x,\hat{t} \sim P_{data}}[log D(x) + \lambda_1 log D(G(x.\hat{t}),\hat{t})]$$
$$+ \lambda_2 L_{rec} + \lambda_3 L_{rec_e} \qquad (4)$$

where λ_1, λ_2 and λ_3 control the importance of additional losses, and t is randomly sampled from a dataset regardless of x. Note that we do not penalize generated outputs using the conditional discriminator in Eq. 3 to instability of training. In our experiment, our objective was enough to produce real images having manipulated attribute.

4   Experiments

Our model is evaluated on the CUB bird [14] and Oxford-102 [17] datasets, comparing with two state-of-the-art approaches SISGAN [2], AttnGAN and TAGAN. on image manipulation using natural language descriptions.

4.1   Datasets

The CUB bird dataset has 8,855 training images (150 species) and 2,933 test images (50 species). Each bird has 10 text descriptions. The Oxford-102 dataset has 8,189 flower images of 102 categories. Each flower has 10 text descriptions.

4.2   Evaluation Metric

We adopt the widely used Inception Score (IS) [15] and *Fréchet* Inception Distance [16] to quantify the performance. For the IS, a pretrained Inception v3 network [18] is used to compute the KL-divergence between the conditional class distribution (generated images) and the marginal class distribution (real images). A large IS indicates that the generated images are of high quality, and each image clearly belongs to a specific class. The FID computes the *Fréchet*   Distance between the features distribution of the generated and real-world images. The features are extracted by a pretrained Inception v3 network. A lower FID implies the generated images are more realistic. However, IS and FID only focus on one aspect of this problem. We also use manipulative precision (MP) [32] to measure the quality of generation and reconstruction. The larger the MP, the higher the image sharpness and the text image similarity.

4.3   Quantitative Results

Table 1. Quantitative comparison.

Method	CUB				Oxford-102			
	IS	FID	L_2 error	MP	IS	FID	L_2 error	MP
SISGAN	–	–	0.30	0.23	–	–	0.29	0.41
AttnGAN	–	–	0.25	0.27	–	–	0.32	0.46
TAGAN	5.35	31.09	0.15	0.25	3.94	55.01	0.16	0.40
Ours	5.24	**26.39**	**0.10**	**0.36**	**4.12**	**50.56**	**0.12**	**0.51**

Table 1 shows the quantitative results of our method and several state-of-the-art GAN models that have achieved remarkable advances in text to image modification. From the second column of the table we can see that, our method reports improvements in IS (from 3.94 to 4.12) on Oxford-102 dataset compared to the most recent state-of-the-art method TAGAN. However, the IS score of our method on CUB dataset has decreased, which likely because the image of CUB dataset is relatively simple and the edge of bird is relatively clear. The additional edge information added in our network is not very effective for datasets with clear edges. Our method remarkably decreases the FID score from 31.09 to 26.39 on CUB dataset and 55.01 to 50.56 compared to TAGAN. Compared with the CUB dataset, the Oxford-102 dataset is more challenging because the background is more complex. Our superior performances indicate that is able to synthesize accurate images with complex background. The superiority and effectiveness of our proposed method are demonstrated by the extensive quantitative evaluation results that the method is able able to generate high quality images with better semantic consistency, both for the images with many detailed attributes and more complex images.

It can be seen from Table 1 that although the IS score of the method proposed in this paper is slightly lower than TAGAN on CUB data set, all other scores on CUB and oxford-102 dataset is better than TAGAN. Therefore, we can preliminarily get the conclusion that the images generated by the method proposed in this paper are more real and reasonable. As shown in Table 1, there is no score except L_2 error of SISGAN and AttnGAN. This is because these two methods are used in text to image generation and our task is text to image modification. So it is incomparable between them.

4.4   Qualitative Results

Fig. 3. Examples of diverse image generation by changing some words in the input text (in red) (Color figure online)

Generalization Ability. Figure 3 shows qualitative results of our method on CUB. In most cases, the visual attributes of images are accurately changed according to the text. It can be seen that by changing a part of text, the network will generate the corresponding picture. For example, if we replace the word "white belly" with the word "yellow belly" in the text, the network will generate a picture that replaces the color of bird belly from white to yellow while keeping other areas unchanged.

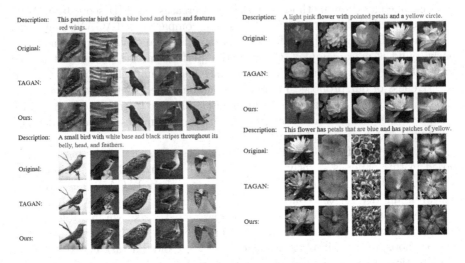

Fig. 4. Qualitative comparison of three methods on the CUB bird and Oxford-102 datasets

Comparison. Figure 4(a), 4(b) compares the generation effect of our method and baseline on Oxford-102 and CUB datasets.

It can be seen that TAGAN can modify the image according to the text, but the modified area is not that accurate. The image generated by TAGAN has an obvious problem of blurred edges. As we can see in Fig. 4(b), the shape of some flowers generated by TAGAN are changed. Tagan also lose some detailed information such as texture. For example, when TAGAN generates a picture of a bird, the bird's eyes and the texture of feathers will become blurred or even lost. And when TAGAN generates a picture of flowers, the texture of petals and patches will be lost. TAGAN is also easier to modify information irrelevant to text, such as background. For example, in some pictures, the background of flowers is solid color, but in the pictures generated by TAGAN, the background of flowers is composed of green leaves and other information.

We can easily see from the Fig. 4(a), 4(b) that the method proposed in this paper can modify the image according to the text more accurately, and can better retain the background, shape and other information irrelevant to the text. As shown in Fig. 4(a), the method proposed in this paper better retains the texture of feathers in the generation process, and does not lose important information such as bird's eyes. As shown in the Fig. 4(b), the petals and stamens did not change the shape of the petals and the texture of the stamens while changing the color. And the background generated by the proposed method in the process of image modification is almost the same as the original image.

5 Conclusions

In this paper, we proposed a method for text-guided image modification. This method focus on the edge of original image, fuse edge information and text information, generate more clear and accurate images. Extensive experimental results demonstrate the superiority of our method, in terms of both the effectiveness of image manipulation and the capability of generating high-quality results.

References

1. Goodfellow, I., Pouget-Abadie, J., Mirza, M., Xu, B., Warde-Farley, D., Ozair, S.: Generative Adversarial Nets. In: NIPS, pp. 2672–2680 (2014)
2. Dong, H., Yu, S., Wu, C.,: Semantic Image Synthesis via Adversarial Learning. In: ICCV, pp. 5707–5715 (2017) 10.1109/iccv.2017.608
3. Nam, S., Kim, Y., Kim, S.J.: Text-Adaptive Generative Adversarial Networks: Manipulating Images with Natural Language. In: NeurIPS, pp. 42–51 (2018)
4. Geirhos, R., Rubisch, P., Michaelis, C.: ImageNet-trained CNNs are biased towards texture; increasing shape bias improves accuracy and robustness. In: ICLR (2019)
5. Reed, S., Akata, Z., Yan, X., Logeswaran, L., Schiele, B., Lee, H.: Generative adversarial text to image synthesis. In: ICML, pp. 1060–1069 (2016)
6. Zhang, H., Xu, T., Li, H., Zhang, S., Wang, X., Huang, X., Metaxas, D.N.: Stackgan: Text to photo-realistic image synthesis with stacked generative adversarial networks. In: Proceedings of the IEEE international conference on computer vision, pp. 5907–5915 (2017) 10.1109/iccv.2017.629
7. Xu, T., Zhang, P., Huang, Q., Zhang, H., Gan, Z., Huang, X., He, X.: Attngan: Fine-grained text to image generation with attentional generative adversarial networks. In: Proceedings of the IEEE Conference on Computer Vision and Pattern Recognition, pp. 1316–1324 (2018)
8. Yu, Y., Gong, Z., Zhong, P., Shan, J.: Unsupervised representation learning with deep convolutional neural network for remote sensing images. In: Zhao, Y., Kong, X., Taubman, D. (eds.) ICIG 2017. LNCS, vol. 10667, pp. 97–108. Springer, Cham (2017). https://doi.org/10.1007/978-3-319-71589-6_9
9. Chen, Q., Koltun, V.: Photographic image synthesis with cascaded refinement networks. In: Proceedings of the IEEE International Conference on Computer Vision, pp. 1511–1520 (2017)
10. Isola, P., Zhu, J. Y., Zhou, T., Efros, A.A.: Image-to-image translation with conditional adversarial networks. In: Proceedings of the IEEE Conference on Computer Vision and Pattern Recognition, pp. 1125–1134 (2017)
11. Wang, T. C., Liu, M. Y., Zhu, J. Y., Tao, A., Kautz, J., Catanzaro, B.: High-resolution image synthesis and semantic manipulation with conditional GANs. In: Proceedings of the IEEE Conference on Computer Vision and Pattern Recognition, pp. 8798–8807 (2018) https://doi.org/10.1109/cvpr.2018.00917
12. Liu, M. Y., Tuzel, O.: Coupled generative adversarial networks. In: Advances in Neural Information Processing Systems, vol. 29 (2016)
13. Zhu, J.Y., Park, T., Isola, P., Efros, A.A.: Unpaired image-to-image translation using cycle-consistent adversarial networks. In: Proceedings of the IEEE International Conference on Computer Vision, pp. 2223–2232 (2017)
14. Catherine, W., Steve, B., Peter, W., Pietro, P., Serge B.: The caltech-ucsd birds-200-2011dataset (2011)

15. Salimans, T., Goodfellow, I., Zaremba, W., Cheung, V., Radford, A., Chen, X.: Improved techniques for training GANs. In: Advances in Neural Information Processing Systems, vol. 29 (2016)
16. Heusel, M., Ramsauer, H., Unterthiner, T., Nessler, B., Hochreiter, S.: Gans trained by a two time-scale update rule converge to a local nash equilibrium. In: Advances in Neural Information Processing Systems, vol. 30 (2017)
17. Nilsback, M.E., Zisserman, A.: Automated flower classification over a large number of classes. In: 2008 Sixth Indian Conference on Computer Vision, Graphics & Image Processing, pp. 722–729 (2008)
18. Szegedy, C., Vanhoucke, V., Ioffe, S., Shlens, J., Wojna, Z.: Rethinking the inception architecture for computer vision. In: Proceedings of the IEEE Conference on Computer Vision and Pattern Recognition, pp. 2818–2826 (2016)
19. Karras, T., Laine, S., Aila, T.: A style-based generator architecture for generative adversarial networks. In: Proceedings of the IEEE/CVF Conference on Computer Vision and Pattern Recognition, pp. 4401–4410 (2019) https://doi.org/10.1109/cvpr.2019.00453
20. Yu, Y., Gong, Z., Zhong, P., Shan, J.: Unsupervised representation learning with deep convolutional neural network for remote sensing images. In: Zhao, Y., Kong, X., Taubman, D. (eds.) ICIG 2017. LNCS, vol. 10667, pp. 97–108. Springer, Cham (2017). https://doi.org/10.1007/978-3-319-71589-6_9
21. Liu, X., Yin, G., Shao, J., Wang, X.: Learning to predict layout-to-image conditional convolutions for semantic image synthesis. In: Advances in Neural Information Processing Systems, vol. 32 (2019)
22. Yin, G., Liu, B., Sheng, L., Yu, N., Wang, X., Shao, J.: Semantics disentangling for text-to-image generation. In: Proceedings of the IEEE/CVF Conference on Computer Vision and Pattern Recognition, pp. 2327–2336 (2019)
23. Tao, M., et al.: Df-gan: Deep fusion generative adversarial networks for text-to-image synthesis. arXiv preprint arXiv:2008.05865(2020)
24. He, Z., Zuo, W., Kan, M., Shan, S., Chen, X.: Arbitrary facial attribute editing: Only change what you want. arXiv preprint arXiv:1711.10678, vol. 1(3) (2017)
25. Iizuka, S., Simo-Serra, E., Ishikawa, H.: Let there be color! Joint end-to-end learning of global and local image priors for automatic image colorization with simultaneous classification. ACM Trans. Graph. (ToG) **35**(4), 1–11 (2016)
26. Pathak, D., Krahenbuhl, P., Donahue, J., Darrell, T., Efros, A.A.: Context encoders: Feature learning by inpainting. In: Proceedings of the IEEE Conference on Computer Vision and Pattern Recognition, pp. 2536–2544 (2016)
27. Zhu, J.-Y., Krähenbühl, P., Shechtman, E., Efros, A.A.: Generative visual manipulation on the natural image manifold. In: Leibe, B., Matas, J., Sebe, N., Welling, M. (eds.) ECCV 2016. LNCS, vol. 9909, pp. 597–613. Springer, Cham (2016). https://doi.org/10.1007/978-3-319-46454-1_36
28. Gatys, L.A., Ecker, A.S., Bethge, M.: Image style transfer using convolutional neural networks. In: Proceedings of the IEEE Conference on Computer Vision and Pattern Recognition, pp. 2414–2423 (2016)
29. Johnson, Justin, Alahi, Alexandre, Fei-Fei, Li.: Perceptual losses for real-time style transfer and super-resolution. In: Leibe, Bastian, Matas, Jiri, Sebe, Nicu, Welling, Max (eds.) ECCV 2016. LNCS, vol. 9906, pp. 694–711. Springer, Cham (2016). https://doi.org/10.1007/978-3-319-46475-6_43
30. Isola, P., Zhu, J. Y., Zhou, T., Efros, A.A.: Image-to-image translation with conditional adversarial networks. In: Proceedings of the IEEE Conference on Computer Vision and Pattern Recognition, pp. 1125–1134 (2017)

31. Lample, G., Zeghidour, N., Usunier, N., Bordes, A., Denoyer, L., Ranzato, M.A.: Fader networks: Manipulating images by sliding attributes. In: Advances in Neural Information Processing Systems, vol. 30 (2017)
32. Li, B., Qi, X., Lukasiewicz, T., Torr, P.H.: ManiGAN: Text-guided image manipulation. In: Proceedings of the IEEE/CVF Conference on Computer Vision and Pattern Recognition, pp. 7880–7889 (2020)
33. Liao, W., Hu, K., Yang, M.Y., Rosenhahn, B.: Text to image generation with semantic-spatial aware GAN. In: Proceedings of the IEEE/CVF Conference on Computer Vision and Pattern Recognition, pp. 18187–18196 (2022)
34. Esser, P., Rombach, R., Ommer, B.: Taming transformers for high-resolution image synthesis. In: Proceedings of the IEEE/CVF conference on computer vision and pattern recognition, pp. 12873–12883 (2021). https://doi.org/10.1109/cvpr46437.2021.01268
35. Van Den Oord, A., Vinyals, O.: Neural discrete representation learning. In: Advances in Neural Information Processing Systems, vol. 30 (2017)
36. Ramesh, A., Pavlov, M., Goh, G., Gray, S., Voss, C., Radford, A., Sutskever, I.: Zero-shot text-to-image generation. In: International Conference on Machine Learning, pp. 8821–8831. PMLR (2021)
37. Ding, M., et al.: Cogview: Mastering text-to-image generation via transformers. Advances in Neural Information Processing Systems **34**, 19822–19835 (2021)

Industrial IoT Network Security Situation Prediction Based on Improved SSA-BiLSTM

Ke Xiao, Yueyao Zhang$^{(\boxtimes)}$, Yunhua He, Gang Xu, and Chao Wang

North China University of Technology, Beijing 100144, China
zhangyueyao61@sina.com

Abstract. The industrial Internet of Things (IIoT) can provide production management services for customers, but also faces cyber-attacks and security issues. The network security situation prediction describes the security status of the network from a holistic perspective for the coming period. Existing network security situation prediction models suffer from low prediction accuracy and do not apply to industrial IoT scenarios. To address the above problems, an ISSA-BiLSTM-based security situation prediction model for industrial IoT is proposed. Firstly, a situational assessment index system is proposed for the characteristics of industrial IoT, and the real situational values of the used industrial IoT datasets are calculated based on this index system. Besides, the opposition-based learning and Lévy flight strategy are introduced to improve the sparrow search algorithm (SSA) to avoid it from falling into local optimum. At last, we use the improved SSA (ISSA) to search for optimality of the relevant parameters of the BiLSTM model to ensure the accuracy of the prediction. With simulation experiments, we verify that the ISSA-BiLSTM model has smaller errors and higher fitness.

Keywords: Industrial IoT · Situation prediction · BiLSTM neural networks · Sparrow search algorithm · Lévy flight strategy

1 Introduction

The Industrial Internet of Things, as the representative technology of the fourth industrial revolution, drives economic efficiency and fuels the booming global manufacturing industry. Industrial manufacturers can easily improve productivity and quality, as well as enhance business agility through IoT [1]. However, IoT adoption faces security challenges.

The Snake ransomware attacked the processes and related files of industrial control systems (ICS) in 2020. A malicious cyber attack on the computer system of the Macao Health Bureau in China affected the normal operation of systems such as health codes, medical vouchers, COVID-19 vaccines and nucleic acid testing in 2021 [2]. Industrial IoT devices are vulnerable to cyber attacks, and a single security protection facility cannot achieve comprehensive monitoring of

© The Author(s), under exclusive license to Springer Nature Singapore Pte Ltd. 2022
H. Ma et al. (Eds.): CWSN 2022, CCIS 1715, pp. 212–224, 2022.
https://doi.org/10.1007/978-981-19-8350-4_17

the overall situation. Therefore, it is crucial to design models that reflect the overall industrial IoT security situation.

The network security situation prediction has been proposed to solve this problem. First of all, we establish a system of indicators reflecting the current network security situation, and assess the overall state of the network based on these indicators. Then use the historical network security situation values to predict the development trend of the network security situation in the future period, so that network security administrators can use them to prevent possible network attacks in advance and make effective planning and more scientific decisions.

Traditional network security situation prediction methods include Bayesian networks [3], game theory [4], and gray theory [5] models. However, the trend of network security situation change is nonlinear and time-varying, and the prediction accuracy of many classical prediction methods is not satisfactory. At this stage, the solution combining network security situation prediction technology and artificial intelligence (AI) has become one of the research focuses in academia and industry. Tang et al. [6] proposed an ELM network model based on an improved particle swarm algorithm which improved the prediction accuracy and speed of the ELM network. Wang [7] demonstrated the performance of radial basis function (RBF) networks with particle swarm optimization through comparative experiments. Zhang et al. [8] proposed a sigmoid weighted linear element and cuckoo search algorithm which improve the prediction accuracy and reduce the training time of the LSTM network. Wei et al. [9] proposed an NSSP model based on security posture factor prediction. The model mainly analyzes the dynamic changes of attack information, vulnerability information, and defense measures, and performs the posture prediction from both host and network levels. In summary, the backward and forward correlation on time-series data is not considered in network security situation prediction, however, network attacks show certain regularity in time series, and this deficiency inhibits the prediction effect.

BiLSTM network has dynamic memory property and can make full use of the information in time series data. It is considered as one of the feasible solutions to solve the problem of insufficient accuracy in network security situation prediction. In addition, there are differences between industrial IoT and traditional networks. The industrial Internet of Things devices generate and consume data, which involves transferring data back and forth between various devices [14]. The network data generated when many industrial devices communicate with each other is different from the traditional network data. Various network datasets, for example, KDDCUP99, NSL-KDD, UNSW-NB15 and ISCX, were generated for evaluating IDSs; however, they do not include any specific characteristics of IoT/IIoT applications. Therefore, it is important to propose a network security situation prediction model applicable to industrial IoT.

We propose a BiLSTM network model based on an improved sparrow search algorithm. Firstly, to address the problem that there is no real situational value in the industrial IoT dataset, an improved fuzzy hierarchical analysis proposed is used to obtain the situational value with reference to the index system and the industrial IoT data feature set. In the ISSA-BiLSTM model, the sparrow search algorithm is optimized by the reverse contrastive learning and Lévy flight strategy to balance the local and global search ability and accelerate the model convergence. In addition, a dropout layer is added after Bilstm to improve the generalization ability.

The contributions of this paper are summarized as follows.

1) We propose a situational assessment index system with industrial IoT characteristics, based on which we calculate the true situational values of the used industrial IoT datasets.
2) We introduce the opposition-based learning and Lévy flight strategy into the sparrow search algorithm to avoid the SSA from falling into local optimum and accelerate the convergence.
3) We use the improved sparrow search algorithm for the BiLSTM model to perform parameter search optimization, and finally, through experiments, we demonstrate the prediction accuracy of ISSA-BiLSTM model.

The remainder of the paper is organized as follows. Section 2 presents the BiLSTM network and sparrow search algorithm, with Sect. 3 detailing the process of industrial IoT security situation prediction. Section 4 conducts the experimental analysis. At last, the paper is concluded in Sect. 5.

2   Research Methods

2.1   Bidirectional Long Short-Term Memory Network

LSTM is a one-way extraction of sequential information [10]. While the BiLSTM network consists of two LSTM layers superimposed in the forward and reverse directions, the output value is determined by both the forward and reverse layers. Figure 1 illustrates its basic structure.

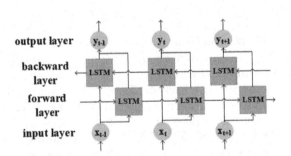

Fig. 1. The basic structure of BiLSTM model

2.2   Sparrow Search Algorithm

The sparrow search algorithm is a new heuristic swarm optimization algorithm proposed by Xue et al. [11] through the foraging behavior of sparrows. Sparrows as discoverers provide foraging areas and directions for all followers [12], the discoverer's position is updated with an expression such as the following equation.

$$X_{i,j}^{t+1} = \begin{cases} X_{i,j}^t \cdot exp\left(\frac{-i}{\alpha \cdot iter_{max}}\right), & R_2 < ST \\ X_{i,j}^t + Q \cdot L, & R_2 >= ST \end{cases} \qquad (1)$$

$X_{i,j}^{t+1}$ represents the value of the jth dimension of the ith sparrow at iteration t + 1 at iteration t. α and Q are random numbers. L denotes a $1 \times d$ all-1 matrix. If $R_2 < ST$, this indicates that the surrounding area is safe.

The equation for updating the location of followers is as follows.

$$X_{i,j}^{t+1} = \begin{cases} Q \cdot exp\left(\frac{X_{worst}^t - X_{i,j}^t}{i^2}\right), & i > \frac{2}{n} \\ X_P^{t+1} + |X_{i,j}^t - X_P^{t+1}| \cdot A^+ \cdot L, & other \end{cases} \qquad (2)$$

X_{worst}^t represents the global worst position. A denotes a $1 * d$ matrix with internal elements randomly assigned 1 or -1. When $i > n/2$, it means that the ith follower with poorer fitness value needs to fly in other directions to find food.

The warners generally represent 10% to 20% of the population and their location is updated with the following equation.

$$X_{i,j}^{t+1} = \begin{cases} X_{best}^t + \beta \cdot |X_{i,j}^t - X_{best}^t|, & f_i > f_g \\ X_{i,j}^t + K \cdot \left(\frac{X_{i,j}^t - X_{worst}^t}{(f_i - f_w) + \varepsilon}\right), & f_i = f_g \end{cases} \qquad (3)$$

X_{best}^t represents the global best position. β and K are step control parameters. f_i denotes the fitness of the sparrow. When $f_i > f_g$ indicates that the sparrow is vulnerable to predator attack, when $f_i = f_g$ indicates that sparrows in the middle of the population sparrows need to move closer to the other sparrows.

3   Industrial IoT Network Security Situation Forecast

The industrial IoT security situation prediction first requires collecting industrial IoT data, and establishing a situation assessment index system that reflects the correlation between industrial IoT data and protocol characteristics. Then the industrial IoT dataset is pre-processed in a time slice of 20 min, and the real posture values are evaluated as training labels for the industrial IoT dataset using this index system and the improved AHP method. In addition, the pre-processed samples are divided by the sliding window method, and finally the ISSA-BiLSTM model is used to train and predict the posture values in the next time slice. The flow of industrial IoT security situation prediction is shown in Fig. 2.

Fig. 2. The flow of industrial IoT security situation prediction.

3.1 Industrial IoT Dataset Description

Traditional network security situation prediction commonly uses network intrusion detection datasets for experiments. However, the network data generated by IoT devices communicating with each other is different from traditional network data and has its unique data characteristics. Therefore, it is unreasonable if the intrusion detection dataset is chosen to reflect the overall network condition of the IoT.

The experiment uses the next-generation IoT and IIoT dataset TON_IoT [13], which were collected from a realistic large-scale network designed by the University of New South Wales Canberra Network's IoT Lab and others. The datasets including several normal and cyber-attack events were collected from the IoT network in a parallel processing manner.

The network data collected in TON_IoT contains 46 features and 9 types of attack behaviors. We select the Train_Test_Network.csv file in the official website dataset as the sample set, which contains 461043 pieces of data.

3.2 Industrial IoT Network Security Situation Value

The Train_Test_Network.csv file in TON_IoT does not have the real situation value, so we consider the idea of constructing the situation indicator system and the features in the IoT protocol in paper [14], and then construct the IIoT security situation assessment index system as shown in Table 1.

Table 1. IIoT security situation assessment index system

Guidelines	Indicators
Operational dimension	Device asset value, operating system version information, time of the packet connections
Fragile dimension	Severity of vulnerability, number of open ports, network topology
Stability dimension	Subnet traffic variation rate, total subnet traffic, peak subnet traffic, source bytes
Threat dimension	Security event history frequency, number of alarms, total length of subnet packet IP headers, destination bytes

The TON_IoT dataset has too much data, so we cannot use the dataset directly and need to process it further. By comprehensively measuring the number of samples within the dataset and the feature information that each sample can contain, we divided the dataset into 215 time slices according to the length of each time slice of 20 minutes in this paper. Then mine the data on each time slice and perform the extraction of situational elements according to Table 1, and finally calculate the value of each indicator in the indicator layer. Since the sample set constructed in this paper does not have the true situation values, the situation evaluation algorithm proposed by Luan et al. [15] is used to generate the situation values in this paper, and the generated situational values are shown in Fig. 3.

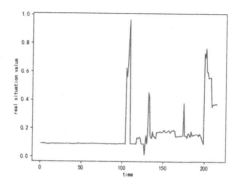

Fig. 3. Real situation values of TON_IoT network.

3.3   Sliding Window Method to Divide the Sample Set

In this paper, we set the sliding window size as $m + 1$, then the n samples can be divided into a test sample set structure according to Table 2.

Table 2. Prediction sample set structure

Sample number	Input samples	Output data
1	$(x_1, x_2, ..., x_m)$	x_{m+1}
2	$(x_2, x_3, ..., x_{m+1})$	x_{m+2}
...	...	...
$n - m$	$(x_{n-m}, x_{n-m+1}, ..., x_{n-1})$	x_n

There are 215 samples in total in this experiment, and $215 - (m + 1) + 1$ samples are formed by the sliding window method (size $m+1$, sliding one unit at a time). The number of neurons in the input and output layers of the BiLSTM network corresponds to the number of input samples and output data, so the number of neurons in the input layer is set to m and the number of neurons in the output layer is set to 1.

3.4   Construction of BiLSTM Model

The BiLSTM model used in this paper is shown in Fig. 4.

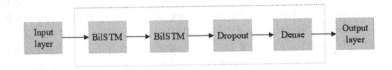

Fig. 4. BiLSTM model.

1) The two BiLSTM layers can make full use of the before-and-after information in the time-series data to achieve better prediction results.
2) The dropout layer avoids overfitting and improves generalization.
3) The dense layer transforms the output dimension and obtains the predicted values.

3.5   Improved Sparrow Search Algorithm

Opposition-Based Learning Strategy. The initial population of the sparrow search algorithm is randomly generated, and the sparrow positions may be too aggregated or dispersed, leading to slow convergence of the algorithm. Therefore, we introduce the Opposition-Based Learning (OBL) [16] strategy proposed by Tizhoosh to improve the population quality and obtain the initial population with better adaptation.

Suppose the initial population $\mathbf{X} = x_1, x_2, \ldots, x_n$ is generated randomly. X corresponds to the inverse population $\overline{X}$ defined as $\overline{X} = Ub + Lb - X$, and Ub and Lb are the upper and lower bounds of the search space, respectively. Merge the populations X and $\overline{X}$, sort the $2n$ sparrow individuals in ascending order according to their fitness values, and select the top n sparrow individuals with fitness values as the initial population.

Lévy Flight Strategy. To address the problem that SSA is prone to local optimality [17,18], we introduce the Lévy flight strategy [19], which is a non-Gaussian stochastic gait whose step size obeys a heavy-tailed probability distribution. Lévy flight is characterized by a long period of small steps and occasional large steps [20]. When searching for the optimal solution, Lévy flight can not only perform local search in short distances but also global search in long distances. Therefore, when searching for the optimal solution, Lévy flight can balance the local and global search ability and solve the problem that the standard SSA algorithm tends to fall into local optimum. We introduce the Lévy flight strategy in the follower position update formula to improve the global search capability. The improved formula is as follows.

$$X_{i,j}^{t+1} = \begin{cases} Q \cdot exp\left(\frac{X_{worst}^t - X_{i,j}^t}{i^2}\right), & i > \frac{2}{n} \\ X_P^{t+1} + X_P^{t+1} \otimes Lévy(d), & other \end{cases} \tag{4}$$

The Lévy flight strategy is as follows. Both $r_3(r_3 \in [0,1])$ and $r_4(r_4 \in [0,1])$ are random numbers, and the value of ξ can be taken as 1.5.

$$Lévy\,(x) = 0.01 \times \frac{r_3 \times \sigma}{|r_4|^{\frac{1}{\xi}}} \qquad (5)$$

σ is calculated as follows $\Gamma\,(x) = (x-1)!$

$$\sigma = \left(\frac{\Gamma\,(1+\xi) \times sin\left(\frac{\pi\xi}{2}\right)}{\Gamma\left(\frac{1+\xi}{2}\right) \times \xi \times 2^{\frac{\xi-1}{2}}} \right)^{\frac{1}{\xi}} \qquad (6)$$

3.6 Steps of ISSA-BiLSTM Model Situation Prediction

The ISSA-BiLSTM model is to optimize the relevant parameters of BiLSTM based on the fast optimization-seeking capability of the ISSA. The specific steps for constructing the ISSA-BiLSTM model are as follows:

- Step 1 sets the window value m and divide the dataset into a test set and training set in the ratio of 8:2.
- Step 2 initializes the relevant parameters of the sparrow search algorithm.
- Step 3 sets the dimensions of sparrows to represent the number of cells in the first and second hidden layers, the number of model iterations, the learning rate, and the proportion of discarded layers in the BiLSTM model. An opposition-based learning strategy is introduced to initialize the sparrow population.
- Step 4 sets the fitness function of the sparrow search algorithm, calculates the fitness of each sparrow in the population, and obtains the best individual.
- Step 5 updates the producer position according to Eq. (3), introduces Lévy flight strategy to update the follower position according to Eq. (6), and updates the warning position according to Eq. (5).
- Step 6 proceeds to step 7 if the maximum number of iterations is reached, and if not, continues to iterate step 5.
- Step 7 assigns the obtained optimal parameters to the BiLSTM model and obtains the posture prediction results.

The flow chart of ISSA-BiLSTM model industrial IoT network security situation prediction is shown in Fig. 5.

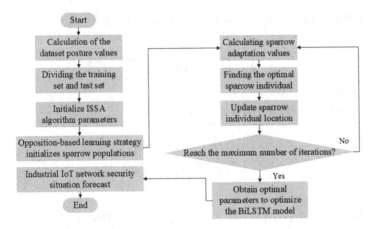

Fig. 5. ISSA-BiLSTM model prediction process.

4   Experiment

To verify the predictive ability of all models proposed in this paper, four typical regression evaluation metrics were selected to evaluate each model, which are mean square error (MSE), mean absolute error (MAE), root mean square error ($RMSE$), and coefficient of goodness of fit (R^2). The formulas of these four evaluation metrics are shown below.

$$MSE = \frac{1}{N} \sum_{i=1}^{N} (y_i - \hat{y}_i)^2 \tag{7}$$

$$MAE = \frac{1}{N} \sum_{i=1}^{N} |y_i - \hat{y}_i| \times 100\% \tag{8}$$

$$RMSE = \sqrt{\frac{1}{N} \sum_{i=1}^{N} (y_i - \hat{y}_i)^2} \tag{9}$$

$$R^2 = 1 - \frac{\sum_{i=1}^{N} (y_i - \hat{y}_i)^2}{\sum_{i=1}^{N} (y_i - \bar{y}_i)^2} \tag{10}$$

where N is the number of samples, y_i denotes the true posture value, $\hat{y}_i$ denotes the predicted posture value, and $\bar{y}_i$ denotes the average of the true posture values. The smaller the value of the error, the better the model performance is. $R^2 \in [0, 1]$, the closer its value is to 1, the better the fit of the model.

In order to verify the prediction effectiveness of each model, experiments were conducted at the window values of 4 and 6, respectively. The window value of 4 means that the situational values of the first three time periods are used to predict the situational values of the latter one. When the window value is 4, we compare the ISSA-BiLSTM model proposed in this paper with the IPSO-LSTM model proposed in another paper [10]. The prediction results of each model are shown in Fig. 6, and the absolute errors between the predicted and true values of each model are shown in Fig. 7.

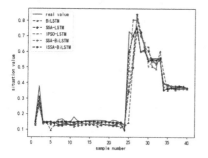 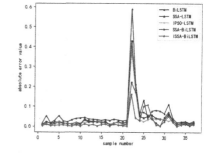

Fig. 6. Comparison of prediction results (window value of 4).

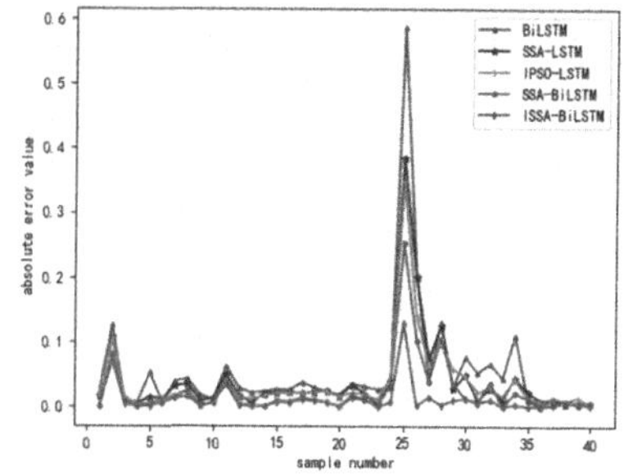

Fig. 7. Absolute error comparison (window value of 4).

From the above two figures, it can be seen that the predicted situational values of the ISSA-BiLSTM model proposed in this paper almost fit the real situational values, and the remaining four models have some fitting bias.

When the window value is 6, we compare the ISSA-BiLSTM model proposed in this paper with the IPSO-LSTM model proposed in another paper [10]. The prediction results of each model are shown in Fig. 8, and the absolute errors between the predicted and true values of each model are shown in Fig. 9.

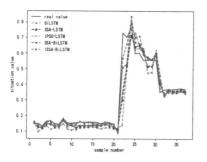

Fig. 8. Comparison of prediction results (window value of 6).

Fig. 9. Absolute error comparison (window value of 6).

From the above two figures, it can be seen that the ISSA-BiLSTM model proposed in this paper fits better than the remaining four models.

The evaluation metrics for each model with windows value of 4 and 6 are shown in Table 3 below.

Table 3. Comparison of evaluation indicators of different models

Window value	Evaluation indexes	MSE	MAE	RMSE	R^2
4	BiLSTM	0.011783	0.053730	0.108552	0.746588
	SSA-LSTM	0.006034	0.040027	0.077679	0.860211
	IPSO-LSTM	0.004670	0.035883	0.068340	0.890909
	SSA-BiLSTM	0.002217	0.024023	0.047093	0.946835
	ISSA-BiLSTM	0.000885	0.013589	0.029758	0.986332
6	BiLSTM	0.012951	0.061997	0.113805	0.737988
	SSA-LSTM	0.006638	0.039835	0.081479	0.857593
	IPSO-LSTM	0.005208	0.033925	0.072168	0.886749
	SSA-BiLSTM	0.002913	0.031643	0.053976	0.933424
	ISSA-BiLSTM	0.001554	0.020190	0.039429	0.964423

When the window values are 4 and 6, the MSE, MAE and RMSE values of the ISSA-BiLSTM model proposed in this paper are lower than those of the BiLSTM, SSA-LSTM, IPSO-LSTM and SSA-BiLSTM models, respectively, and the fitting coefficient R^2 is higher than those of the other four models. Therefore, the ISSA-BiLSTM model is superior to the other four models.

A comparison of the fit of the predicted values of the different models with the true situation values is shown in Fig. 10.

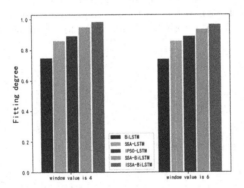

Fig. 10. Comparison of the fitting degree of different models.

The comparative analysis of the experimental results shows that the ISSA-BiLSTM model proposed in this paper outperforms the remaining four models in terms of prediction accuracy when the sliding window value is fixed. When the sliding window value is not fixed, it is more appropriate to choose three historical situation values to predict the situation value of the next period.

5   Conclusion

In this paper, we propose an ISSA-BiLSTM-based approach for industrial IoT security situation prediction. A situational assessment index system is proposed to calculate the true situational values. In the construction of the model, opposition-based learning and Lévy flight strategy are introduced to optimize the sparrow search algorithm for the drawback that the SSA is prone to fall into local optimum. Finally, after experimental comparison, the ISSA-BiLSTM model proposed in this paper has a better prediction effect than the rest of the models.

References

1. Lohiya, R., Thakkar, A.: Application domains, evaluation data sets, and research challenges of IoT: a systematic review. IEEE Internet Things J. **8**(11), 8774–8798 (2020)
2. Pathak, N., Deb, P.K., Mukherjee, A., Misra, S.: IoT-to-the-rescue: a survey of IoT solutions for COVID-19-like pandemics. IEEE Internet Things J. **8**(17), 13145–13164 (2021)
3. Okutan, A., Yang, S.J., McConky, K.: Predicting cyber attacks with Bayesian networks using unconventional signals. In: Proceedings of the 12th Annual Conference on Cyber and Information Security Research, pp. 1–4 (2017)
4. Abdlhamed, M., Kifayat, K., Shi, Q., Hurst, W.: A system for intrusion prediction in cloud computing. In: Proceedings of the International Conference on Internet of Things and Cloud Computing, pp. 1–9 (2016)
5. Leau, Y.B., Manickam, S.: A novel adaptive grey verhulst model for network security situation prediction. Int. J. Adv. Comput. Sci. Appl. **7**(1) (2016)
6. Tang, Y., Li, C., Song, Y.: Network security situation prediction based on improved particle swarm optimization and extreme learning machine. J. Comput. Appl. **41**(3), 768 (2021)
7. Wang, G.: Comparative study on different neural networks for network security situation prediction. Secur. Priv. **4**(1), e138 (2021)
8. Zhang, H., Kang, C., Xiao, Y.: Research on network security situation awareness based on the LSTM-DT model. Sensors **21**(14), 4788 (2021)
9. Hu, W., Liu, J., Guo, H., Li, J., Zhao, X., Zhang, M.: Network security situation prediction model based on security situation factors. In: 2021 IEEE Sixth International Conference on Data Science in Cyberspace (DSC), pp. 23–31 (2021)
10. Yang, X., Jia, Y.: IPSO-LSTM: a new internet security situation prediction model. In: ICMLCA 2021 - 2nd International Conference on Machine Learning and Computer Application, pp. 1–5 (2021)
11. Xue, J., Shen, B.: A novel swarm intelligence optimization approach: sparrow search algorithm. Syst. Sci. Control Eng. **8**(1), 22–34 (2020)
12. Liang, Q., Chen, B., Wu, H., Han, M.: A novel modified sparrow search algorithm based on adaptive weight and improved boundary constraints. In: 2021 IEEE 6th International Conference on Computer and Communication Systems (ICCCS), pp. 104–109 (2021)
13. Moustafa, N.: TON_IoT datasets (2019). https://doi.org/10.21227/fesz-dm97. Accessed 17 May 2022

14. Ahmad, M., Riaz, Q., Zeeshan, M., Tahir, H., Haider, S.A., Khan, M.S.: Intrusion detection in Internet of Things using supervised machine learning based on application and transport layer features using UNSW-NB15 data-set. EURASIP J. Wirel. Commun. Netw. **2021**(1), 1–23 (2021)

15. Luan, D., Tan, X.: EWM-IFAHP: an improved network security situation assessment model. In: ICMLCA 2021 - 2nd International Conference on Machine Learning and Computer Application, pp. 1–6 (2021)

16. Tizhoosh, H.R.: Opposition-based learning: a new scheme for machine intelligence. In: International Conference on Computational Intelligence for Modelling, Control and Automation and International Conference on Intelligent Agents, Web Technologies and Internet Commerce (CIMCA-IAWTIC 2006), vol. 1, pp. 695–701 (2005)

17. Chengtian, O., Yujia, L., Donglin, Z.: An adaptive chaotic sparrow search optimization algorithm. In: 2021 IEEE 2nd International Conference on Big Data, Artificial Intelligence and Internet of Things Engineering (ICBAIE), pp. 76–82 (2021)

18. Hu, C., Liu, G., Li, M.: A network security situation prediction method based on SA-SSA. In: 2021 14th International Symposium on Computational Intelligence and Design (ISCID), pp. 105–110 (2021)

19. Mirjalili, S.: Dragonfly algorithm: a new meta-heuristic optimization technique for solving single-objective, discrete, and multi-objective problems. Neural Comput. Appl. **27**(4), 1053–1073 (2016). https://doi.org/10.1007/s00521-015-1920-1

20. Zhao, J., Gao, Z.M.: The improved equilibrium optimization algorithm with Lévy flight. In: 2020 5th International Conference on Computer and Communication Systems (ICCCS), pp. 352–355 (2020)

Author Index

Printed in the United States
by Baker & Taylor Publisher Services